The Seven-Year Stretch

The Seven-Year Stretch

How Families Work Together to Grow Through Adolescence

Laura S. Kastner, Ph.D.,

AND

Jennifer F. Wyatt, Ph.D.

HOUGHTON MIFFLIN COMPANY

BOSTON · NEW YORK

1997

TO OUR NEXT GENERATION
Cameron and Lindley
Megan, Molly, Andy, and Jay

————

For information about permission to reproduce
selections from this book, write to
Permissions, Houghton Mifflin Company,
215 Park Avenue South, New York,
New York 10003.

For information about this and other
Houghton Mifflin trade and reference books
and multimedia products,
visit The Bookstore at Houghton Mifflin
on the World Wide Web at
http://www.hmco.com/trade/.

Library of Congress Cataloging-in-Publication Data
Kastner, Laura Scribner.
The seven-year stretch : how families work together
to grow through adolescence / Laura S. Kastner
and Jennifer F. Wyatt.
p.   cm.
"A Marc Jaffe book."
Includes bibliographical references.
ISBN 0-395-73526-2
1. Parent and teenager — United States. 2. Adolescent
psychology.   I. Wyatt, Jennifer Fugett. II. Title.
HQ799.15.K37   1997
649'.125 — dc21   96-48027   CIP

Printed in the United States of America

Book design by Joyce Weston

QUM 10 9 8 7 6 5 4 3 2 1

Contents

___

Acknowledgments

I am grateful to many mentors who have inspired me and encouraged me along my path: Mavis Hetherington, Mary Ainsworth, and Dickon Reppucci at the University of Virginia; faculty in pediatrics, child psychiatry, and adolescent medicine at the University of Washington; and all the families who have shared with me their inner workings, their troubles, their capabilities, and their healing ways. My deepest gratitude goes to my parents and siblings, who originally gave me a reverence for family, and to my husband, Philip Mease, and our children, who teach me daily about the work, humor, respect, patience, cherishing, humility, and goodwill that constitute family. — *Laura Kastner*

I've had the good fortune to have been born into a caring family and to have been educated by thoughtful minds. My love of language and inclination to write owe a debt to these influences. I also thank the whole Wyatt clan with its lively, loving presence; educators who have shaped my thinking and especially my children's teachers at the Bush School; my children, who provide me with the most fascinating and valuable job known to humankind; and my husband, Scott, whose unwavering belief buoys my spirit. — *Jennifer Wyatt*

Our mutual appreciation goes to our agent, Pam Bernstein; to our initial editor, Gail Winston, who guided our thinking early on; to our editor Marc Jaffe, who shepherded the project through to completion; to friends, fellow writers, and colleagues who talked us through this project; to members of our book club who listened and held our hands; to the individuals who participated in a survey for the book and shared their stories; and to the parents and professionals who waded through multiple drafts, participated in review sessions, and offered pivotal insights that strengthened our book.

A Note from the Authors

This book was written by Laura Kastner and Jenny Wyatt collaboratively. It would be more appropriate to use the third person "we" as the authorial voice in the text, for we created each page together. Ultimately, for clarity's sake, we made the decision to speak to readers from the first person, since Laura Kastner is the psychologist whose knowledge, insights, and personal clinical experiences are represented in the book.

Jenny Wyatt's background in writing and parenting made her the indispensable expresser and translator of ideas in this book. We see this book as a mutual creation of two people talking, drafting, meeting with parent/psychologist reviewer groups, and redrafting. A process produced this book, whose outcome is the result of Jenny Wyatt's writing, Laura Kastner's professional experience, and the thoughtful input of a multitude of families who speak through us.

Introduction

___

The Stretch Begins

I WAS shuffling my notes from a talk I'd just given to a group of parents, when I noticed a mom, visibly shaken, approaching the podium. Sighing dishearteningly, the mom voiced concerns about "peer pressure" and our "consumerist society" before broaching the problem preoccupying her. In a clothing store, her fourteen-year-old daughter had been caught shoplifting with some other girls. As I listened to the mom, I heard two diametrically opposed reactions to the crisis. First came the stern words of the accusing mom: "My daughter is a thief. I'm angry enough to ground her for the rest of my life." Next, the plaintive explanation of the excusing mom: "There's so much pressure on kids today. She's completely humiliated. My heart breaks for her."

A behavior like shoplifting could be as simple as an isolated risk-taking incident, which calls for one type of parental response, or as complex as a symptom of deep anger and family dysfunction, which suggests an entirely different intervention. How does one know which it is? What's a parent to do? Describing her quandary, the mom struck a chord that rings repeatedly among parents today: "I went to school to prepare for a job, but there's no school to teach us how to be parents. I don't know what to do."

Everyone is stretched by adolescence. Many parents who haven't been near a child-rearing section of a bookstore since their child's early years find themselves again wandering the aisles seeking out guidance. Not since pregnancy have many felt such anxious anticipation about changes brewing in the household. For nearly twenty years I've worked as a clinical psychologist; I continue to be struck by how daunting parenting an adolescent can sometimes be, but I'm also inspired by the growth that occurs as families work through their challenges.

Perhaps you're a parent of a teenager and you've experienced a distressing incident, a drinking episode, for example. Perhaps you're perplexed over new behaviors, like a smart mouth, a first serious boyfriend or girlfriend, or a tendency to regard you as superfluous. Maybe your child isn't an adolescent yet, but you want to brace yourself for these years reputed to be so trying. Whatever the case, the seven-year period roughly corresponding with the junior high and high school years is a unique stretch of the parenting journey, which calls for an expanded repertoire of skills and new insights. No longer will a simple technique — like pulling out a popsicle — work to affect the moment positively. Because teenagers are more complex beings, parenting involves greater thoughtfulness, greater creativity, and a deeper understanding of what makes kids this age tick, especially given their complicated, sometimes frightening environment.

What would you do if, for example:

- your teenage son pulls the classic adolescent stunt of telling you he's spending the night with a friend, when he has every intention of attending a rock concert in another part of the state?
- your child undergoes a major academic slump and whatever you do seems to make it worse?
- you've tried to give your child everything you thought he needed, but his constant demands make you wonder if you've created an emotional terrorist?
- your son clams up when you try to talk to him and you worry you've lost him?
- daily life with your daughter has become one long screaming match?
- you have major worries about your child moving into a "bad" peer group?
- your teenage daughter appears to be on the verge of having sex with her boyfriend?
- you have evidence indicating that your child is using drugs?
- your child doesn't look as if she's going to be able to leave home successfully after high school?

And what if your problem is compounded by the fact that you and your spouse have vastly different ideas about how to handle a predicament, even though you know you're supposed to parent together as a united front? Or you're a single parent and you feel as if you're flying by the seat of your pants without a road map or another adult to help you find your way?

The above scenarios are a sampling of the some two-dozen detailed family vignettes you'll read about in *The Seven-Year Stretch*. Some of these adolescent behaviors occur in very healthy families, dealing with the typical stuff of the teenage years, while others are part of a more entrenched, destructive situation. As an adolescent and family therapist, I often encounter parents wondering whether a particular dilemma they're facing with their child is "normal" or cause for alarm. Therapists such as myself have a number of ways of assessing problems, as we winnow out important considerations and determine what to do in a given situation. We look not only at the individual adolescent behavior, but at the richer mix of dynamics within the family. A large constellation of variables and life circumstances — biological, sociocultural, interpersonal, and developmental — can be at play, even with a behavior that at first glance may seem to pertain only to the adolescent. *The Seven-Year Stretch* provides parents with a wide-angle lens through which to view adolescence. It invites parents to open up their perspective on what happens during this critical child-rearing stretch and acquire some new tools for handling their own adolescent and family issues.

Over the past thirty years, a vast body of psychological literature and research has illuminated the parental and familial factors associated with family health and with family dysfunction, but most of this information has remained in the hands of specialists like myself, instead of in the homes of the "users." Though humans are never an entirely predictable lot, research has told us what kinds of parenting behaviors tend to yield certain outcomes in offspring. This book draws on many of the leading schools of psychology/psychiatry: developmental theory, object relations theory, attachment theory, cognitive-behavioral theory, and, importantly, family systems theory. In large part, information from theory and research has been built into the characterization of families in the vignettes in order to illustrate theory in action.

The vignettes in *The Seven-Year Stretch* are fictionalized composites of real families, whose sources are many: families I saw at the adolescent clinic at the University of Washington in Seattle, where I have taught for the past seventeen years; families I treated in various clinical settings and in my private practice; families who responded to a survey conducted for this book; and families I met in workshops and in a variety of other informal settings.

The public lectures and workshops I have given over the years have provided me with valuable insights into the experiences of ordinary families — their dilemmas, crises, and joys in parenting an adolescent.

People I've worked with in therapy who have attended my presentations have joked with me about their fears of having their particular stories described in my case examples, then expressed relief in not having their fears realized. In these talks, as in this book, I have kept strict confidentiality. On the other hand, many people previously unknown to me have come up to me after a presentation, asking how I could have described their family so perfectly having never met them. The answer is that there truly are some classic patterns that family therapists know like the backs of their hands, and interested parents can benefit from learning about them.

Any number of disturbing social issues — increased violence in society, demands on families and schools, concerns about educational standards, less parental supervision in homes — make this an uneasy time to be parenting an adolescent. Our lives are full of stress. In the face of all there is to make us anxious, parents today seem more passionate than ever about doing a good job and more conscious of the effects of their parenting on their children. A view I share with many teenagers and colleagues in the field of adolescent health is that some books and media stories about adolescence focus exclusively on serious problems like drug use, violence, and mental disorders, without appreciating the many adolescents and parents who are doing well and thriving during the teenage years.

Studies in various health disciplines have indicated that 10 to 20 percent of adolescents have significant psychiatric problems (the smaller or larger percentage depends largely on socioeconomic factors). Researchers who survey the general population estimate that of the remaining 80 to 90 percent of adolescents without psychopathology, 10 to 20 percent sail through adolescence with relative ease; and the remaining 60 to 70 percent experience occasional problems and crises but will come out basically well adjusted.[1] *The Seven-Year Stretch* contains stories across this whole continuum, not just the pathological end. And, more importantly, it seeks to strike a balance between alerting parents to the dangers that truly do exist and reassuring them that families often possess the necessary strengths to raise their adolescents successfully.

Chapters begin with high-functioning, healthy families confronted by a puzzling adolescent behavior or a problem that has arisen. Related explanatory material delves into why and how the family was able to deal effectively with the issue at hand. As each chapter progresses, the families portrayed are grappling with more deep-seated problems. In the vignettes where adolescents and families are in moderate trouble, explanations are given and solutions are suggested. The small number of stories of dysfunctional families are offered mainly to show parents all that can be involved in such situations rather than to advise extensively on what these families should do, for families with severe problems will need to pursue professional help.

Families with significant problems bring along with them a tangled skein of causes and forces exacerbating their situations. By exposing these variables we demystify the experience of the highly troubled adolescent. An overarching purpose of all the vignettes is to help parents identify where they are vulnerable and where they are not, when they have work to do and when they can cast aside fears, draw on their family strengths, and enjoy their adolescent.

Even in the healthiest of families, there are many layers to examine, for we are all — parents and their children alike — uniquely and imperfectly formed out of our genetics, our environment, and our significant relationships with others, past and present. My experience in working with a broad range of families tells me that parents are interested in exploring those many layers in a way that can help them improve their parenting. Once we've gained insight into the intricate workings of who we are as parents, how we function as families, and how we influence our adolescents, more choices open up to us. Admittedly, parenting an adolescent involves a lot of stretching, flexing and adapting, but many moms and dads find it a very gratifying and engaging stage of child rearing.

Families struggling with poverty, psychiatric disorders, and any of a host of personal problems will be more likely to be overloaded with stressors and experience difficulties with their adolescents. Nonetheless, all families, including the very healthiest, will face challenges while raising a teenager. A critical difference is the healthy family's capacity to harness their strengths, help their adolescent develop critical competencies, and grow together through their life experiences.

1

"Trust Me"

*Goal: Trust your adolescents most of the time
and recognize when you shouldn't.*

EARNESTLY, angrily, pleadingly — in as many tones of voice as the light spectrum has colors — our adolescents ask us to trust them. No matter how said, this phrase has a deeply desirable inner ring to it. Like love, trust is something we hope to give and get, yet it is such an abstract, intangible, and lofty ideal that the skeptic dwelling in each of us feels uncomfortably boxed in by an open-ended request for trust.

Sensing that the ability to trust is some kind of parental test, we might respond reflexively to our adolescent, "Of course I trust you," then proceed with actions or ambivalent statements that negate what we've just declared: "Of course I trust you to drive carefully, but you still can't take my car." "I trust you, but not your friends." Most teenagers are clever enough to retort, "If you really trusted me, you wouldn't worry about my friends." And, they have a point. In extreme cases, some parents, enraged at their adolescent, brandish the weapon of "I can't trust you anymore."

Why does trust have such resonance? Why does it come up again and again as one of those strong valence words in parenting? Although trust is a central theme throughout child rearing, to understand its full impact on parenting during adolescence, we need to expand the scope of analysis to include our own upbringing, early parent-child interactions, and the internalized "trust compass" parents and children each bring with them into the teenage years. Trusting runs very deep. Our ability to trust involves our innermost instincts, and it reaches back to experiences we (who are now parents) had as babies and children. Learning to trust others and to trust ourselves is "our first developmental task."[1]

Newborns begin to develop the internal equipment to trust when someone responds to their biological and emotional needs. Described in its purest form, a baby sends a cue that she is hungry, or tired, or needs to be held in a particular way, and, ideally, a parent or a committed caregiver responds. In this first relationship between the baby and parent (or caregiver), the foundation for trust is laid. This relationship serves as a prototype for much of what the baby intuits about trust. If the baby had language, she might say, "People are basically reliable. They tend to pull through when you need them." And the baby also learns to trust herself. "I was right to send that cue because I got what I needed."

If all goes well, the baby learns to rely on herself, on others, and the external world as a pretty good place, most of the time. Obviously, there will be occasions when the baby's needs are frustrated, so she adjusts her thinking to the quality of the response received. Importantly, the baby's innate temperament and biology and environmental factors affect the interaction. The baby starts to acquire what psychologists call a secure base if there are overall patterns of dependability, warmth, steadiness, and continuity in caregiving. Fast-forwarding through time, we can imagine the baby, turned child, turned adolescent, turned adult and parent, learning a lot more about who and when to trust.

Though we come into the world with instincts to love, bond, and seek relationships, the extent to which we are able to trust others and trust ourselves is largely acquired. Likewise, trusting is not confined to a moment in time when a judgment must be made, like whether we should trust our adolescent not to drink at a party. Our ability to trust loops back through the history of our relationship with our parents and our children. Within each of us, trust has an ongoing, multigenerational story.

An Inner Certainty

If early attachments and experiences with others we care about have been basically responsive and secure, we develop a capacity to trust ourselves and others. In the 1960s, Mary Ainsworth and John Bowlby began developing an area of theory and research about early parent-child relationships called "attachment theory."[2] Building on Ainsworth and Bowlby's pioneering work, researchers have investigated how the security or insecurity of early attachments influences later emotional adjustment. The quality of our early attachments has a powerful impact; secure attachment is associated with highly desirable qualities — social competency, flexibility, self-reliance, and curiosity — many of which dovetail with trust.

As Erik Erikson so aptly wrote, trust is "an inner certainty." It means we believe in our ability to make good judgments, and we see ourselves as trustworthy. By the time we're parents, we've internalized a model into the fabric of our being; we've formed some kind of personal theory (usually more felt than articulated) about trusting other people and trusting ourselves, and in all likelihood, we've passed this operating model and set of expectations along to our children.

A parent who trusts herself and is trustworthy has the internal equipment to believe others are capable of the same. Like mirroring images — "I recognize it in myself; I recognize it in you" — a trustworthy parent has an easier time extending trust to her child. In turn, children are quick to recognize when they are being trusted and will respond positively, for it feeds their self-worth and gives them confidence. Being trusted, they become increasingly capable of living up to expectations. From generation to generation, the "inner certainty" of being trustworthy and trusting others develops and cycles.

All said, what's passed along is not necessarily a direct legacy, for the lines between past and present can diverge. As Selma Fraiberg put it, "History is not destiny."[3] Even though we have each been shaped by our attachment and childhood history, it does not determine our lives or our children's. In the absence of strong parental attachments, someone else (a teacher, a relative, a friend's parent, a neighborhood mentor) may have come in to provide support. Because people tend to be fairly adaptable, we're able to build personal structures to compensate for weak foundations. Fraiberg maintained that we have the capacity to "banish the ghosts from the nursery," and build on what was beneficial from our pasts. We can face our memories, draw on our adaptability, and make efforts to create a secure, responsive kind of parenting by choice.

By the time we're parents of adolescents, our early experiences can be murky, as memory reconstructs reality. Indeed, researchers have found that *how* parents remembered their own childhood attachments was more important in understanding their behavior toward their children than what the history actually was.[4] Even if their memories were somewhat painful, parents who were able to recall their past tended to convey security to their children.

If parents carry within them a lack of self-trust, it can manifest itself in dramatic ways during a child's adolescence, compared to other times in a child's development. Adolescents can end up rattling their parents' foundations because the judgment calls become more difficult, the stakes are higher, and our anxiety can gyrate us more than ever.

Adolescence is sometimes referred to as a child's "second autonomy" because, similar to a child's second year of life, adolescents face the task of distinguishing and differentiating themselves from their parents. The difference between a two-year-old and an adolescent is, of course, immense; instead of squawking no (which means, "I know I am separate and unique if I don't do what you want"), our teenagers show disdain for our beliefs, our policies, and us in varied and painful ways: "You don't have a clue. . . . You don't understand me. . . . Why are you never on my side. . . . You don't even know me. . . . Just leave me alone. I need my space." Parents often wonder whether such rebuffs are part of normal adolescent differentiation or whether they reflect a deeper rift in the relationship. As a general rule, if other aspects of an adolescent's life are stable, there is a good chance a remark like those above, occasionally sprinkled into an otherwise relatively positive relationship, is the noise of differentiation. If, however, parents lack self-trust, they may be unduly disturbed by their adolescent's rejecting messages, even when they are basically benign. And if a parent has an extremely poor attachment history (particularly one not dealt with, like a history of unacknowledged abuse), there is a greater likelihood that the parent's and child's internal trust compasses are haywire and these adolescent noises may indeed signify problems.

The Many Faces of Trust

The adolescent who says "Trust me" needs to have her imperative translated. "Trust me" sometimes means "I need your respect" or "I need you to see me as competent." But it can also mean, "I want what I want!" When should we trust our adolescents, say yes to the reasonable freedoms they request, and bid them a trusting good-bye? When should we wonder about our naiveté, fret over their capacity for risk-taking adventures, and halt them in their tracks? How do we know whether a particular "trust me" reflects a sincere need or is code to get them what they want? Herein lies part of the challenge of parenting an adolescent.

Trust is a ricocheting phenomenon: parent to adolescent, adolescent to parent, parent to parent, and back again. And, it's all about mutuality. Consider these variations on trust:

- Adolescents want to be trusted by their parents. ("I want my parents to know that I am responsible and capable.")
- Adolescents want to trust themselves and their judgments. ("I can rely on myself to make good decisions.")
- Adolescents want to trust their parents. ("My parents aren't going to fail me. They're on my side most of the time.")
- Parents want to trust their adolescent. ("I trust my child to make decisions that will keep him/her safe.")
- Parents want to trust themselves and their own judgments. ("I'm doing the right thing by my child, even if it means contending with some resistance.")
- Parents want to be trusted by their adolescents. ("I want my adolescent to understand that I'm acting in his/her best interest.")

The blanket term "trust" is, in actuality, multivectored; it's a back and forth action and reaction. Trust's source, as attachment theory tells us, runs very deep within us; what could be more alluring than the "inner certainty" of trusting? But, of course, we also don't want to be overly romantic, unrealistic, and moralistic. Good kids still push the limits, lie occasionally, and experiment with various larks as an intrinsic part of adolescence.

What, then, is a usable parental guideline and goal? From a developmental perspective, the more mature the adolescent, the more we are usually able to trust them to act competently and independently, but this guideline must go hand in hand with evidence that their behavior is generally trustworthy. If a teenager is not evidencing trustworthy conduct, we need to take a closer look at our parenting, the family dynamics, and the adolescent's individual issues.

Parents should have very high expectations of themselves and others; however, if a family member comes up short, don't assume trust has been broken irrevocably. Too often, when there's a lapse in trustworthiness, we move to an extreme and declare that we'll never trust the person again. We want to avoid taking on "large-chunk" concepts like trust, honesty, unfaltering love, and expecting the impossible. These are beacons, and we try hard for them. We can set our standards high, but no so high as to demand perfection. *Once we acknowledge and accept that trusting "mostly" is as good as it gets in human relations, we are easier on ourselves and our children.*

The three vignettes in this chapter depict parents — successfully and unsuccessfully — working on the goal of trusting an adolescent "most of the time." The first story came to me through a mother named Stella, who attended one of my parenting workshops and told the group about her son going to a rock concert on the sly. We explored her experience at length in the workshop because of her productive resolution of the crisis. My retelling of Stella's interaction with her son is a close version of what she told the group. Although the vignette focuses primarily on the issue of trust, Stella's family reflects many principles of healthy functioning.

What Is This Thing Called Trust? Stella and Chris

Pleasant news rarely comes in the form of a late evening phone call. Hanging up the receiver, Stella leaned against the wall to steady herself. She had just learned that her reliable, conscientious son Chris deceived her, consciously and deliberately. Seventeen-year-old Chris had told Stella he was sleeping over at Jason's house, but instead he attended a concert in another part of the state and was spending the night in a motel with several friends.

Of all people, Jason's mother, whom Stella considers highly competitive, had phoned. "I know if it were me, I'd want to know," she had begun. "My daughter just told me that Chris told you he was at our house overnight. Not true. Five of the boys in the class drove over to the concert." Though Stella was truly grateful to be clued in — it's what parents are supposed to do for each other after all — this mother's insinuating manner made it hard to take.

Stella's husband was out of town, which left her alone with a vertigo-like reaction, as physical as it was emotional, in her struggle to make sense of Chris's behavior. Now that she knew the truth, should she call her son at the motel? Jason's mother had assured her the boys were safe (Jason had called her), but this did little to calm her mushrooming fears. "He drove two hours to the concert with Jason, and Jason has only had his license a few months. What are his parents thinking about, handing over so much responsibility to an inexperienced driver!" she thought to herself.

Stella's fear mated with anger. "I trusted Chris, and this is where I end up. How could I have been so blindsided? I must not know my own kid. If he is pulling stunts like this, there's no end to what he might be into." As the hours passed, Stella imagined worst-possible scenarios. "What else could be happening? There are drugs at concerts. Even if he's with his friends, everybody knows how things can get out of control."

After a night of little sleep, Stella fidgeted as she waited for her son to arrive home. To reassure herself, she checked in with some of the other mothers whose judgments she trusts. While matters didn't appear as grave as they had in the middle of the night, she remained upset. Because she wanted to see how her son handled the situation, she formed no exact plan of punishment.

One look at Chris coming up the walkway, and Stella started to feel more sure of herself. Stella met him in the hallway before he could dash upstairs to his bedroom. Somewhat too cheerfully, he greeted his mom with a big "Oh, hi!"

Unable to resist a small dig, Stella said, "Hi, Chris. You look really tired."

"We didn't get much sleep at Jason's house."

"Stop right there, Chris," she stated calmly and directly. "I know you didn't spend the night with Jason. You've been at a concert."

Chris was panicked, at a loss for words. He averted his gaze from his mother to the stairway.

Stella filled in the awkward silence. "I also know you spent the night in a motel room."

"Who told you this?"

She was reluctant to disclose her source, but nonetheless admitted, "Jason's mother called me."

Flushed and taken aback with shame, Chris said, "I've blown it big time. What are you going to do?"

"Obviously, this is a real violation of my trust in you."

"Now you'll never trust me again," mumbled Chris beleagueredly.

"Never's too long," Stella retorted. "Frankly, it would be impossible for me to trust your every moment's decision. I am very upset about this, and I'm disappointed that you lied to us."

"I guess I'm grounded."

"Grounding sounds right for starters." Stella paused, trying not to let the silence force her into saying too much too soon. Her self-dialogue was actively advising her to breathe deeply and give Chris time to absorb his dilemma. Although she wanted to keep him talking, she didn't want to press too hard too fast, which might trigger the escape Chris so transparently craved. After a few seconds had passed she continued, "What happened, Chris? This isn't the kind of thing I'd expect you to do."

"My favorite bands were there. Everyone else's parents were cool about it. I didn't want to lie, but I really wanted to go."

"Why didn't we talk about this? Why didn't you ask?"

"Why should I ask? I already knew the answer," said Chris, beginning to get angry himself. "I knew you'd say no. You and Dad didn't let me drive to the state basketball tournament with Casey last month."

"Look, that was a five-hour drive over the mountains in the winter. I stand by that decision. But, I didn't realize how much that call was going to affect you, and that you'd sacrifice our trust in you for something like this."

"What trust is there to sacrifice?" responded Chris, his pitch rising. "How much trust are you putting in me when you treat me like a twelve-year-old? We got the room because we didn't want to drive back late at night in the concert traffic. But — no — you're not giving me any credit for that. I just decided, 'Why even try to play by their rules? There's no payoff. I don't get to do anything.'"

"O.K., O.K., I get your point. What you've just done doesn't exactly inspire me to let you try new things. In fact, now I feel like we need to move the fence in and monitor what's going on more carefully. We're going to have to figure out a way for you to show us that you're responsible, so we can regain trust and eventually say yes."

"Great," Chris angrily retorted. "Now you're going to be stricter than ever."

"Yes, for a while, because of what just happened. I'm not comfortable pushing the fence back right now. I think you should be grounded for two weeks and after that we'll set up a check-in system for a month. When you've shown us you're back on track, we'll negotiate more freedom. I hear what you're saying to me. I'm sorry you felt like it was fruitless to try to talk to me about freedoms you thought were reasonable. But, don't take the back door. You've got to come through the front door and keep it open so we can prevent future problems like this."

From Black and White to Shades of Gray

Upon first learning of Chris's deception, Stella's world was turned upside down. Her ability to trust was temporarily eclipsed by doubt and fear. Stella's initial reaction was, at once, a little excessive and all too human. What parent wouldn't be overwrought upon discovering her child devised a scam of this type? In moments of great anxiety, we have a tendency to shift into primitive black or white thinking, which for Stella meant "My son, who was so good before, is now all bad." Neither was or is true, of course, though panic made the loss of the good son feel real. Instead of a balanced analysis of what Chris's action meant, Stella worried the extremes. But if we let anxiety drive our response to a crisis, the situation is likely to deteriorate.

Though Stella had been thrown, when she saw her son safely home, an internal toggle switch adjusted her anxiety. No longer black or white, her reality became gray, her mindset more troubled than condemning. Notice the contrast between the potentially explosive language Stella released in the middle of the night and the more neutral, less threatening interchange with her son the next morning. For example, "If he's pulling stunts like this, there's no end to what else he might be into" became instead a question for Chris, "What happened? This isn't the kind of thing I'd expect you to do." Angry though Stella was — all sins are *not* forgiven — there were no screaming reprimands, no putdowns, and no rejecting statements.

When dealing with an adolescent's slip-ups, guard against black/white thinking and avoid venting fears and fantasies, because this depicts them as worse than they actually are. Chris's action was an isolated incident and not a chronic pattern, so Stella took care not to overstate what happened. Because Stella and Chris's relationship is thriving and healthy, Stella relied on their history together to ease her into a balanced perspective, which is a prerequisite for a productive discussion. Other parents may need an external prompt to regain footing, such as talking with a spouse or friend or taking a good long walk. When parents find themselves on the brink of a confrontation sure to explode, they can postpone the talk. A good option is to say something like, "I'm too angry to talk about this now," so the interaction is not severed in a rejecting way. (Know thyself, however; some people stew and grow angrier as time passes.)

Chris lied twice — initially about going to Jason's and again when

Stella commented on how tired he looked. Stella handled these lies beautifully. *When confronting an adolescent, present all the information you have, rather than entrapping them with contrived inquiries to see whether they will continue to lie.* When parents have the goods on their teenager, they can be tempted to see if their son or daughter will confess or is audacious enough to lie more. This does a child an injustice because it encourages continued deception. Most kids and even some adults will scramble desperately in an entrapped situation to avoid trouble.

If Stella had said, "Hi, Chris. Did you have fun at Jason's house?" there is a very low probability Chris would have responded, "Well, now that you ask, I wasn't at Jason's house." Chris would have kept his cover by saying, "Yeah, it was O.K." He would have perpetuated the original lie, ratcheting up his infraction. In this case, Stella would also have been culpable and dishonest because she did not come clean with the known facts at the beginning of the conversation.

Learning from a Lie

Because Stella let all lies die a quick death, she moved quickly to the heart of the problem. (She also swallowed Chris's exaggerated claim that he "never gets to do anything.") The lie was symptomatic of a deeper issue between Chris and his parents — that of freedom and responsibility, a topic to be more fully explored in the next chapter. Some parents go into a tailspin over the immorality of lying and react with a limited approach. The essence of their message is you did wrong; you lied; how dare you lie to me; you're a bad kid; you can't be trusted; you deserve to be punished.

Nothing is learned. Certainly parents don't want to sanction lying, for honesty is one of the virtues we want our children to take into adulthood. Nonetheless, teenagers will occasionally lie to get what they want *and* they can still grow up to be honest, especially if they have parents who are honest and who work with their child, as Stella did, if a lie is discovered.

Stella neither dismissed the lie nor focused solely on it. She opened up the situation rather than closing it down. Instead of moralizing, she tried to understand the situation. The dialogue between Chris and Stella proceeded well because:

- Stella focused on the facts and suspended judgment until she heard Chris out. She knew that Chris was basically trustworthy. Attending the concert was a strategic error rather than a deep and significant character flaw. Stella's manner communicated to Chris that he could trust her, and she established a communication bridge with her son that provided access to his pent-up feelings.

- Chris wanted to explain himself. He was angry at his parents because he felt they set up the necessity for subterfuge with their restrictions.

If a child feels totally lambasted during a parent-child confrontation, he will be less likely to talk frankly about what is on his mind. Parents have to restrain themselves from going on and on about how disappointed they are, how wrong the child was to lie, because moralizing shuts teenagers off. "Oh, no, not another lecture," they groan to themselves. When an adolescent violates trust, parents will learn more about the underlying reasons and motivations if they listen, exercise patience, and let the adolescent do most of the talking.

The crux of Chris's dilemma rested in his statement "I didn't want to lie, but I really wanted to go." From his perspective, he had no good way out. Dilemmas of this kind explain why a lot of good kids lie. Chris believed he should be able to go to the concert, and he believed his parents were too strict. According to this typical adolescent convoluted thinking, two wrongs neutralized each other. His rationale was, my parents have behaved in a way I think is wrong, so I feel entitled to wrong back. Chris didn't really believe it was morally right to lie, but his anger and indignation motivated him to legitimize his disobedient action. Just as Chris broke his parents' trust by going to the concert, he felt that his parents broke trust by not being reasonable enough to let him go. He did not trust his parents to hear how desperate his need for more freedom was. By not being rigidly high-minded and punitive, Stella gained insight into some of the pressures on her son and into the effects of her parenting behavior. *This is one of the truisms of interpersonal relations: when we stop insisting that we are 100 percent right, we can listen better and learn from another's point of view and experience. Trust yourself and your judgments mostly, but never believe you are so right that you become unwilling to make some adjustments.*

Stella was humble enough to apologize and admit to playing a part in the crisis at hand: "I didn't realize how much that decision [that is, a previous no to the state basketball tournament] was going to affect you. . . . I'm sorry you felt like it was fruitless to try to talk to me about freedoms you thought were reasonable."

As a parent of the '90s, Stella needed to be a little more sensitive to the mores of the time and to her son's readiness for more freedom. One of the topics we explored in the workshop wherein I met Stella was the effect of parental background on childrearing. Stella had been brought up in a traditional white middle-class family. Her relationship with her parents had been secure and responsive, providing her with a sense of self-trust. She recalled living contentedly within a strict behavioral code that allowed for little independence. In raising her own son, she doled out freedoms with much deliberation, trusting that because her parents operated this way, she would do best to follow suit. Though Stella's husband was not directly involved in the situation, from what I gathered from Stella, his theories on parenting were in sync with hers. They both knew that competence is expanded with trust and incremental responsibilities, but they'd overlooked Chris's recent need to stretch in new ways.

Chris was probably right in assuming his parents wouldn't have allowed him to go to the concert. As parents, we sometimes sail along thinking all is well, until our kids' behavior wakes us up. Chris was sobered by what he had done, yet he also made a little dent in his parents' tendency to hold their line. The point is, we can't say no again and again and sit back and feel smug about our firmness when our teenagers feel our decisions are unjust. Open communication will allow us to find out what their needs and perspectives are so that we can attempt the eternally difficult task of bridging our preferences with theirs. The parent's job is always to listen, consider, and mediate wishes. Though self-trust is critical to childrearing, we can all use some fine-tuning.

Returning to Trust Most of the Time

Regardless of the fact that Chris could justify his behavior and was upset at having injured his credibility, he clearly showed poor judgment in choosing to lie. *Typically, discipline that follows misbehavior in a trustworthy teenager like Chris should be highly dependent on the quality of the dialogue that occurs during the confrontation.* Usually, the more remorse a child shows, the less punitive a parent will need to be because the teen is self-administering part of his own punishment. This is one of the benefits of self-generated guilt. In its best form, it's about learning from a mistake and self-correcting. Why would parents want to upstage this natural, internal process by overdosing with their punishment?

Chris was grounded for two weeks, and for a month thereafter, his parents kept close tabs on his comings and goings, which served as Chris's reparations for his misdeed. By following through with these consequences, Chris could reestablish himself as competent, reliable, and trustworthy in his parents' eyes. Once Chris carried out the terms of his punishment successfully and his parents felt more confident in him, he would then be in the position to negotiate for more freedom.

Of all that needed to happen in the wake of Chris's concert spree, the most critical agenda item was to return to trust "most of the time" — the chapter's goal. As they spoke, Stella rejected Chris's disheartened claim, "Now you'll never trust me again." This was a serious incident, not a catastrophe, and, as such, a modicum of distrust would shadow their relationship for a short period. Stella replied to Chris, "Never's too long . . . it would be impossible for me to trust your every moment's decision."

Trust is not a monolithic absolute. Because it is multifaceted, accept your child as a human being. Neither extend blanket trust nor view a small degree of distrust as unacceptable. Stella accepted that her adolescent might not always make the right decision. Her job as a parent is to help him through mistakes and help him avoid serious, life-threatening situations. Through her body language and positive tone, Stella separated trust from respect; in spite of what happened, she continued to value Chris's inherent worth.

Sometimes it's more palatable to adolescents if we make note of their vulnerability in impersonal terms, with a comment like, "I expect a range of decision making from someone your age. Adolescents are often put in situations when they're not able to make the best choices." What a relief for parents to advertise their humane acceptance of imperfection and slip-ups, especially since we so often send messages to others that we expect perfection. If trust (the foundation for human relationships) depended upon perfection, relationships would inherently self-destruct.

Much was accomplished between Stella and Chris because they did not get locked into his violation of trust exclusively. Profound work takes place on the edge of childrearing, in crisis situations. After the initial pain and insult of Chris's misdeed had subsided, Stella and Chris were able to rebuild their connection in a way that created closeness and ultimately greater trust. Chris's parents were resensitized to his need to be trusted with greater freedoms. They fortified the foundation of their relationship, which will help them survive the next adolescent challenge.

Tough Parenting Calls: To Trust or Not to Trust That a Teenager Can Stay Safe

Going to a rock concert two hours away and staying in a motel is borderline and risky for a seventeen-year-old. Far from being an automatic yes or no, this is *exactly* the kind of difficult decision that adolescents push parents to make. Some parents (like Stella) deliver an automatic no; others may not bat an eye before saying yes; and parents caught in the middle may want some criteria for judging whether an adolescent's request is reasonable. Tough parenting calls invariably crop up when teenagers get their driver's licenses, which diminishes parental control. With borderline areas, we want to advance rather than retreat, cultivating as much information as possible. Ultimately, what drives this type of decision is a parent's experience with her particular child and feelings of trustworthiness. Using the concert quandary as a model, parents can modify the questions below to fit the judgment call they're facing:

- Has your teenager attended local concerts before? Has she been open about what goes on at these events and discussed ways of staying safe and out of trouble?
- Has your teenager stayed clear of drugs and alcohol? What about the friends accompanying your child?
- Has your teenager demonstrated an awareness of risks involved and shown herself capable of making good judgments in the past? Has she basically stayed out of trouble thus far? Has she avoided getting caught up in a risk-taking syndrome that is keeping you awake at night?
- Is your teenager willing to negotiate on who, when, and how the car trip can be handled? How long has the driver had a license, and what types of driving experience has she had? Will your teenager check in by phone a couple of times during the trip? Is she staying at a reputable motel in a safe neighborhood? Has she successfully vaulted the hurdle of prior independent overnights?

A yes to questions like these means there's an opening for consenting. Likewise, there is a perfectly reasonable scenario for refusing.

Trusting an adolescent means taking reasonable, carefully determined risks.

Sometimes, before imposing restrictions, we need to take our own anxiety temperatures so we can determine how much of our motivation for holding the line is actually our own unwillingness to stretch, regardless of how capable our teenagers have demonstrated themselves to be. How much easier on our nerves it would be if we could simply shake our heads and keep them safe at home! It can help to apply this analogy: parents of a three-year-old usually have to hold their breath as their vulnerable daughter hangs upside down on the jungle gym. She may injure herself, but chances are she'll pull herself back up safely, so the parents let her dangle in order to gain confidence and competence for bigger playgrounds to come. As the parent of an adolescent, we need to continue to stretch, play the odds, and feel a little anxious when we consent to something that involves risk.

What does it take to let them dangle? To trust someone, we must have confidence in them; we need to see them as dependable and reliable; we need a history of experience with that person and his judgments — and we need Erikson's "inner certainty." To trust, parents come full circle through their own attachment history with their parents, their own upbringing, their own internalized model for trusting themselves and others, which their child has most likely internalized. Without an "inner certainty," parents often resort to too much control, which teenagers are likely to experience as oppressive.

Knowing yourself and your family history will help you assess your trust threshold. If your parenting style is relaxed compared to that of peer parents (for example, you are too trusting, perhaps a bit gullible, and not questioning any of your teenager's requests), extend your antenna. Be more vigilant. Motivate yourself to take action if there is cause for distrust.

On the other hand, you may have a background that engenders certain anxieties. If, for example, your brother lost sight in one eye when he was hit by a beer bottle at a fraternity party, you're going to be nervous when your child goes to parties, and you'll need to adjust for it.

For everyday kinds of decisions regarding a teenager's whereabouts and behaviors, instead of either constant monitoring or trusting, a useful compromise is a technique known as spot checks. If you've never kept track of what's in your liquor cabinet, take a measurement once in a while. If you haven't talked to parents of your child's friends for a while, give someone a call. If you haven't stayed up to greet your teenager at curfew for a while, make an effort. Even with now-and-then checks, parents may lose a little popularity with their adolescent, but part of a parent's job is to take some heat.

Early, Mid-, and Late Adolescence

Ideally, a parent's ability to trust a teenager increases with the teenager's age, for they should be internalizing more of their own moral code as they mature. Adolescence, which begins prior to the teenage years and actually extends beyond them, is not one period but rather a series of developmental phases, usually broken down into three.

Early adolescence roughly coincides with the middle school years. During this time, they are growing rapidly — physically, cognitively, and emotionally — and a major task is to adapt to those changes. Parents of early adolescents continue to provide a fair amount of structure for their children, in terms of planning activities, setting time limits, and defining behavioral parameters, though it should be less than in elementary school. Early adolescents are more or less expected to comply with what parents think is best for them, for we don't yet trust that middle schoolers can navigate by their own standards. Increasingly, however, we extend greater independence to them in certain areas, in order to develop their capacity to make decisions and build competence and self-reliance.

Although middle schoolers, compared to younger children, have a far greater appreciation for "the right thing to do" (for example, taking responsibility for homework, obeying rules, apologizing after a misdeed, coordinating one's personal desires with those of others), they also struggle with their egocentrism and their strong need to be more independent, especially from parents. Middle schoolers are sometimes desperate for acceptance from peers, so they will act impulsively and do things they would not think of doing on their own — break rules, be cruel to others, show off, or be rude. They will act wrongly, even while knowing what's right; hence, the common parental refrain, "You should know better." Blessedly, both egocentrism and peer conformity dwindle in high school, but can resurface at any moment during adolescence.

A second phase, called middle adolescence, coincides with the early high school years. Challenges during middle adolescence include developing self-reliance and greater psychological independence from parents, developing deeper friendships with peers, and handling them responsibly. As high school progresses, there should be less direct supervision, less overseeing of school projects, and less control over friend choices, money, time, and leisure activities. Though restricting privileges and adding extra chores are common disciplinary maneuvers, we shape and influence our adolescents through discussions, role modeling, and structuring the home environment. Because they have a more highly developed conscience and sophisticated understanding of social relationships and mutuality, we are increasingly more able to use reasoning, negotiation, and fairly abstract statements about life expectations in our explanations of why we want to see more or less of a certain behavior.

Late adolescence, the third phase, begins around the last year of high school and extends into the twenties. This phase includes launching from home and continues until young people have achieved a relatively clear sense of personal identity and committed themselves to some specific value system and life goals.

A Portrait of Distrust: Diane, Harris, Ashley, and Gordy Winbush

Not all families have the wherewithal to reach the other side of a breach in trust. That Stella maneuvered successfully through the crisis created by Chris's deception had everything to do with the fact that the family operated from a stable, healthy base and that Chris was ashamed and appalled by his own wrongdoing. The family was resilient, respectful of one another, and confident of its ability to solve problems together. In his overall adolescent life, Chris was doing well; he did not have slipping grades, questionable friends, and a troublesome attitude. In other words, Chris was not Gordy, a fourteen-year-old who shuffled head down into my office behind his parents; thus, the intervention required for Gordy's lapses in trustworthiness was very different from that with Chris, though the goal of resuming trust most of the time remained a constant.

Diane Winbush, Gordy's mother, made the appointment over the phone, explaining how worried she was about her son's marginal school performance and truancy, which had recently precipitated a huge family blowup. Diane described Gordy as messy, disrespectful, and a chronic liar. Raising him had been far more difficult than raising her older daughter, Ashley, now a freshman in college at a prestigious East Coast university. I stopped Diane from telling me too much, for in such situations I prefer my clients to explain their views in one another's presence. That way, the identified patient (the one perceived to have the problem) feels more control and is able to challenge the presentation of the facts. Also, family interaction patterns may hint at what is contributing to the problem.

For the Winbush family's first session, all parties, except daughter Ashley, were present: Diane, Caucasian, a successful professional; Harris, her husband, African American, an executive recruiter with his own business who worked long hours; and Gordy, biracial and an eagle-eyed observer beneath his air of nonchalance. A slice of this session encapsulates their family dynamic.

Diane [nervously; eyes dart from Gordy to Harris]: I know Gordy doesn't want to be here, but he's had trouble in school lately. He's not turning his homework in, and they called us in for a conference because he's just had his eighth unexcused absence.

Gordy: That's bull. I'm in class. They just count me absent because I'm late. It's not my fault my locker is so far from my classes. Plus, those teachers enjoy marking me late. It's their form of entertainment.

Diane: Oh, Gordy, you know you're loitering in the halls. You don't make an effort to be on time.

Gordy [mock shuddering]: Right, Mom, I'm *loitering,* like a bum in the park. That's what you think, of course. I'm also shooting up and pushing drugs. Why not tell the shrink that one too!

Diane [to LK]: See what I deal with? There is absolutely no way to communicate with him. We have a total breakdown in trust. I can't trust him to do his homework, to go to class, to lock the front door, or to carry on a civil conversation. Sometimes he calls me at the office, and I can't even trust him to be there when I call back!

Gordy [laughing cynically]: Yeah, two hours later you call me back. Why would I be there?

LK: Gordy, your mom uses the word "trust" a lot. What does it mean to you when she says she can't trust you?

Gordy: It means I'm a total fuck-up. They treat me like I'm the scum of the earth.

Diane: But Gordy, that's not true! We are just frustrated with the way you abuse our home, our trust, and our efforts to reach out to you.

Gordy looked at me with a face that said See? I held his gaze and said with my eyes, Yes, I see.

LK: Mr. Winbush, what is your perception of the problem here?

Harris: Well, it's pretty much like she says.

LK: You seem to kind of sit back and let them go at it.

For the first time in the session, Gordy was growing attentive, watching me address his parents' issues.

Harris: Well, that's sort of the way it usually goes. They both get at each other a lot.

LK [said to Diane]: What's it like for you — with your husband observing, I mean?

Diane: It drives me crazy. I do all the dirty work attending to all the problems that go on with Gordy, and he sits back like the Buddha, just watching it all.

LK: What would you like from him?

Diane [exasperated]: Well, a little more support, of course!

Harris [turning to Diane]: Yeah, but whenever I do try to help, you either cut me off at the knees and tell me I'm coming on too strong or tell me somehow I'm doing it all wrong.

Diane [to LK]: It's just that his temper seems out of control sometimes.

Harris [harshly to Diane]: Yeah, to you, maybe. But see — either I'm a lazy Buddha or "out of control." It's no win with you!

Gordy: Yeah, Mom. You're all over everybody. The only one that doesn't give you constant heart attacks is prissy perfect Ashley. She can do no wrong.

Diane: She never speaks ill of you. How dare you —

LK [interrupting]: You were watching your parents pretty closely there, Gordy — before you chimed in to side with your dad. What would happen if you didn't jump in like that?

Gordy: I don't know. I guess we'd get to watch them drive each other crazy — like Mom said.

LK [to Gordy]: How helpful of you to draw off the fire. It seems like you are pretty good at drawing a lot of fire, what with the school calling your mom about all your absences and incomplete homework and so on.

Gordy: Yeah, I guess that's what I'm real good at — drawing fire.

Without question, Diane had viable reasons for not trusting Gordy: He didn't do his homework; he loitered in the halls and skipped classes; he left house doors unlocked as he exited; he wasn't home when he was supposed to be, and he seemed incapable of carrying on a civil conversation with his parents. The frustration that builds up within parents in these kinds of situations can be overwhelming. Although it was not the case in the Winbush family, some parents distance from their children because they are unable to handle the pain of having their child "turn out" like this.

Nonetheless, Gordy's behavior was not without motivation, which becomes apparent in the evaluation session excerpt. What is destructive about the above dialogue is not just Diane's overt criticism, but also her more indirect blaming. When Gordy said, "I'm a total fuck-up," Diane incriminated herself by virtue of trying to reassure her son. She responded, "That's not true! We are just frustrated with the way you abuse our home, our trust, and our efforts to reach out to you." In the nicest of manners, she listed all his violations, confirming through the subtext of her message that he is the family screw-up.

Gordy heard Diane's statements as an attack. Matters in the Winbush family had deteriorated to the point that Gordy experienced much of his home life as a toxin to his system. He was furious with how little good his parents saw in him, and he felt so shamed that he had moved to protect himself through a bulwark of defensiveness. Nonetheless, Gordy played an important role in his family, in addition to causing them a lot of grief.

In many cases a particular child will function as the black sheep of the family, and as such draw the fire away from other significant family problems. I reframed the picture of Gordy by emphasizing his role as the family lightning rod. I did not want to confirm the picture of him as the cause of all the family pain and suffering. Even Gordy recognized his parents might "drive each other crazy" without him. The purpose of this "reframing" was to stimulate the process of getting to another side of Gordy.

This snippet of dialogue suggests that this family lacks a history of respect for one another, of having good times together, of mutual high regard. Clearly, what was happening in the Winbush family was not only about Gordy. Admittedly, Diane and Harris couldn't trust their son, but had they given Gordy reason to trust them?

Family Systems Theory

Ever since Freud began to codify the notion of the unconscious mind through psychoanalytic theory in the early 1900s, various models for understanding human behavior have been forwarded. Unlike psychoanalytic theory, family systems theory does not examine conflict strictly in terms of the individual psyche. Family system theorists, whose ranks have steadily increased over the past twenty-five years, believe that to understand what's going on with an individual, we need to explore the larger network of relationships of which he or she is a part. When problems arise in the family "ecosystem," everyone is affected or involved in some way, and everyone can be part of the solution.[5]

Patterns of interaction between family members become a primary focus for family systems theorists, seeking to analyze family structure — who is close to whom, who reacts to whom, who has power, whether the parents have hierarchical rank above the children, whether "boundaries" exist to organize roles and behaviors of family members in healthy, productive ways. Patterns are studied over time to figure out the function of certain behaviors, and, as in the Winbush family, seemingly maladaptive behaviors, like Gordy's conduct problems, often turn out to have adaptive functions; in his case, they served to keep the focus on him and "draw off fire" from his parents' conflicts. Gordy does not act up consciously to get clinical attention or to get his father more involved, but his behavior ends up having this beneficial side effect. Sometimes, because two or three generations of patterns have influenced a specific adolescent and family situation, we delve into "family-of-origin" issues to determine how patterns of the present evolved from those of the past. Within some families, patterns of substance use, teenage pregnancy, or incest have uncanny ways of being maintained from generation to generation through modeling, denial, high tolerance for deviance, and various responses that reinforce repetition.

When systems theorists analyze how the family as a whole operates, they seek to identify all the patterns that constitute the family "homeostasis" — the fairly steady state of equilibrium a family maintains. One of the ironies of the way human systems tend to work is that even though an individual's problems or life circumstances may create a certain amount of chaos, there is also a certain predictability of patterns. Families with problems often have ingrained behaviors that assume a life of their own despite the pain they cause. When this happens, parents lose flexibility, perspective, and creativity, and negative feelings abound. The cry I frequently hear in these situations is, "Help, we are stuck," and indeed they often are. A family crisis can serve as a shaking-up point for examining how each person's behaviors affect one another. With or without a therapist, in the wake of a dramatic event families often determine to change their ways. Should a family come into therapy, however, one of the therapist's objectives is to change the family homeostasis and interrupt the dysfunctional patterns, which is exactly what needed to happen in the Winbush family.

When Logical Parental Actions and Reactions Aren't Working

Anger and hostility swirling about them, Gordy and his family were like a gathering storm. Unless real changes in family function occurred, problems were likely to deepen. Fortunately, the Winbushes sought consultation, and over the next eighteen months, we worked together primarily on three areas: to shift everyone's focus away from Gordy as the "boy who could not be trusted" and lay open the larger patterns that were hindering all family members; to intervene behaviorally with Gordy and get him back on track at home and in school; to rebalance the family system, bring Harris in, and relieve Diane of all the responsibility for Gordy.

In all fairness to Diane and Harris, whose personal and marital issues had exacerbated Gordy's problems, it should be said up front that Gordy had never been an easy child. As a baby, he was frequently agitated; as a toddler, active and distractible; as a young child, sensitive, demanding, and poor at adapting to change; and as a student, kindergarten through his current eighth-grade year, frequently labeled "uncooperative" and "difficult" by teachers. Attention deficit disorder had been ruled out because he had no difficulty sustaining attention. Throughout his childhood, Gordy had had lots of friends, and had always been demanding about getting together with them because he was so easily bored. Diane spoke the truth when she said that raising Gordy had been difficult: some kids *are* tougher than others to parent because of who they are temperamentally and biologically.[6]

Children like Gordy are called spirited or hard-to-parent because they require better than average behavioral management skills in the parents and a striking amount of creative engineering in the home so that the child still gets the message he's "mostly good" even though his behavior is likely to pull bad reactions out of everyone. Though a hard-to-parent child requires additional patience, foresight, consistency, and follow-through, if parents are able to spend a lot of time with him and set up situations oriented to his strengths (say, interpersonal skills or intuitiveness), he stands a good chance of feeling secure and cherished. Often, whether or not such a child does well is not simply a matter of his temperament but also of his temperament as it interacts with a particular parent's; a good fit can make all the difference. Because Diane was rather intense and exacting, she was not equipped intuitively to understand her son's needs.

By the time I saw the Winbush family, Gordy was going out of his way to keep his "bad boy" label intact. Not only was he lying with great proficiency to teachers and parents alike, he showed little remorse for doing so. Moreover, his situation at school was made more difficult because he had a mild learning disorder (revealed through testing). Though he had a growing interest in computers, he didn't like his teachers; he didn't like school; and he didn't want to be there.

One of the methods of family systems therapy is to identify what we call feedback loops. Understanding how feedback loops work can help everyone avoid the trap of blaming; for example, Gordy's behavior "caused" his parents to fight, or conversely, Gordy's parents' behavior "caused" Gordy to act hatefully. *As conceptualized, in a feedback loop, every action begets a reaction, and the responses mutually reinforce one another to create a cycle that repeats itself over time.*

Problematic feedback loops in the Winbush family were pervasive. One example: Gordy misbehaved, and Diane reacted negatively, which sent the message back to Gordy that he is a bad kid (not just a challenging one). With all his insecurities about his learning problems and how his mother feels about him, he acted even worse, which stimulated greater reactivity and stronger negativity from Diane. Another pattern: Diane was so impassioned about Gordy that Harris took a passive role to keep Gordy from feeling that everyone was against him, but this caused Diane to feel abandoned and solely accountable for Gordy's discipline, so she became hotter and angrier, which distanced Harris even further. Even Ashley played a role: the more upset Diane was with the men in the family, the more sympathetic Ashley felt toward her mom. Ashley tried to compensate for the family hardships on her mom by being a perfect child and by being close to her mother, which caused Gordy to resent his sister and behave meanly toward her. Diane moved to protect Ashley and to show her appreciation to Ashley for her support, which furthered Gordy's belief that his mom loves Ashley and not him.

When families have one child who has a spirited temperament and another with an adaptable temperament, it is easy to fall into the trap of conveying to the spirited one that he is less loved and valued. From a systems point of view, we might say that most family systems simply can't afford two kids acting out at the same time. Almost necessarily, when one child is on the hot seat, the other represses her impulses to act out and basks in the role of the valued "good kid." Despite one child's behavioral havoc and the other child's curbing in of herself, there is a kind of stability at work in such families because the pattern reinforces itself, as the spirited child receives all the negative parental feedback and the good kid receives the positive. The dynamic stays in this uneasy equilibrium — until, that is, the problem child gets better and then, quite often, the roles reverse and the "good" kid lets loose with some necessary and healthy developmental havoc of her own.

Even if a family has several spirited children, the kids often alternate being on the hot seat over the weeks, months, or years, particularly when the family is healthy and flexible enough to address problems as they crop up with each child. To a lesser degree, this kind of rotation happens in families with children of all temperaments, as individual kids go through their developmental transitions and cause various problems for their families. The challenge for parents is to deal deftly with the child who is creating ruffles and still have energy for the other children and their developmental business. If one child stays on the hot seat for an extended time — as was the case with Gordy — it could be a sign that all is not well in the family.

Everything that everyone was doing in the Winbush family was both logical and understandable, but it wasn't working. I often advise parents that a warning sign to get professional help is when they're doing the natural thing, given the situation, but the net result is worsening everyone's behavior. *When families feel "stuck" and in despair, therapists often advise parents, Whatever you're doing as parents to solve the problem, as logical as it may seem to you, don't keep doing the same thing, because it's likely reinforcing the problem.* Imagine how counterintuitive it would be for Diane to lighten up on Gordy, for Harris to become more involved in parenting Gordy, and for Diane to stop protecting Ashley, but these were some of the new directions the family needed to pursue.

No child can tolerate a stream of criticism without reacting. In her effort to correct Gordy's ways, Diane had developed a shotgun-like approach, scattering complaints broadly — his room, friends, his homework, his appearance. Because Diane was not engaging in blatant name-calling or explosive tirades, Gordy was not able to point a finger and say, "Look at how abusive my mother is." Nevertheless, her tone and her steady focus on what was "wrong" with her son expressed her irritation and sense of futility.

A parent who chooses all the battles at once becomes the oppressor. Naturally, the adolescent feels motivated to retaliate against the oppressor, and, in the ensuing negativity cycle, the parent douses the flame of any desire the child might have to improve his situation. Even though trust was Diane's major obsession, it had become just one more criticism to level against Gordy. Trust had almost ceased to have a distinctive meaning in this overall mutually contemptuous situation.

Though Diane had occasionally complimented Gordy, his experience of his interactions with his mother was, as a ratio, one hundred criticisms to one positive aside. In his mind, he was not getting credit for all the good things he was doing. Unfortunately, with things as they were, praise from Diane would have been disingenuous because she wasn't able to see his good side at that time. His parents couldn't hide their higher regard for Ashley. Treating Gordy as a miserable disappointment had validated his worst fears about himself; indeed, Gordy had bought into the portrait painted of him by his parents and teachers. He had a terrible self-image, and kids who feel this way about themselves rarely improve. Angry and resentful of the skewering he had received over the last fourteen years, he now had the gratification of gaining a kind of revenge by acting out. Without Ashley around to provide solace for Diane, she began to suffer even more from the intense warfare with Gordy, which probably contributed to the heating up of the situation and their decision to pursue therapy.

Straightaway, I encouraged Diane to refrain from addressing Gordy's each and every bad habit. *To make progress in a difficult situation, parents need to pick their top issue(s) and focus on concrete behaviors.* If Diane can have success in one area and start some positive feedback loops, other negative behaviors may naturally subside. It's all too easy for any of us to unintentionally send degrading messages to our adolescents. Teenagers read our faces well; they are highly aware of the parental hawkeye and the repertoire of nonverbal admonitions. Prods such as "Have you done your homework yet?" "How long have you been watching TV?" "Would you clean up the family room? It's filled with your stuff" or "When is the last time you washed your hair?" are implied complaints. Not that we should remove these phrases from our vocabulary entirely; it's a matter of the ratio of negative to positive. Parents need to make themselves accountable for communicating in positive ways to their child without being gratuitous or saccharine. Though praising can be tricky, parents need to find where their children are soaring and be genuinely impressed.

Quid Pro Quo: Cutting a Deal with a Recalcitrant Teen

What is often ironic about family predicaments like the Winbushes' is that everyone wants to get to the same place. No clashing objectives, Diane and Harris wanted to be able to trust Gordy to do his homework and behave more respectfully without having to nag him constantly, just as Gordy wanted nothing more than to get his mother off his back. Though setting up a system to monitor Gordy's schoolwork and attendance closely was not going to solve the family's dysfunctional patterns, it would begin to steer his behavior in another direction while therapy ferreted out deeper problems.

Once we established that everyone had the same goal, we cut a deal to get there: Gordy had to complete all schoolwork on time and receive grades of C or better, which would not be easy for him because of his deeply entrenched pattern of slacking off. Diane and Harris had to agree not to hassle Gordy about his schoolwork, which was a particular challenge for Diane, who had agonized over Gordy all these years.

Gordy's parents had plenty of data indicating he needed a tangible framework to hold him accountable for his schoolwork; a merely verbal set of expectations would be inadequate at this point. The Winbushes worked with the school to create a framework to supervise Gordy's school performance, though initially this structure had to be more cumbersome than anyone wanted.

Given Gordy's track record, his parents couldn't trust him to do his schoolwork on his own, but the goal of getting there remained a constant. For two months, Gordy had to collect weekly signatures from his teachers indicating that — as stated above — all his homework was in and his performance was C-level or better. Gordy had to turn the signatures in to Harris, not Diane, an important detail covered in the next section. All of Gordy's weekend privileges and extra computer time were contingent upon his getting the necessary signatures. The point was to create an airtight system and then *not* to talk about it. Diane and Harris needed to tolerate Gordy's anger about this structure and not loosen up until Gordy demonstrated he could be trusted to uphold his end of the deal.

Why would defiant Gordy ever cooperate with this kind of scheme? Kids hate having to get signatures from teachers they don't particularly like. My experience is that they're willing to suffer through it because they know this system also puts their parents on the line. When I introduce this system with families, we spend half the session covering the mechanics of what the adolescent has to do and possible loopholes; if he comes home with classic lame excuses like he can't find a teacher or the dog ate the signatures, he loses privileges automatically. Then we focus the other half of the session on the parents — their slip-ups and negative body language — for they are under contract not to say a word to their child about homework. Equal time and equal pressure on the child and his parents: quid pro quo.

Trust is mutual: Gordy needed to be more trustworthy in his school perform-ance and his parents needed to be more trustworthy in providing an affirmative home environment. The system described here created a path for Gordy to be successful in school, a notion that had been utterly foreign to him. All too aware of his failure in school, he had been avoiding schoolwork — playing Nintendo, chewing up time on the computer, taking lots of naps. He was furious with his parents and depressed about his role as the family screw-up. His thinking was, "What if I really tried in school and still did poorly? I'd never get good grades anyway." Gordy resented his peers and especially his older sister, who seemed to breeze through school. Gordy's learning profile made high achievement difficult, particularly in his traditional school environment. Importantly, Diane and Harris had to acknowledge that for Gordy, C or better indicated success.

Family Restructure: Bringing in Dad and
Excusing Mom from the Frontline

Even though the Winbushes had reduced their negativity and addressed some of Gordy's needs at school, there remained an imbalance in the family system.

Because Diane tried to solve Gordy's problems on her own, she had become the parent in conflict with Gordy. She felt abandoned by Harris, who was underinvolved in parenting. Ashley had become more of a coparent for her mother than a sister to Gordy, and Gordy had become the family black sheep, expressing the dysfunction of the entire family system. Gordy "successfully failed" in enough ways that Diane and Harris became desperate enough to seek help, and once in therapy were persuaded to work together to find a solution.

With the newly introduced structure, Harris could no longer be the drop-out parent because he had to hold Gordy accountable for collecting his teachers' signatures. *Fathers who are overwhelmed by the emotional intensity or demands of their home life will often overwork in order to control what they can control.* In therapy situations, I often hear men say, "Work is what I know how to do. I go home and I can't seem to do anything right." Because they feel ineffective on the emotional front, the only way such men can be "good guys" is to retreat to work. While some men overwork because they can't say no, Harris acknowledged that he viewed work as an escape.

Although the school plan gave Diane the involvement she supposedly wanted from Harris, she was so anxious about achievement and Harris's ability to "stay on top of things" (as she put it), she had a tough time relinquishing control. Therapy focused on ways that Diane could pull back, remove her feet from the fire, and spend some low-key, nonjudgmental time with Gordy, which would serve to balance out the stringency of Gordy's school regimen.

Once Diane and Harris looked eye-to-eye in their parenting, they also had to work out some marital thorns. It had been more comfortable for them to drift apart, but Gordy's problems unveiled this fact: neither Diane nor Harris trusted each other as parents. Often, when fathers deal themselves out of active parenting, the implication is that they are leaving this valuable job to the mother because they trust her in this role. In many situations, however, fathers may not actually support the parenting approach of their spouses, but they don't want to confront the problem directly — either because they don't know what to do, don't trust their own instincts, are avoiding dreaded conflict, or are trying to deny that the spouse's parenting approach may be as damaging as they suspect.

Melding with the cultural tradition of "father knows best" as head of household is the myth that "mother knows best" with regard to parenting. *The reality is that both mothers and fathers have strengths and weaknesses, good and erroneous instincts, and biased assumptions, and this is why two parents working together as a team tends to enrich the system and provide necessary checks and balances.* In many cases, as in the Winbush family, parental differences can precipitate a withdrawal of the father and bring about single parenting by the mother, by default, and one germ of this dynamic is distrust. The chief reason for a father's removed role in the family structure is cultural tradition. Harris also faced the additional challenge of struggling with an egalitarian marriage with a white woman.

Family-of-Origin Issues: Shadows of the Past on Parenting

Often, solutions to relationship problems become clearer by delving into the past. *Family-of-origin issues, as they are commonly called, come into play when we carry unresolved difficulties from the past into present.* Family-of-origin baggage often drives errors in parenting, and those errors, in turn, create problems in a child, which can become more intensely felt during adolescence.

Diane's deep love for her son had come through in a skewed way because she worried obsessively about "the bad egg." Her younger brother had suffered from a learning disorder far more severe than Gordy's. Because it was undiagnosed and because Diane's family was too overwhelmed to stay on top of his needs, her brother failed at school, at work, and in relationships, and ended up destitute on the street. That "seeds can go bad" haunted Diane from day one with Gordy.

In a word, Diane identified Gordy with her brother. Her distrust in Gordy had been fueled by his disruptive behavior in school and on the playground and by all the negative feedback about him from teachers and other parents. Moreover, she worried about his identity problems as a biracial child. Will the world fully accept him? How will he be treated in a larger social context? At one point during therapy, Diane recalled a fourth-grade school conference wherein two teachers took Gordy to task rather ruthlessly for not following directions on a test. Though by this time teachers and parents alike knew of Gordy's learning problems (he probably didn't understand the directions), Diane was nonetheless unable to serve as Gordy's advocate and defend him in the face of the teachers' indictments. Paralyzed by anxiety, Diane panicked, "Oh, no, my son is my brother." Because her education had been her ticket to success, she fretted openly about Gordy not making it into college, while also pointing out how Ashley's efforts were paying off for her.

Another issue in Diane's background harkened back to her mother's smoldering life problems. A '50s mom who wished she could have gone to college, Diane's mother had little outlet for her energy and intelligence. Although she had provided Diane with a relatively secure attachment, other issues had intervened to affect Diane. Her father had died in his early forties from poorly managed diabetes; her mother experienced life chiefly as a series of regrets and losses. While growing up, Diane, hoping to compensate for her mother's unhappiness and disappointments, worked diligently to make her mother proud of her, much as Ashley did now. Diane was a "model child," whose most independent achievement was marrying Harris. Their biracial marriage created a rift in her relationship with her mother, but also helped her spring loose of the midwestern town that might have kept her back.

Diane met Harris in college, where he was an affable, though sometimes angry, athlete whose expansive, confident style appealed to her. Diane was attracted to his African American heritage and his warm family. Marrying Harris provided her with some of the liveliness she lacked. Harris, in turn, was drawn to Diane's poised and studious demeanor. In their child-rearing years, however, their styles started to polarize: Diane's seriousness and diligence distanced Harris, who thought the kids needed some space; Harris's laissez-faire style annoyed Diane, and she multiplied her efforts to address Gordy's deficits. Diane filled in for what she perceived to be Harris's lapses, in the same way she had attempted to compensate for her mother's problems.

Harris grew to deplore Diane's fretting and fussing. From his point of view, her scrutinizing of Gordy was obsessive and "too white." In the matriarchal structure of his family of origin, his mother had governed with a warm, confident hand. To offset what he called during therapy Diane's "worrywartism," he had vacillated between minimizing Gordy's problems and criticizing him for his "laziness." Down deep, Harris was actually just as ashamed of Gordy as Diane was, perhaps even more. As is true for many middle-class African American males, shaming the family is seen as a major violation of code, because a premium is put on maintaining an image of social respectability.[7] Harris had been the highly valued son in his family, pushed to achieve, and he felt pressure to provide materially for his family, in spite of (and maybe because of) Diane's equal earning power. Initially in our therapy, Harris was reluctant to express the pressures he faced related to race and racism, but the exploration paid off because it revealed links to his anger. He and Diane became united in their discussion of feelings multiracial couples have about the perceived ignorance and meanness of those who oppose multiracial marriages.[8]

Though Harris was cool on the surface, his temper frequently got the better of him. Whenever Diane and Harris attempted to discuss Gordy, they invariably disagreed, and before long, Harris would end up "blasting everyone in sight," as Diane put it. Ultimately, she gave up trying to share her concerns with her husband. Harris's health had also been a factor in their marital dynamics. With a history of heart disease in his family, Harris had become increasingly self-absorbed and worried about his physical well-being. Diane feared that Harris would die an early death, as her father had, and as a protective measure, she avoided burdening him with more direct conflict. But, as Harris revealed six months into therapy, he had been far more distressed by their earlier submerged marital difficulties than by the process of restructure, direct discussion, and change.

Many issues emerged gradually during the course of family therapy with Diane, Harris, Gordy, and Ashley (when she came home from college on visits). Ashley spoke of the burdens of being the "perfect" child, her sadness in missing her brother, who had turned against her, and her anger over her parents' ineffectiveness with Gordy. Diane and Harris sorted out their marital issues, determining what they could live with and what had to change. Harris became the permanent link between Gordy and his school routine, while Diane stayed out — as best she could. She made real efforts to be less intense and do fun things with Gordy. Recognizing that Gordy was suffering from poor a self-image, she made herself responsible for containing her anxiety about Gordy.

Harris and Gordy built a stronger father-son bond. Over the summer (while I was still seeing the family in therapy), Gordy worked at his father's office. I had been hesitant about this arrangement, since employment of family members can be risky. But sometimes father does know best; Harris put a coworker in charge of his son, and Gordy flourished. Without the negative cloud of school difficulties over his head, Gordy was able to use his intelligence, motivation, and computer skills, and his parents were encouraged. Sometimes, kids like Gordy, who have solid intellectual capacities but also minor learning disabilities that make school difficult, find that certain job situations can tap into their strengths.

As Diane and Harris opened their eyes and saw Gordy for who he was, they began to appreciate his many good qualities. Harris and Diane concluded that things could be worse. Gordy had not dropped out of school; he was not doing drugs; he was not in detention day after day — though they had been treating him as if he was. Despite the difficulties, Diane and Harris began to trust each other as parents and to trust Gordy to do well enough in school. Once Gordy felt the support of a functioning family system, his behavior took an upswing. Although Gordy's school performance improved, his parents were careful not to up the ante from C's to B's as their goal. Gordy recognized that his parents cared and were making real efforts, and this made all the difference in the fortunate outcome of this case.

Lying, Cheating, Check Forging: Trust Abandoned. Ann, Martin, and Fiona Haas

As troublesome as the situation was with Gordy prior to therapy, the Winbushes were parents who were deeply concerned about their son and who remained committed to each other, in spite of significant marital strife. Though their attempts to deal with Gordy had been misguided, their intentions were honest. Seeking help, they earnestly probed into their backgrounds and motivations and made the necessary changes to keep their family together. The following, highly abbreviated overview of the severely troubled Haas family illustrates the relative health of the Winbush family. The Haas family is included as a point of contrast to families represented in this book that are struggling hard but have not yet abandoned hope, as the Haases basically had.

The major difference between the Winbushes and the Haases involves levels of hostility, rigidity, and chaotic functioning. In the Haas family, there was an insensitivity to each other's suffering and a true withdrawal of love between some of the family members. Unlike the Winbush family's story, this vignette lacks a happy resolve. Utterly miserable together, the Haases could not mobilize for the process of therapy.

From the outset, danger signals were glaring. Central to the Haas family story and to many others where the situation deteriorates to the point of total breakdown, Ann and Martin Haas were in total denial about the extent and seriousness of their long-festering problems. Up until the time fifteen-year-old Fiona entered adolescence, everything had been "just fine," the parents said. It was Fiona's stormy adolescence that had stirred things up in their otherwise "satisfactory" (Martin's word) family. Having ignored the destructive dynamics within the family for nearly two decades, the Haases now lived from crisis to crisis. A fuller history revealed that damaging patterns had evolved over the entire span of Ann and Martin's marriage; fault lines had been forming beneath the surface and an earthquake was imminent.

When Fiona was caught in an act too obvious to overlook — check forging — her parents marched her into my office in a spirit of incrimination, though it was clear from the outset they lacked the resolve to face their problems. Fiona's run-in with the law served only to reinforce Ann's and Martin's unfortunate mantra: we can't trust Fiona. From the parents' point of view, Fiona was the agent of destruction. If only she were trustworthy, the family could revert to its former "happier" state.

At the beginning of the first session, I observed Ann and Martin both launch rather brutally into Fiona, who sat back with a look of utter contempt on her face. The family's present impasse was supposedly all about Fiona's badness and untrustworthiness. Problems her parents listed included lying, drinking, smoking, aggressive/violent tendencies, laziness, promiscuity, skipping school, and stealing. Although Fiona's profile suggested conduct disorder (a persistent pattern of law breaking and disregard for social code), I also suspected depression, but the brevity of therapy did not allow me to pierce through her wall of hostility. When she did speak, Fiona was as sharp-tongued as adolescents get. Her language was so raunchy that even I — who have been fully exposed to teenagers using the F-word — was taken aback.

After some time, Ann began to ease off on her criticism. As she did so, Martin gained velocity, charging full speed ahead, including Ann in his litany of complaints. "Ann is too lax with Fiona. That's the real problem here. She doesn't discipline her properly. She doesn't demand enough respect," he stated with conviction. This telling shift was characteristic of what was happening in the family macrocosmically.

Ann was a very smart, amiable, "people" person. Although confident in many ways, she was extremely self-conscious of her weight, which I gauged to be close to 200 pounds on a five-foot-eight-inch frame. Fiona had inherited her mother's body type. Some years ago, Ann had started her own small retailing business, which had expanded into a national chain. Publicity about Ann's "entrepreneurial spirit" and her success had been extremely positive, and she made a very handsome income. Of northern European descent, Martin was circumspect, slim, an avid runner, and rigid in his beliefs about willpower. He believed his wife had the potential to be slim, if only she would put her mind to it. As for Martin's career, in his position as a midlevel, state government employee, he had basically plateaued. He sought consolation by running track with a vengeance.

I saw Martin, Ann, and Fiona only four times over two months (with four broken appointments due to Fiona's runaways and refusals to attend) before they quit, but the basic dynamic that led to their bottoming out as a family was apparent from the first session. Whenever Fiona did something outrageous, both parents would lambaste her, but as soon as Martin's back was turned, Ann would rush to rescue Fiona. This infuriated Martin, who felt Ann should be harder on her. The relationship between Ann and Fiona was more like two adolescents rather than parent and child. Because they had many personality features in common, they would fight like banshees; then in order to make up, they would escape for larks together — off to the video store or shopping. Ann identified with her daughter's weight problems, felt her pain, and indulged her by supplying her with a room full of things and a closet full of clothes. The family's background was sketchy to me because I spent only a brief time with them, but from comments made, I speculated that there had been earlier insecure attachment patterns given their erratic emotional responses, the level of disconnection from feelings, and the insensitivity pervasive in the family.

Ann functioned as Fiona's lifeline, but the line would snap precipitously. Sometimes her mom would "save" her from her father's stormy tirades; other times she would fail her by siding with Martin. Ann described her predicament this way: "When I side with Fiona, I get bashed by Martin; when I side with my husband, I abandon my child." When I saw them, Ann was in the untenable position of choosing between her child and her husband. Whenever she spoke up for Fiona during a session, she attracted more of Martin's scorn for both of them.

Things had deteriorated to the point that Martin was physically and emotionally abusing his wife and daughter. Their home was a battle zone. The Haas family engaged in mutually coercive actions toward one another, which are typical of families who have children with conduct disorder. In these families, members initiate attacks, retaliate with counterattacks, and keep the attacks going, with more frequent cycles and cycles of longer duration than families without aggressive children. Martin was capable of humiliating, rejecting, and threatening Ann and Fiona with his power. He was disgusted by their appearance, saying, "How can you live with yourselves like that!" But his tyrannical abuse of power also seemed to carry a message. Ann's success in her business and her ultimate choice to support Fiona left Martin feeling powerless.

Polarization: When Differences Become Magnified

To some degree, at some point, and on some topic, all parents experience polarization. Two different people who share over the years the daunting enterprise of coparenting and the process of deciding the right approach to complex anxiety-producing parenting challenges are bound to have contrasting opinions, which produce occasional unresolved conflicts. *In all marriages, there will be issues on which parents agree to disagree, though ideally they will continue to work toward a mutually satisfactory solution. If parents react to each other instead of addressing the conflict, they often move to more extreme positions, causing polarization.* Polarization will be portrayed in vignettes in this book many times and in various forms because it is one of the most common stressors parents experience.

In this tragic scenario, Ann and Martin had become severely polarized. Martin had reacted to his wife's loving, compassionate nature, viewing her as emotionally "sloppy." Whenever Ann rushed to Fiona's rescue, Martin felt as if he had to compensate by being the disciplinary force in the family. Furthermore, he was jealous and threatened by the alliance between Ann and Fiona.

Ann, on the other hand, had failed to appreciate both Martin's emotional vulnerability regarding this alliance and his efforts in their early child-rearing years to contribute the structure necessary to provide limits and consistency for Fiona. Ann sided with her daughter against what she saw as his essential hardness. Over time, Martin became ever more rigid in dealing with Fiona, while Ann became softer and softer, until they were, indeed, at opposite poles.

To have survived as a couple, Ann and Martin — very different people from the start — would have had to learn to work with their dissimilarities and appreciate what the other brought to the marriage, which is often far easier said than done. Instead, they reacted against those differences, judging them as something negative to be controlled rather than to be incorporated into the marital dynamic. As recognizable and classic as this pattern may be, couples become trapped in it time and again.

Instead of facing the problems in her marriage, Ann sought solace in companionship with her daughter, functioning more as a friend than a mother. Ever off to open a new store, Ann was preoccupied with her own life and was insensitive to Martin's discouragement in his job. And Martin was incapable of seeing that he was using his daughter to express his disappointment with his career and marriage. Fiona was a safer target for Martin, emasculated by his wife's success and embittered by his ineffectiveness at work and home, so she became a stand-in for everything he resented about Ann — her joie de vivre, her success, her capacity to love. Rather than deal with his issues with his wife directly, Martin reacted to Fiona. With her cigarettes, her mouthiness, her excessive weight, and her messiness, Fiona attracted all of Martin's voltage, and it reached explosive proportions. As conflicts within the family escalated, Fiona's behavior increasingly reflected the emotional rejection and vile contempt leveled at her by her father and the absence of firm parental support. Fiona was receiving no coherent, consistent parenting to guide her through the challenges of adolescence. So overwhelmed were her parents by their own issues and problems that Fiona had become a neglected child.

More often than not, when patients leave my practice abruptly I remain in the dark about subsequent events in their lives. With this case, however, I was contacted by colleague of mine, who two years later obtained a "release of information" from the Haases. Through the Haases' consent, this colleague and I were able to share patient information. I learned that shortly after the Haases left therapy, Fiona was hospitalized because of a suicide attempt. She ultimately left high school to work in a bead shop. I also learned that Ann had been having an affair for many years. She divorced Martin, who became acutely depressed initially but remarried shortly thereafter.

This account provides an overview of what happens in severely dysfunctional families. Ann and Martin had been convinced that Fiona's "lack of trustworthiness" was their major problem, but the loss of trust was far more pervasive than the parents realized. Early in their marriage, Ann and Martin had begun drifting apart. Thus, the core issue was marital difficulties rather than Fiona's acting out, which was more of a symptom than a cause of the family breakdown. No one in the family could trust anyone else; least of all could Fiona trust her parents. The Haases' story is about trust, but it's about many other things that went wrong in their family over many years. In these situations teenagers can wind up in desperate straits.

No one ever knows for sure why teenagers go awry, but there is always more to it than the simplistic generalizations we hear: "She went bad because she gave in to peer pressure." "She had low self-esteem." When adolescents have the problems of a Gordy or the outcome of a Fiona, it's unlikely to be a fluke. Most adolescent problems have deep roots. To help us understand the interplay of factors that can lead up to a crisis during adolescence, we explore specific characteristics of an adolescent, along with identifiable family patterns, which can often be traced back through the generations. As the stories of Gordy and Fiona demonstrate, when there is a breakdown in trust, numerous causal factors exist — biological, generational, marital, environmental, and ones lodged in years of problematic interactional patterns. The reasons are multifaceted and often observable. If families looking in the mirror see these patterns, I urge them to address their problems. If not, then parents should consider what may seem inconceivable in the '90s: keep up all the hard work and guidance it takes to raise an adolescent, but also trust that your adolescent has it within him or herself to turn out *mostly* fine.

2

Adjusting Control and Freedom

*Goal: Allow your adolescent to become increasingly
independent, while adjusting limits according
to your child's needs.*

A LABEL applied to a family can be
off-putting and inexact; indeed, the fuller stories of Chris and Stella, the
Winbushes, and the Haases reveal more about their family functioning
than is implied in their clinical descriptions of optimal, midrange, and
dysfunctional. Nonetheless, each family has a fairly stable way of operating, which master clinicians and researchers could describe and label if
they observed us for many hours at home, in therapy, or in a lab situation.
We all have highs and lows, days when we feel wonderful as parents and
days when we consider ourselves basket cases as we respond to varying
circumstances. However, on the whole, over a period of time, our behaviors fall within a limited range and assume certain predictable patterns.

Different types of families, for example, tend to handle power, discipline, and control in particular ways. On every parent's list of concerns
during adolescence are preoccupying questions about control versus freedom: How much control should I maintain? When do I loosen up? How
much freedom is too much freedom? When do I pull in? Answers to these
questions hinge on our particular parenting style. In healthy/optimally
functioning families like Chris's, parents maintain their authority, but also
respect their adolescent's need for autonomy. Based on their child's age
and record of competence, such families hold the line on bids for excessive latitude, while also negotiating toward new privileges. Healthy parents
accept that their children will have negative feelings about them when

they refuse freedoms, even if the freedom denied is quite reasonable from the parent's perspective. Although the parents are clearly in control, there is an ongoing give and take with an adolescent, directly mediated and directly communicated.

Midrange families like the Winbushes prior to therapy are more ineffective in their decision making. Such parents are often too rigid and controlling; typically they don't trust their adolescent or understand his need for behavioral independence. Often, couples in midrange families have clashing opinions and experience turmoil in parenting as a team — thus specific questions about control of and freedom for an adolescent become entangled in a larger morass of parental strife. In general, negotiation between parent and child, as well as between parent and parent, is a struggle. In highly dysfunctional families like the Haases, power struggles often prevail. What we are most likely to observe in a dysfunctional family is a chaotic pattern, which vacillates between total neglect and permissiveness, followed by periods of extreme control, rage, and, potentially, abuse.

Many researchers, with varying emphases and different theoretical approaches, have described and categorized families. Among them is W. Robert Beavers, whose continuum of family functioning inspired some of the organization of this book.[1] Vignettes in each chapter, which proceed from stories about families who are functioning optimally to families who are in deeper trouble, bring to life some of the influential processes that determine how our children will proceed through adolescence. The concept of a continuum assumes that families generally operate within a certain range, but that movement along a continuum is possible, as families adapt to change.

For their longitudinal research, Beavers and his colleagues devised a rating scale to describe five different types of families: optimal, adequate, midrange, borderline dysfunctional, and severely dysfunctional. One of the key concepts Beavers references below is boundaries, a term widely used in the mental health field because virtually all of our interactions with others can be interpreted in terms of the kinds of boundaries we have. *In the simplest of terms, boundaries organize how we relate to others. They pertain to the separateness we maintain between self and other, which can range from too open and vulnerable to what others think and feel to too closed off.* Boundaries help us figure out distinctly who we are, what we believe, what we feel, and what our responsibilities are so that we are not overcontrolled by or merged with another's identity, role, beliefs, or feelings.

Healthy boundaries are firm borders but not rigid walls; they allow consideration of others' feelings and feedback so that growth and intimacy can occur. The critical concept of boundaries will be further explained and explored throughout the book.

Beavers's system for categorizing family competence makes these distinctions:

Optimal families: Clear boundaries; flexible but organized family functioning; individual choice and ambivalence respected; warmth, intimacy, humor, optimism

Adequate families: Relatively clear boundaries; negotiating occurs but with pain; ambivalence reluctantly recognized; some periods of warmth and sharing interspersed with control struggles

Midrange families: Relatively clear communication; constant effort at control; loving means controlling; distancing; anger; anxiety or depression; ambivalence handled by repression

Borderline dysfunctional families: Tyrannical control; boundaries fluctuate from poor to rigid; distancing; depression; outbursts of rage

Severely dysfunctional families: Poor boundaries; confused communication; lack of shared attentional focus; chaotic family functioning; despair; lack of empathy; denial of ambivalence

As this model makes clear, parental control is one of the defining features of who we are as parents. Control pertains not only to how closely we supervise our children, but to our use or abuse of power within our family in a global sense. Are we sensitive to our children's need for autonomy? Do we allow and trust their input into the decisions we make about their lives? Do we maintain control of ourselves even when our adolescent is making increased bids for control? Are we comfortable sharing control with a spouse? The further down the competence ladder we move, the more we see just about every parenting strength, including effective control, dwindle.

The following vignettes show three different families adjusting the reins of control and freedom with their adolescents. As is true throughout this book, these stories tie together a particular type of family functioning with frequently associated adolescent behavior, illustrating the impact of how we parent on our children. The first story depicts healthy functioning. The second story is of an adequate to midrange family, and the third is midrange to borderline dysfunctional. The situations in this chapter pertain to the broad workings of control within families, rather than to specific risk-taking behaviors, like sneaking out, drinking, or fast driving, which will be covered in Chapter 7.

Dee Howard came to see me for therapy a handful of times because of some issues she was dealing with at work. A head nurse at a large hospital, she consulted with me over some problems between her and an administrator. Of African American descent, she is the single parent of two daughters. Her husband left the family when the children were young — a significant risk factor for families — but the strength of Dee's relationships with her large extended family helped fill the void.

During consultation, Dee told me about an incident with her daughter, Maya, which I retell below. Within healthy families, parental control can look almost easy because this pattern of functioning tends to engender respect, compliance, and competence in children. When parents in optimal families ask their children to do chores or they explain why they can't permit something, parental control often appears simpler, cleaner, and more effective — especially from an outsider's perspective. Behind this relative ease is a history of ongoing effort, since within even the healthiest of families, children will balk and become angry. Dee shows how deftly a parent can exercise control, in spite of plenty of adolescent resistance.

Skillful Handling of Adolescent Resistance: Dee, Maya, and Aleisha Howard

If the kitchen is the heart of the home, it can also become the setting for heated family discussions. Dee, a single parent of sixteen-year-old Maya and nine-year-old Aleisha, was making dinner one July evening after work, when Maya passed through the kitchen to find out when it would be ready. Only the day before, Maya had returned from overnight camp, where she had been free as a summer's breeze from her family's customary restraints and expectations. These circumstances set the stage for a mother–daughter head-on, which had as its core issue one of the most persistent of parental quandaries: parental control.

Looking up from the salad she was preparing, Dee asked Maya to babysit Saturday night for Aleisha. The request rubbed Maya the wrong way. On the heels of her recent camp experience, she wanted continued fun and independence! Like many basically solid, responsible teenagers, Maya knows how to resist adroitly. Because boisterous rebellion is not her style, she introduced lots of static into the conversation.

"Aleisha is so obnoxious when I sit for her. You have no idea, Mom. She ignores me. I can't get her to go to bed. If she is going to act like this, I don't think I should have to sit for her," said Maya.

Dee maintained a steady tone: "We'll set you two down together for a talk after dinner. Peel the carrots, please."

"But, Mom, it doesn't work," responded Maya, carrots in hand. "Last time I sat, she kept picking up the phone when I was on it and burping and singing. It was gross. None of my other friends has to sit."

"We've been here before, Maya. You need to limit the amount of time you talk on the phone when you sit. Five-minute calls, that's it. But let's back up here, now. This is really beside the point. Move away from the sink so I can drain the noodles. O.K., so we're going to have a talk about what goes on between you and Aleisha after dinner — "

Maya interrupted, "Isn't this Aleisha's night to set the table? You did it for her! That's not fair. She is turning into such a brat. You ask me to babysit, and she gets away with not helping. I can't handle her. Why doesn't Aleisha spend the night with a friend Saturday night?"

The discussion between Dee and Maya teetered; Maya would not commit to babysitting. It was up to Dee, as the parent, to keep matters on track. Having let the conversation digress to other topics (Aleisha's misbehavior, Maya's phone limits while sitting, Aleisha's not setting the table), Dee next made an effort to refocus it by reminding Maya that helping with her sister was one of her family responsibilities. She reiterated her request for Maya to sit Saturday night, but Maya still refused to be pinned down. She announced that she was going out Friday night and had plans to go shopping with a friend on Saturday, so she would be too tired Saturday night. With every passing second, Maya's tone became more impassioned.

"I haven't seen my friends for such a long time, and something might be happening Saturday night that I don't know about. You're not letting me have any social life!" said Maya, slamming the vegetable peeler down on the kitchen counter.

"Tell me about Friday night, Maya. Where are you going and who is going with you? Were you planning on asking to use the car?" The dialogue between mother and daughter drifted further and further from the babysitting request.

"Mom, Anna has the car, and we're going out. I'm sixteen years old. I don't think I need you to help me plan my weekends."

Dee kept it light: "I don't think you need me to do that either. You've been doing a real good job. I know it's important to you to see your friends, and I hope you have a good time doing that Friday night and Saturday during the day. I'm counting on you to fill me in on your plans with your friends when you figure them out. I need that information. I'm also counting on you to save Saturday night for sitting. Let's get this food on the table."

Throwing her head back like a thoroughbred horse, Maya sputtered, "You are so grouchy! I can't wait until I go away to college."

Dee countered the outburst by affirming her daughter's wish: "Well, girl, I'm sure college will be great for you. After all the good experience you've had balancing your responsibilities with your fun, I'm sure you'll be able to handle the freedom of being away from home."

"I'm going to hate every single minute of babysitting!"

Dee refrained from responding to Maya's last little nip, as she called Aleisha to join them for dinner.

The Holy Triad of Parenting

Dee's and Maya's conversation represents a common predicament: Dee needed to impose certain controls over her daughter, and Maya reacted to them, intensifying "smart mouth" and all. Essentially, Dee had two parental missions:

1. to get Maya to agree to do something that encroached on her "freedom," that is, to babysit, and as the conversation thickened (as they invariably do with adolescents);
2. to make clear to her daughter that she needed information about her plans for Friday night, at a time when Maya was not forthcoming. And these she accomplished.

The key to success in a parent-child power struggle is to keep sight of what needs to be controlled in a particular situation versus what doesn't need to be controlled. Freedom and control is a primal parent/adolescent struggle, with parents typically vying for more control and adolescents pushing for more freedom. Once we step back from an argument's radiating heat, we can be amazed to discover how many of our angry encounters with our teenagers are basically a tug of war for control. While in the midst of a skirmish, parents sometimes need to stop and reflect, "What is this argument about? Is it only about washing the dinner dishes? using the car? seeing an R-rated movie? or is there another dynamic being played out here?" Typically, there's an umbrella process, such as a need for more independence, involved, and this larger dynamic is what we want to be conscious of as we choose our parental response. It's like heeding the river's big currents and flow rather than being fooled by surface eddies.

The specific issue under debate is usually less critical than the way in which we manage, or fail to manage, the tug of war. What are we like, as we tell our teenagers, "Yes, you may," or "No, you may not"? Is there destructive muscling of power? Is aggressive shouting a predominant tactic? Any tenacious clinging or sudden caving in on the parent's part? It can help to think of words to describe a parent's manner and attitude in these situations because the process of *how* we struggle with our adolescents is as important as many of the details of our family rules and policies.

As she interacts with Maya, Dee represents not only optimal family functioning, but also a parenting style described by Diana Baumrind as "the authoritative parent."[2] Baumrind was able to establish that certain parenting attributes are associated with successful adolescent adjustment. The three all-important qualities of the authoritative parent are high control, high warmth, and open communication. The qualities are a package, in that each one is necessary for a successful outcome, and together they constitute the holy triad of parenting:

Permissive	Authoritative	Authoritarian
Low Control	High Control	Excessive Control
	High Warmth	Low Warmth
	Open Communication	Low Communication

The Holy Triad of Authoritative Parenting,
Part I: Thoughtful Control

Upon returning home from camp and re-entering the world of parent control, Maya felt oppressed and constrained. Her saucy behavior was backwash from her experience of unfettered freedom from Mom, but, camp or no camp, teenagers often perceive themselves as hemmed-in and react accordingly. As sympathetic as Dee was, she maintained her authority by making sure her daughter fulfilled her family obligation to babysit.

On a continuum, authoritative parents like Dee are located midpoint between permissive parents on one end and authoritarian parents on the other end.

Permissive	Authoritative	Authoritarian
Low control	High control	Excessive control

The authoritative parent exercises control judiciously — to teach, guide, and support — rather than to wield power for the sake of wielding power. As a sixteen-year-old, Maya is still learning to control herself, and she continues to accept some external control from her mother. Clearly, she has been brought up to see the link between being responsible and earning privileges like going to camp, since some part of her feels bound to help, even as she sends up a smoke screen, searching for extenuating reasons why she can't sit: "Aleisha bugs me. . . . I haven't seen my friends. . . . Something might come up."

In contrast to Dee, permissive parents sustain a family structure of low control where pretty much anything goes. Though permissive parents vary in their involvement with their children (some are overly involved and others are disengaged), their key feature is that they don't act hierarchically and responsibly to give their children the structure they need.

Permissiveness and flexibility are not synonymous, though it could be said that permissive parents are exaggeratedly flexible to the point of laxity. Flexibility refers to the positive trait of healthy families who adapt to the changing needs of family members as they grow and to changing circumstances as they arise, such as illness or unemployment. Parents in permissive families can be very accepting and affirming, but under the guise of communication they may explain, defend, and reason so much with their children that firm limits and family policies aren't enforced.

Authoritarian parents, at the opposite pole, are "give/go" parents: "I give the order, you go do it!" Authoritarians are not interested in dialogue, negotiation, or the feelings of the adolescent, and they tend to adhere to a rigid set of standards. Baumrind's studies found that children in both permissive and authoritarian families were significantly less competent when compared to children in authoritative homes. In permissive families, children were found to be less achievement oriented. Boys reared in authoritarian households were hostile and resistive, while girls tended to be dependent and submissive, relative to those in authoritative homes.

As an authoritative parent, Dee had the choice of flexing and taking Maya up on the suggestion that Aleisha spend the night with a friend, or not flexing and insisting that Maya sit for Aleisha. Unswayed by the romance of reunion with her daughter returning from camp, Dee decided to override her daughter's pleas and reinforce the family expectation. Only too easily might Dee have deliberated, "Maya's resistance is causing a hassle and making me weary. Maybe I should let babysitting slide so I don't have to put up with her flack. It's been a long day, and I have to get dinner on the table."

Before deciding to yield to our children's wants, we need to ask, "In whose interest am I acting when I change my mind or plans: my own, because I can no longer tolerate the barrage of negative emotions, or my child's, because there is some larger purpose to be served?" Though she took no enjoyment in her daughter's protest, Dee recognized it was probably not in Maya's best interest to be flexible at this time because the structure of the family — the balance of control and freedom — needed to be reasserted. Otherwise, what would happen the next weekend? Wouldn't Maya push for the same free rein? And wouldn't the battle be even tougher?

Dee's background explains why she was able to keep her wits in the face of her daughter's protest. First of all, Dee knows that, as a single parent, she has no partner to help out with day-to-day domestic tasks. Her nearby extended family generously pitches in, but she still has to be both mother and father for her two children. Dee doesn't want to overburden her daughters, so she guards against asking too much from them in the way of chores. On the other hand, she has noticed, somewhat critically, how few responsibilities her children's friends seem to have. Dee values responsibility; she recalls having taken care of her brothers and sisters and contributing to the household as she grew up. Helping out was not a hardship because it made her feel included in the family and did not significantly interfere with the fun she had growing up. As Dee explained to me, "It's right that Maya helps because I know she also has plenty of time to be with her friends." Though sensitive to her daughter's social needs, Dee responded pragmatically to her daughter's squawking.

At a deeper level, Dee remained relatively unruffled in this situation because she trusts her parenting instincts. As a rule, she delivers her calls confidently because she is raising her children in much the same way she was raised. Her own mother was securely in control and insisted on routine chores, which Dee now sees as positive. In a sense, each of us attended a kind of parenting school, and a very powerful one at that, based on the way we were raised and the experiences we had growing up.

When we become parents, it is very likely we will repeat many of the parenting practices we experienced as children, or if we disagreed with them, we may swing to the other extreme. If we were generally comfortable with the way we were raised, we accept the likeness between past and present, admittedly with some chagrin, modification, and perhaps even resistance on fine points. As with Dee, when we have a workable past to draw on, we usually feel surer in our judgments. It's the parent who wants to be significantly different from her own parents who has it tough because she often lacks the internal navigation system to guide her decisions and judgments.

Dee's authority and control shone through in another important way. She was not in the least apologetic about asking the five questions that are every parent's right to know.

The big five questions are:

- Where are you going?
- Who are you going with?
- How will you get there and back (i.e., who is driving)?
- When will you be home?
- Will you call me if your plans change?

Teenagers are often indignant about these questions, as they do, after all, close in on their thirst for unbridled rein. Nonetheless, they are more likely to cooperate and supply us with answers to these important questions if we are not intrusive or prying with all the small inquiries that lie in-between the big five. As parents, we can tell our adolescents to stand on notice: we expect certain information about their plans and their means of transportation. Then, we have to impose a little self-discipline and refrain from interrogating our teens about other areas of their lives. Since teens will clam up and probably won't answer questions about their friends or their friends' parents anyway, we might as well stick to what is legitimate to know. Remember: teens control their parents by keeping information to themselves.

The Holy Triad,
Part II: High Warmth

Tolerant and affectionate, Dee's warmth radiated throughout the interchange. Importantly, Dee adjusted for her daughter's emotions, cutting her some slack for her imperfect attitude. On a continuum, warm parents are found midpoint between enmeshed parents, whose own emotional life is fused with their child's, and disengaged parents, who have neither empathy for their child's feelings nor a grasp of their developmental needs. In family interaction studies, parental warmth has been identified as a necessary ingredient in the mix of parenting strengths contributing to strong self-esteem and self-confidence in adolescents.[3]

Symbiotic	Warm	Cold
Enmeshed	Appropriately engaged	Disengaged

Because Maya is usually a plucky, resilient child, Dee noted the attitude change and adjusted her own expectations. What could she realistically expect from a teenager in a peevish mood? (We might ask this same question of any family member stressed by work or rebounding from a run-in with a friend or coworker.) Dee sensed that her daughter felt coerced and imposed upon, particularly as Maya reflected nostalgically and, no doubt somewhat inaccurately, about camp freedom. How odd it would be if Maya didn't occasionally balk at sitting for her little sister. Maya's negative attitude directly reflects her proliferating negative feelings, and because Dee has clear boundaries, she is not overly affected by her daughter's mood and behavior. Appropriately empathetic, Dee had enough confidence and self-esteem to stay afloat in the presence of Maya's undertow. She trusted that her relationship with her daughter remains sound and that Maya would calm down and be responsible, as she has in the past. Empathy, confidence, clear boundaries, and trust are what enabled Dee to be warm.

Instead of reacting to Maya's spark of negativity, Dee reached into their relationship and responded to the good part of Maya. Dee knew that even if the "good" Maya was overshadowed by an of-the-moment outburst, it was still there to access.

As parents, we can at any moment draw on positive ways our child has behaved in the past and respond to who we know our child to be rather than to the negative behavior confronting us. Parents who are securely attached to their children and who have a whole history of being responsive and sensitive to them are in a better position to tap into the good than those who've had a rocky relationship. A sound history and inner security provides parents with the former successes and the positive relationship to draw on, if only in their hearts and mind, so that they can face significant adversity in the moment with their adolescent and maintain parental presence.

Faced with Maya's accusations and criticism ("I don't need you to help me plan my weekends"), Dee countered positively, acknowledging her daughter's solid track record: "You've been doing a good job balancing your freedom with your responsibilities. . . . I hope you have a good time." When Maya ranted about wanting to go away to college, Dee maintained a jocular tone, and without missing a beat, affirmed that Maya will be able to handle college. By introducing positive charges, Dee short-circuited a potential negative/negative cycle. Such cycles are often triggered by a knee-jerk negative response to someone else's negativity. And, of critical importance, Dee avoided humiliating her daughter — an ugly but common tactic for seizing the upper hand.

Unlike Dee, many parents lack a history of positive relating with their adolescent to draw on when they're "under fire," and they lose control. In some cases, a fiery temper or a reactive tendency is a cultural variable that works in combination with the larger parenting style of which it is a part. In other cases, loss of control is a significant problem. Obviously there are degrees of anger and upset, since none of us can remain composed all of the time. As unflappable as Dee was under the above circumstances, she, too, loses her "cool" now and then, for it is hard to maintain focus and stay respectful when someone is as provocative and rude as Maya was. As parents, our goals are to be "mostly" authoritative, "mostly" warm, and "mostly" in control.

The Holy Triad,
Part III: Open Communication

Notice how clearly and directly Dee spelled out her expectations of her daughter. "I'm counting on you to fill me in on your plans. . . . I'm counting on you to save Saturday night for sitting." Maya, on the other hand, had an interest in venting her need for freedom and avoiding commitment, so she diverted the conversation to her sister's uncivil phone interruptions. Dee listened and responded to Maya's concerns about her sister's behavior. She neither closed down communication over the sibling issue, nor did she become distracted by it; instead she tabled the conversation until they could deal with it in a more productive and concrete way, presumably after dinner. When matters started to veer off into a discussion about phone limits, Dee caught herself.

As typified by Dee, open communication is the happy medium between unrestrained response to every conversational nuance and communication shutdown. We might imagine the dialogue of parents at either end of these two extremes, one chiding her daughter, "I'm so concerned about your attitude. Why are you acting like this? You're hurting your sister's feelings when you refuse to sit" and the other declaring, "You're babysitting Saturday night, and I don't want to hear another word about it!"

Excessive Communication	Open Communication	Closed Communication
Confused	Clear	Shutdown

Of the many positive ways Dee acted and reacted, the clincher was that she did not take the bait of her daughter's angry assertions. She was not over-controlling, even as she deftly sidestepped and directed the flow of conversation with Maya.

How easily might the conversation between Dee and Maya have escalated had Dee tried to control her daughter's every wayward comment and emotion and tried to bring her around to seeing it her mother's way. Notice how much Dee didn't respond to: Maya deemed her sister a brat and her mother a grouch; she accused Dee of being unfair, of trying to plan her life, and of thwarting her social life. No doubt Dee had to summon her self-control to keep from barking back comments like, "You are being utterly ungrateful. After I paid all that money to send you to camp and now you won't even sit for your sister!" or "Now wait just a minute young lady, you're lucky to have a mother who cares about you, and all you want to do is go away" or "How dare you speak to me like that. This is a very reasonable request." For all of the importance of high communication, we sometimes need to remind ourselves of the opposite — the importance of being silent. Good communication involves knowing what to say and what not to say.

Maya became defiant, if not a little hostile to her mother, but in Dee's judgment she did not cross a critical line. Dee made this call because she knows and understands her daughter. Healthy parents have an innate ability to sense when to press an issue and when to back off. In some other conversation, Dee might have been more controlling of her daughter's disrespectful language, but she recognized that too many other balls were now in the air. Were she to focus on Maya's bad attitude, she might have lost track of what she needed to accomplish in this interchange.

Although Dee was not flexible about babysitting, she flexibly relegated her daughter's wayward emotions to low priority. A parent who would keep after her daughter in this situation is trying to do more than have her daughter sit: she is also trying to coerce her daughter into *wanting* to sit, which may be an impossibility. With a firm psychological boundary to her daughter's animosity in place, Dee could accept her daughter's ambivalence about submitting to a chore she didn't particularly enjoy, just as she also accepted her daughter's ambivalence toward her.

At that particular moment, Maya probably didn't like her mother very much. *This is one of the big secrets of child rearing: sometimes our kids dislike us. During adolescence, it can feel downright loathsome — even in loving families.* Because parents in healthy families realize their children will have moments of soaring appreciation mixed with moments of aversion, they find it best to steady themselves, mobilize their sense of humor, and not expect unadulterated adoration and admiration from their children.

If we've been intentional and conscientious in our parenting, we can be comfortable with their dislike and know that it is temporary and only a part of a mostly loving relationship. Our self-trust has to keep us going during these lapses of rapport with our teenager. Dee let Maya have the last word, in her protest that she was going to hate every minute of babysitting. Maybe she did.

Some Guidelines for Creating Family Policies

Parents of adolescents often seek prescriptions for how much freedom and how much control is appropriate, but, unfortunately, with abstractions like these, there's no pouring them into a vial to measure the ideal dosage. Issues of control and freedom govern a whole range of questions that can crop up during adolescence: What is an acceptable curfew? Is it O.K. to leave my son and his girlfriend alone in the house? At what age can I go out of town overnight and leave my adolescent in charge of herself and the house? Should I let my son use my new car or will it tempt him to drag race? Should I let my middle-school daughter take a ride with a high school boy?

As with different families, so with the nuances of their reactions to these questions; to respond usually requires consideration of the specific family context. Parents often devote enormous amounts of energy searching for the "right" answer to a parental quandary, when — life being a complicated matter — few policies apply universally. We're faced with essay questions, not multiple choice ones. A range of acceptability exists, for we must always think in terms of different kids with different needs and different families with different values. Sometimes, while parents are faltering — perhaps arguing with each other trying to determine the "perfect" policy — the question goes begging and the teenager finds enough of a policy hole to drive a truck through.

The process for determining a family rule usually includes more than one step, depending on the issue at hand. Let's say, for example, you're trying to determine a reasonable curfew for your sixteen-year-old daughter. Perhaps you are the mom, and you feel comfortable with 11:00. Your daughter wants to push it to midnight, and your spouse is leaning toward the later time. Since this is a policy with room for potential negotiation, you might devise a three- or four-step process:

- Do initial groundwork
- Hold a parent "summit" meeting (divorced parents can confer with a former spouse or not; different rules in different households can also work)
- Discuss the issue with the teenager; convey your decision clearly

- Debrief with the other parent, and/or agree to renegotiate with the teenager at a later date.

Although parents want to be efficient in their deliberations, few decisions are as urgent as teenagers make them out to be. It is well within a parent's right to say something like, "I haven't had time to think this through. I'm not ready to answer this question right now, but it's still very much on my mind and I'll have a response by [a set time]."

Some thoughts on the groundwork:

- Interview several parents whose judgment you trust and use it as an opportunity to test out your ideas. The process of discussing your issue with others can help your ideas crystallize. ("I like the fact that family X makes exceptions for big events, but keeps the curfew relatively early for most nights.")

- Try not to make your decisions in a vacuum, but don't be timid about sticking with your values if it is important to you. ("I can see the advantage of offering an elastic curfew, but I'm not sure I'm personally comfortable with that. I know I might be out of line with other parents, but I'm willing to take the time and effort to enforce my values, even though I know my daughter will resist.")

- Gather as much objective information as possible about how your teenager is handling freedoms in other areas of her life — with school, extracurricular activities, family responsibilities — so you have some larger picture of your child's competence and maturity level. What kinds of situations has she mastered? What needs do you see? Is this a time to pull in the reins or let them out?

- Think back on what your parents might have done and make sure you are neither reacting to their errors nor passing along a parenting style you don't want to sustain. ("My parents were always so strict, so . . ." At this point, you could flip either way.)

Once you've done some groundwork, it can be beneficial to hold a parents' summit meeting, as a further check and balance. Together, parents can determine their range and latitude so they can meet with the adolescent as a united front.

Some thoughts on the parent summit meeting:

- As you move toward a decision, keep in mind that policies are about competency, developed progressively. Children wade; they dog paddle; then they swim, learning one stroke at a time. Policies should start in a place that allows for growth. (If you move to midnight at sixteen, where do you go at seventeen?)

- Moreover, teenagers become competent when parents stretch, sometimes uncomfortably so, allowing for trial and error and judgment on the teenager's part. A key parallel process occurs: teenagers learn self-control *only* when parents gradually relinquish control. They learn how to handle their stride without parental reining in at the same, constant monitoring level.

- Should you consent to the issue under negotiation, what is the worst possible consequence this freedom might carry with it? Is it a potentially lethal issue, one involving cars, for example? The more dangerous the freedom, the more cautiously parents should proceed.

- Whenever possible, try to incorporate the teenager's input and preferences into the policy. This initiates a pattern of responsive parenting and reinforces the teen to participate in negotiation. Moreover, it builds a trust that parents can listen.

Some thoughts on discussing the policy with the teenager:

- Run through the process of how you came to your decision with your teenager. Make it clear that you are not being arbitrary and that you've thought matters through. If you're certain your rule is not negotiable at this time, make that clear from the beginning.

- Keep only one ear (not both) open to your adolescent's point of view. Although it is in her best interest to push for the outer limit, which renders her views automatically suspect, she may have a compelling case to make.

- As you consider your daughter's ideas, remember that a parent's comfort zone is not identical to a teenager's. If you as the parent are completely content with the policy, it's probably not going to be all right with your teenager. (Just because you want to go to bed at 11:00, your teenager may not!)

- Don't expect your teenager to be happy about rules she believes to be too strict. Be prepared to handle her indignation. (Only in an unrealistic portrayal would a daughter say, "Mom and Dad, you're right, my Saturday night curfew should be an hour earlier than everyone else's because I might be too fatigued on Sunday to do an adequate job on my homework.")

- Reassure your teenager that if she masters one level, you will be prepared to move to the next level. Think of this as the carrot: if your daughter shows she can handle a small freedom, reward her competency by augmenting privilege. This puts tension on the teenager to be responsible, and tension on the parent to loosen the reins. ("If you come in at 11:15 for six months, and all goes smoothly, we'll stretch to midnight.")

Depending on how the discussion with the teenager went, parents might want to reconvene to talk about what happened or possibly even vent a little. After hearing the adolescent's perspective, parents might want to reflect on whether they need to make any adjustments to the family rule, and if so, when and how. With any policy, there are two points to keep in mind. The first is to realize that, despite protest, teenagers are often relieved to have rules, when they are fair and consistent. In a pinch, they can call upon their parents' authority or a family policy as a face-saving backup. A second consideration is on an opposite note. When teenagers believe their parents' policies are too restrictive, they will find ways to maneuver around them: teenagers seek the lowest denominator of control. If your daughter's curfew is 11:00 and her best friend's is 1:00, she might seek permission to spend the night with that friend — often.

Power Struggles as Lose/Lose Propositions: Patrick, Maureen, and Allen Madigan

Through the public lectures and school workshops I've given, I've become acquainted with many healthy to midrange families, who then come in for short consultations of one or two sessions. A generation ago, most families of these types would never have considered a visit to a psychologist's office for a "tune up" to help their family run smoother, but these visits can be very productive, particularly when a family has a specific issue to address.

Some parents request a tune up but actually need an overhaul. Such were the circumstances under which I met Patrick and Maureen Madigan, who were functioning at best midrange and occasionally at the dysfunctional level. When someone calls for an appointment, I sometimes have to make a judgment call about which family members to include in the consultation session. If an adolescent is exhibiting significant behavioral symptoms like conduct problems, depression, or failing grades, there is a clear need for him to participate in an evaluation of the problem. But if the problem seems to be more of a parenting issue, asking an adolescent to attend a consultation session can raise hackles and defenses and point the finger at him as "a kid with a problem." Based on the information Maureen gave me about her fourteen-year-old son, Allen, and the reasonable issues she was raising, I didn't feel it was necessary to see Allen — the Madigans' only child — along with his parents. The focus of the Madigans' consultation was their disagreement over how to handle family discipline.

A traditional businessman of Irish descent, Patrick was dragged into therapy by Maureen, in the manner of a parent who insists her erring child come before the psychologist. Patrick's reluctance to deal with their parenting differences put Maureen in the role of the conciliatory good guy and Patrick in the role of the stubborn bad guy, which hinted to me that power plays were an element of the family dynamic. Because Maureen worked as a flight attendant, she was often absent from the home, which gave Patrick a good deal of parenting responsibility. It seemed, however, as if these parents were working two separate shifts, with two different operating manuals.

As is customary in a consultation session, I took down some family history and explored relationships within the family. Maureen's chief complaint was that Patrick was domineering. "He has one way of doing things, and that's his way," commented Maureen. "He won't talk about anything. I'd like to be able to see a little more eye-to-eye and work together as parents."

Patrick immediately took the offense: "Every family has their troubles. Families used to be able to deal with their own, but now you get on a

TV talk show and blab your problems to the world. There's too much talk. We've all gone soft. Whatever happened to a good spanking for a kid every now and then."

Maureen wanted to address a family incident that had occurred several weeks prior to consultation. The incident described to me was a classic one, in that most parents do have some experience with adolescent rebellion. Most of us would hope such power struggles be confined to our bad days rather than to have them be our usual operating procedure, as was the case with Patrick.

At age fourteen, Allen was finishing eighth grade, and a friend was throwing an all-day party at a local amusement park. A month before the "graduation bash" from middle school, Allen's parents had made it clear to him that they would split the cost of the entrance and ticket fees and that he would have to earn his portion of the expenses through extra chores. "Sure, O.K.," Allen had said. But as the weeks went by, he wasn't working on the list of chores. Both parents warned him that he was cooking his own goose and was risking missing the event if he didn't earn the needed money.

Two days before the party, matters reached a feverish pitch. Though Maureen and Patrick wanted their son to be able to attend his party, Patrick's motto was, A deal is a deal. Furious, both parents intensified their threats to Allen, but the final crisis occurred between father and son. During the consultation, I asked Patrick to relate the incident.

"I confronted Allen in his room, telling him that his time was almost up, and he had a lot of work to do. I was trying to be firm, let him know I meant business, and basically, get his rear in gear. Like Maureen said, this party was a big deal. So he tells me to get off his back, real flip. I said to him, 'Do you mean to tell me you're gonna miss this party?' Then he comes back with his plan. What the hell fire was he thinking! He's going to borrow the money from a friend. I thought to myself, 'I don't have to take this crap. He's playing a game with me.' I told him that. I told him I saw through his game. He never intended to earn the money. He was making us sweat it out. At that point I'd had it. I said to him, 'I'll teach you to play games. You can forget borrowing the money. You can forget the party. You can get your ass out in the yard and work for nothing!'"

Patrick adjusted his weight and thrust his chest forward. "Well, things got a little physical after that." Patrick had tried to drag Allen out of his room and into the yard, to no avail. Swearing at the top of his lungs,

Patrick had walked away. For the next three days, father and son avoided each other. Allen didn't go to the party, Patrick was proud to say, but he also acknowledged that even two weeks later, tension between them was palpable.

Maureen offered her perspective on the incident, emphasizing how boxed-in her son had been by Patrick's physical coercion. When I asked Patrick if he thought he had gone too far, he agreed that had been the case, but he felt he had to teach his son a tough lesson. "That's it," said Maureen. "This is what happens all the time — power struggles."

Intervention on Power Struggles

In spite of his forceful, blustery ways, Patrick was exasperated by what had happened. As dogmatic as he was in insisting he'd had to follow through, he conceded, "I may have won the battle with my son because he didn't go to the party, but I'm losing the war." Indeed, this was a lose/lose situation. Allen missed out on an important ritual for his middle school graduation, and the parents missed an opportunity to work with their son on responsible behavior. Parental threats increased at the pace of adolescent resistance. Everyone damaged their rapport with one another, and Patrick lost control, dignity, and trust.

Maureen asked me whether parents have any way out of situations like this. And Patrick, too, seemed curious to hear a response. To answer this question, I needed to take a broader view of the issue. *With any problem, think in terms of prevention, early intervention, and tertiary intervention.* A preventative approach is to maintain a constant outlook on the quality of your relationship with your child and his need for a balance between independence and control. Early intervention would be comprised of efforts to alter an approach, if there is evidence that controls are either too excessive or too lax, or the basic parent-child rapport is subverted. Tertiary intervention, the least desirable of the three, means that extraordinary means must be taken to address the problem because it has become well developed through a pattern of excess or deficit.

From the Madigans' self-described history and parenting philosophy, I had reason to believe that Patrick's parenting style was authoritarian — characterized by high control, low warmth, and low communication. How easy it would be to hear only the story of Allen's behavior and think of him as a spoiled, unreasonable child. Parental expectations are important and earning one's way to special privileges is a good thing, so it's tempting to believe that Allen should be pressed harder for compliance and that he should not get away with his defiance. However, if we focus exclusively on a child's defiance, we fail to acknowledge the understandable resistance an adolescent builds up over the years to a highly controlling parental approach.

By applying techniques of prevention, early intervention, and tertiary intervention to the Madigans' problem, we expand the options for building collaborative family relationships. A preventative approach to further power struggles in their household would be a sweeping review of the "Holy Triad." How does this family measure up with warmth? Is there a strong trusting emotional attachment and positive rapport? As this family communicates, is there negotiation, open flow of conversation, and respectful interchange of ideas and feelings? Do we see clear limits, supervision, and authority — the hallmarks of control? Although authority is important in parent-child interactions, the paradox with any power struggle is that without warmth and communication, parental power is rendered compromised, if not null and void. Patrick was overdosing in the domain of authority, and underdosing in warmth and communication.

In my work with the Madigans, we couldn't retrieve the past to prevent the havoc of the eighth-grade party, but we could use information from what had happened to intervene on issues of control versus autonomy in the family. I saw Patrick and Maureen without their son for ten sessions, in which they retooled their parenting style to become more authoritative rather than authoritarian. We discussed the importance of establishing clear expectations about chores and budgets, for example, and of creating and enforcing limits and policies. Efforts on the rapport and communication fronts were major. Because men are best at shared activities, we searched for noncompetitive, low-key things that Patrick and Allen could do together. Certain kinds of one-on-one outings or trips are a vastly underused method of developing positive feelings. It so happened that Patrick was able to take his son along on a business trip during the summer of our consultations, and it went well.

I stressed to Patrick that he shouldn't necessarily expect his son to talk more to him, but that communication was likely to improve if we revamped the playing field vis-à-vis power, so that their interchanges would occur on more level ground. Patrick "talked to" rather than "talked with" Allen. As we reviewed their conversation dynamics, it appeared that Patrick spoke to his son: 1) to deliver an order or direction, 2) to react to something Allen had done wrong, and 3) to lecture him. During the time I met with the Madigans, I asked Patrick to bring to consultation examples of ways he had interacted with his son that were not one of the above three types. People like Patrick who strenuously assert power often do so out of feelings of powerlessness. It was likely that Allen was resisting his father because communication involved intimidation: I'm the big man and you're the little guy. Allen would be less likely to react to his dad if Patrick mollified his approach. I advised Patrick to share something vulnerable about himself with his son. He didn't need to "spill his guts" or "go soft with talk," ideas that repulsed him. A comment about what he was grappling with at work or a remark about his disappointment about the way a game turned out would serve the purpose. The point was for Patrick to connect with his son on a human level. In the long run, Patrick would have more power if he didn't pursue it directly all the time.

As Patrick tended to these goals, Maureen felt a greater spirit of collaboration in their parenting. Together they reworked their overall parenting approach, and Maureen felt more supported in trying to create a comfortable home environment.

Backed into a Corner

When power struggles in a family become evident, early intervention can help prevent a confrontation from escalating. What could Patrick and Maureen have done early on, as they watched Allen drag his feet on the chores to earn money for the party? It would have been best to fend off the situation through a less controlling parenting style. But when we find ourselves in these predicaments, we can admit to our adolescent that something isn't working and that everyone needs to reconsider the terms involved. As the events unfolded in the Madigan family, all of the tension was focused on whether Allen would or would not do the chores, but Patrick and Maureen were active participants in creating the pinnacle of tension. In other words, Allen was backed into a corner, and his parents had helped move him to that spot. In such situations, parents need to admit their own complicity and show some flexibility.

To exercise early intervention, Patrick and Maureen could have set aside their threats and used comments like these: "We see you're not getting the chores done that will get you the cash for the party. Maybe you would like to renegotiate for a different way to earn money because we may have closed in too hastily on the yard chores. We assume you want to go to the party. We know you have the capability to meet goals like this because we see how you plan ahead on your homework [or an extracurricular activity or on some other commitment]. There must be a good reason you're not getting on with these chores, but to tell you the truth, we're baffled. As days go by, we're getting more concerned that you're not going to make the goal. But, it's your dilemma more than ours, so please let us know what you're proposed plan is for earning the money and we'll talk about it."

Parents fulfill a number of important objectives when they use such an approach. To begin with, they hand back the feelings about failing to deliver on the chores to their son, so that they're not the only ones dwelling on it.

The key is for parents to remove themselves from the power struggle. Threats, emotional pleas, or anger intensify resistance, particularly when there has been a pattern of parent coercion and adolescent passive aggression. Parents can convey their sense of the problem calmly and respectfully, with even a hint of deference that perhaps the original plan was not satisfactory and is open for negotiation. An approach like this refocuses parent expectations on the goal of communication. When the singular goal is behavioral compliance, parents only too readily wind up in a power struggle.

Tertiary intervention on a problem like the Madigans' happens down the line once parent and child are engaged in a screaming match. Again, parents need to realize that they were party to entering into that match. At this point, the parent's sole objective is damage control. Because hurtful words could be said and possibilities for physicality abound, parents need to stop the argument, without either final digging words or an exit that implies one-up. It's imperative for parents to call matters to a halt, saying, "We're not getting anywhere with this. . . . We need to cool off and get back to this later," or some such comment that means time out for everyone.

Some children push for autonomy through defiance. Others resist their parents' agenda through passive aggression. Passive-aggressive adolescents drag their feet and become noncooperative; they express their anger and aggression through passive means. *A basically good adolescent who is resisting parental authority, either actively or passively, is likely to be delivering a message to his parents that he does not feel he has adequate autonomy.* In such situations, parents should look at their parenting style and devise ways to balance their approach. Children who feel overpowered often lack legitimate ways of wielding their own power. Our children can't ground us, put us in a time-out, or otherwise punish us, and because they often lack insight into their own anger and the skills to articulate their complicated feelings, they can't explain the problem. Thus they resort to other behaviors.

Such twitches are sometimes simply part of adolescence. In Allen's case, however, his sullen defiance with the chores was an aggressive declaration of independence. He was, in his own way, matching his father's authoritarian power surges. To unlock horns in these situations, parents need to back up, assess, and readjust. In the short time I saw the Madigans, they began to see changes in Allen, and though it was not easy for Patrick to ease up, he felt encouraged as his relationship with his son became more mutually gratifying and less of a struggle.

"No, You May Not! Well, All Right, You Spoiled Child!" Marilyn, Roy, Larry, and John Sedgwick

Two parents with the best of intentions, Marilyn and Roy Sedgwick were struggling with fifteen-year-old Larry. They were concerned that Larry's acting out would spread like a contagious disease to his little brother, John, who was turning ten. In contrast to the midrange functioning of the Madigan family, the Sedgwicks' parenting style was sliding down the continuum toward the dysfunctional and the chaotic: Larry would be allowed free rein to the point of indulgence, then subjected to overt rage and criticism. Their patterns of functioning were more problematic and more deeply embedded than those of the Madigans.

As is often the case, the Sedgwicks were motivated to seek therapy in the wake of a crisis. The straw that broke the camel's back was a one-time drinking incident at their home, which had occurred while Marilyn, Roy, and John were away overnight. After extensive pleading and bargaining on Larry's part, his parents had allowed him to remain in town and spend the night with a friend, but Larry had managed to sneak back into the house, along with his buddies and a bottle of gin, only to be discovered by neighbors.

Larry was clearly a young man bucking for more independence. When I first met him, he wore a disgusted demeanor that read, "I can run my own life." Conflict between Marilyn, a former teacher with a flaring temper, and Roy, an engineer, was out in the open; they either quarreled or avoided each other much of the time. As Marilyn explained it to me, "I realize Roy and I have trouble setting limits, but Larry's hostile, demanding ways are making us miserable. We're tied up in knots over the way he manipulates us."

The Sedgwicks' inability to say no was pervasive. On a regular basis, Larry violated his curfew, but more often than not his parents would cave in and let him go out again the next weekend because of one extenuating excuse or another. He ignored his chores, which were the basis for a generous allowance, but still found ways to finagle money out of his dad. As Roy put it, "No matter how much we do for Larry, or how reasonable we try to be, he's never appeased. He's always pushing for something."

Although the alcohol crisis had driven the family into therapy, they related to me a predicament that was more representative of their day-to-day battles with their son. The following episode reveals the painful breakdown of parent control and authority.

It was 4:30 on Friday afternoon, and Larry wanted new Nikes for a party that evening. He announced to his mom that he *had* to have new shoes; otherwise he would look like a geek. Seizing the upper hand, Larry had contemptuously criticized his mother for having bought the shoes he was wearing in the first place, "You're clueless, Mom. Do you expect me to wear these lame things?"

Larry insisted they go shoe shopping, and initially Marilyn bore up, explaining that it was late in the day and there would be rush hour traffic. She said she needed to get ready because she and Roy were going out that evening. Reacting to his mother's refusal, Larry launched into a tirade, pressuring his mother into making the trip. He attacked his mother's mood ("You're stressed out. Going to the mall is no big deal"), accused her of being unfair ("Look at your closet full of shoes!"), and went after her for being unsupportive ("You never understand. Why can't you help me?").

Inevitably, Marilyn was unable to stand up to Larry's tantrum. But she was fuming. "O.K.! Get in the car," she screamed. Marilyn gunned the car out of the garage and berated Larry for the entire drive, blaming him, labeling him, and guilt-tripping him. The message was, "You're a spoiled, ungrateful child."

In the mall, Marilyn walked at a fast clip ahead of her son. Into the store they went, barely exchanging a word. As sullen as Larry was, he still managed to find the exact shoes he wanted. Marilyn handed over her credit card; the clerk handed over the shoes; and Marilyn glowered, "Are you happy now?"

Mother and son arrived back home only minutes before Marilyn was supposed to leave again for the evening with her husband. An impassioned Marilyn greeted Roy with renewed anger, as she described Larry's outrageous, insistent behavior. "This is Larry's fault! I had to drive through traffic to get these shoes, and now I'm not going to be able to shower before we go out." Though Roy tried to make peace and smooth things over, he, too, became noticeably upset. Larry, all the while, gave both his parents the silent treatment. Her emotions dilating, Marilyn declared she would take the money for the shoes out of Larry's allowance, though he normally didn't pay for his clothing. As Roy gently questioned Marilyn about this decision, Larry made a hasty exit for a friend's house.

What is missing from this story is as telling as what is present: control, warmth, and communication — the holy triad of authoritative parenting — are nowhere to be found. More adept with language than they were at age two, and more physically imposing, teenagers who throw tantrums can dumbfound their parents. Parents I've worked with who have this problem sometimes label these outbursts "terrorism"; they feel they are being held hostage by their child's behavior, as if he is saying "Give me what I want or I'll harass you and withdraw my love."

A close look at what happened between Marilyn and Larry reveals much. Larry longed for new Nikes so he could be cool at the party. When he didn't get what he wanted, he became frustrated, craving those great shoes. In his mind, his mom stood sentry between the shoes and him, so he lashed out at her. Moreover, she often gave in under pressure, so why not throw a fit?

Marilyn was unable to tolerate the hurt of having someone she deeply loves feel such contempt for her. Larry cut deep, and in truth it is very painful when our adolescents display their disrespect for us. Wounded by Larry's animosity, Marilyn capitulated. As I learned during therapy, relenting over the Nikes was merely an extension of the same struggle she had had enforcing time-outs when Larry was a preschooler.

Having caved in to her son's demands, Marilyn resented Larry for wearing her down, so she, in turn, went ballistic. She was furious at Larry *and* at herself for her own lack of mettle. In the midst of their horrible scene, Marilyn felt beside herself with anger, while Larry felt blamed and guilty for having his way. What kind of badge did those shoes become, and what will Larry be reminded of when he wears them? Quiet and unresponsive as he was, Larry took in his mother's contempt for him — with her references to how "spoiled" and "ungrateful" he was — so he responded with his own contempt. Nobody was happy, even though Larry now owned an expensive new pair of shoes.

An essential question remains: why did Marilyn have a pattern of giving in? When I first saw Marilyn in therapy, she described the many books she'd read on parenting. She knew it was important to set limits, to discipline consistently and authoritatively, but again and again, she inevitably folded — on chores, allowance, on any demand — then she would criticize Larry for *her* lack of resolve. Why?

Marilyn's Blurred Boundaries and Patterns of Indulgence

A fundamental problem in the Sedgwick family concerned lack of boundaries between Marilyn and her son. In the vignette of Dee and Maya earlier in this chapter, Dee is described as having clear boundaries because she was neither pulled into the whirlpool of her daughter's hostility nor was she insensitive to her daughter's feelings.

Boundaries demarcate the separation between any two entities, whether they be between self and other in an internalized sense, between the parental unit and offspring, or between family and the outside world. Even in our most intimate relationships, we need to have our own feelings and not be so close that we feel all of someone else's feelings. When our boundaries are clear and healthy we are aware of others, hear their needs and feelings, but we make choices about how we respond, in an effort to balance our needs and theirs, based on our values, the situation, and the type of relationship. Parent-child boundaries are particularly important within families, for it is highly problematic when a parent is more intimate with, seeks support from, and has more needs met in a relationship with her child than with the other parent (or other adult friends in a divorced situation). Likewise, families need to maintain a boundary between their family unit and the world so that outside demands and distractions do not intrude and take excess energy away from the family.

Boundaries organize how we function both internally and externally.

They delineate the emotional distance we maintain with others, dictating how we relate, what we share, what we don't, and how we behave with others. As represented in this diagram from family systems theory, an individual with appropriate boundaries is open and empathetic to others, but is neither absorbed by them (enmeshed) nor closed off (disengaged).

Disengaged	Clear Boundaries	Enmeshed[4]
inappropriately rigid boundaries	normal range	diffuse boundaries

Marilyn had a weak self-other boundary. While arguing with Larry, her boundaries became so blurred that her son's animosity rushed straight into her heart. Enmeshed with her son, the only view she had of herself was through his angry eyes. A firm boundary would have given Marilyn what she needed to resist Larry's rage and deflect his piercing dart that she is a bad mother for not doing what he defines as good ("Buy me shoes"; or at age two, "I want to watch cartoons, now"). As Larry's image of her merged with her self-image, she became incapable of defining herself as a good parent in her own terms.

Parents secure in their role (other descriptions are strong ego, adequate self-esteem) have the internal structure that allows them to tolerate the negative script from their adolescent without capitulating. So terrorized was Marilyn by Larry's script that it became the "truth" of the moment. Only by having a strong self-image and clear boundaries could she have taken control in a conflict situation and created her own script. "My son will get through this rage and disappointment. I am a good parent for teaching him tantrums don't work. He needs to learn that he can have fun at a party without cool shoes. I'm doing what I need to do, even though this is hard."

Marilyn suffered from problems accompanying enmeshment. At the opposite end of the boundary continuum are parents who are disengaged. In contrast to Larry, children in disengaged families are often inadequately supervised and insufficiently controlled. Parents become disengaged when, for example, they are overwhelmed by stressors like poverty, consumed by their lives outside child rearing, or beleaguered by their own personal problems. For any number of reasons, some parents are unable to provide their children with the structure, the nurturing, and the control they need to make the journey through adolescence safely.

Strewn Baggage and Emotional Vulnerability

How did Marilyn come to have weak boundaries? During therapy, we untangled the skein of Marilyn's upbringing. Marilyn had deep dysfunction in her background and a history of insecure attachment with her parents. No matter how many books she read about what she "should" do as a mother, until she understood her family-of-origin problems they would continue to dog her and impair her parenting.

Like many parents who find it impossible to say "no" and mean it, Marilyn grew up in difficult circumstances. Raised in an impoverished family, she was the youngest of seven children, and she often felt very alone. Her father periodically lost his job, and when unemployed, he drank heavily. Depressed and burned out by the heavy demands on her, Marilyn's mother left Marilyn wafting in the winds of emotional neglect.

Overly invested in Larry, Marilyn carried around rigid, unrealistic notions about motherhood and sons. She yearned to be a parent who could love her son without reserve, and she wanted him to feel wholly loved and cherished. She clung to romantic notions about being the perfect mother and giving her son everything she had never had. A perfectionist, she was very involved in the minutiae of control. She lacked the flexibility to tolerate life's ambiguities, to compromise with her fantasies, and to accept that her son would inevitably be unhappy with some of her parental judgments.

Unable to rebound from her history of deprivation and sorrow, Marilyn moved to control everything in sight, as a defense against fears of chaos. To combat her inner turmoil, things had to look good on the outside — the bed had to be made; events had to progress on schedule; all attitudes had to be in check. She greeted the world with a fragile porcelain smile, but family members experienced the cauldron of her disturbed inner world.

Insecurely attached to her parents as a child, Marilyn had become an adult without feelings of security and self-regard. Dee, from the first story in this chapter, had a "parenting school" inside her that not only guided her but made her comfortable with authority and parent-child conflict. Without a road map for her parenting, Marilyn lacked a working model for relating to her child in a responsive, secure way. Thus, Larry, like his mother, had his own history of nonresponsive parenting and insecure attachment. Faced with Larry's anger, demands, and criticism, Marilyn regressed into sibling-like bickering with her son, unable to give him what he developmentally needed. To become independent, Larry needed to be left alone with some of his minor conflicts, so he could learn to self-soothe and manage the challenge of having less-than-perfect shoes, a situation that was representative of daily interactions. Essentially, the Sedgwicks' indulgence of Larry had functioned as a type of neglect because Larry never developed the self-control and boundaries that he needed.

Confronted with Larry's wrath, Marilyn panicked because her internal dialogue said, "Oh, no! How did this happen despite my best intentions to have a loving relationship?" The paradox was that Marilyn ended up with the kind of relationship with her son she most wanted to avoid: in the heat of their mutual anger, all warmth was lost. Marilyn was desperate with the realization that she had recreated her past. Her own childhood neglect had transformed her intense mothering efforts into a veritable war zone.

In their efforts to cope, people sometimes patch together maladaptive solutions. Like so many people with a dysfunctional past, Marilyn's insecurities led her to isolate herself. Maintaining a rigid boundary between herself and the world, she was devoid of close friendships and social support. Had Marilyn connected more with other people, she might have recognized she was not unique in her problems and parenting difficulties.

Dad's Dilemma

Circumstances within the family were exacerbated by the fact that Roy's mild manner and nonreactive style played against Marilyn's internal fragility, rigidity, and passion. Though Roy tended to be a steady, low-key person, he, too, was coping with family-of-origin fallout, related to his father's early death when Roy was seven. After his father died, Roy and his mother moved in with a hot-tempered aunt. Though he was only a young child, Roy assumed the role of conciliator, soothing his mother when she was upset by his aunt's fury. These unsettling circumstances helped him develop a high threshold for being rattled, but he likewise gained a sensitivity to those under attack.

Having watched his aunt criticize his own mother, Roy empathized with his son and identified with his plight in having to tolerate Marilyn's shrill manner. When Marilyn complained about Larry to Roy, instead of sympathizing with his wife, he worried about how Marilyn was treating his son. His impulse was to rescue Larry from Marilyn's wrath, in the same way he had rescued his own mother. Roy's internal dialogue said, "I wish she'd lay off. How can she be so cruel? I can't let my son down in a time of need." These circumstances brought Roy and Larry into a relationship that was closer than the relationship between Roy and Marilyn. *When a parent and a child have joined together in an overt or covert alliance against the other parent, it is called a cross-boundary coalition. Such a relationship violates the boundary that needs to exist between parents and a child.*

Unwittingly, Roy had undermined Marilyn. Though he often agreed with his wife in her presence, behind closed doors, he sided with Larry. Marilyn sensed the coalition between her son and her husband, and resented not having him on her side. Roy would say O.K. to his wife, then O.K. to his son. In actuality, Roy tended to cave in much more easily than Marilyn, which left most of the parenting in her hands.

It worked with allowances and other efforts to impose control as it worked with the shoes. For example: Larry wouldn't do his chores, thereby forfeiting his allowance; Larry would put up a fuss and Marilyn would respond by getting angry but giving him an advance anyway; Larry still wouldn't make good on his chores; Marilyn would chew him out and make empty threats about taking away his money (which by this time, he would already have spent); Roy would feel guilty about the fracas; when Larry needed more money, Roy would give it to him on the side — and, in the end, Marilyn and Roy decided their son was manipulative. Parents often use the label "manipulative" when they have not successfully established control. Attributing the problem to Larry, both parents had externalized the blame, when, clearly, they had reinforced Larry's tantrums by giving in to his demands.

As with most kids who seem spoiled, Larry was not a happy child, and neither was his brother John. Family sessions were silent, sober, and deficient in humor and warmth. No one in the family was able to express positive feelings — only anger, resentment, and remarks about other family members' failings. Larry even criticized his parents for not setting more limits. "The punishment I get later with your yelling and guilt trips is worse than not getting what I want." It's always surprising to parents when they hear an adolescent express a desire for more limits, given many kids' bucking for free rein, but it is not uncommon for children to know what they need and even let parents know, albeit inconsistently.

For parents like Marilyn and Roy, saying no was no simple matter. The debacle over whether to buy Nikes for Larry was symptomatic of deep underlying issues — uncertainty over asserting control and fear that negative responses to parental judgments meant a lack of love. The Sedgwick family impasse was about parental panic, intense feelings dredged up from the past, avoidance and withdrawal, and unrealistic expectations.

To untangle the knots, Marilyn and Roy had a lot of work to do. Through an extensive therapy process, which took longer than two years, both parents grieved as they addressed their difficult childhoods. By leaving their pasts as their pasts, they were able to figure out that Larry's occasional expressions of anguish and disappointment were not signals for them to be sensitive to him in the way their parents had not been. Larry was more likely to be scarred by their indulgence and lack of effective control than by the type of neglect they feared.

Together, Marilyn and Roy worked on when and how to exert control and how to set rules consistently. They developed strategies to hold ground and hang together in the face of Larry's anger and to help him deal with his frustrations. Roy saw that he needed to move out of the rescuer role and become more directly involved in parenting. Roy and Marilyn made more time for each other to nourish their marriage.

Marilyn came to recognize that her desire to be the perfect mother was driving her inability to provide authority. Once she truly accepted that bumps and bruises, uncertainties and imperfections are a normal part of child rearing, she was able to make better parenting judgments. She made it a priority to create warmth in her interactions with Larry, outside his defiant episodes. Marilyn benefited from building more of a life with friends and from becoming less enmeshed in her role as a parent. Importantly, Marilyn realized that she and her son were locked together in a way that hindered Larry from developing his own internal controls.

As the vignettes in this chapter illustrate, there is no one formula for achieving a balance between parental control and adolescent autonomy. Rather, it's a process adjusted to existing family functioning and honed to the individual family's and adolescent's needs. When Maya Howard of the first vignette flaunted her need for independence and refused to babysit for her little sister, her mother walked the fine line between appreciating her daughter's push for freedom and reinforcing expectations for family responsibility. The Madigans' particular challenge was to modify their controlling authoritarian style to include more warmth and communication. His demands frequently indulged, Larry Sedgwick experienced very little opportunity to learn to govern himself, as his parents struggled with bouts of overcontrolling, caving in, and rescuing.

By listening to our adolescents and staying attentive to their behavior and ours, we can acquire a keen sensitivity to which way we need to temper our parenting — exerting more control and guidance or allowing our child to flex his autonomy muscles. Through this process, we move toward the loving, long-range goal for all parents: to help our adolescents become competent individuals, able to work the reins of control and freedom themselves.

3

A Self of One's Own

*Goal: Support and accept your adolescent's
development of a unique, healthy identity.*

M0ST parents have, at the very least,
a nodding appreciation that something vital happens with identity during
adolescence. In our minds, we run an informal inventory, wondering
whether the changes we see in our teenagers are normal, temporary, or
cause for alarm. Sometimes we're baffled. Indeed, identity stirrings during
these years can be a source of misunderstanding, misinterpretation, and
muddling.

A friend of mine told me of an alarming experience that was a classic
instance of a parent overreacting to her daughter's identity shiftings. This
woman's thirteen-year-old daughter had just broken up with her boyfriend. To some extent, the mom was prepared for some type of emotional
repercussion from the loss of this special relationship. Even though "going
out" and "breaking up" are part of a normal learning curve whereby
adolescents come to understand who they are within a relationship, there
can be significant pain for the parent as well as the teenager when romance goes awry.

My empathetic friend was commiserating with her daughter, distressed over having hurt this boy's feelings by calling it quits. She liked him
as a friend, but didn't want the pressure of having a boyfriend. In truth, the
mom was relieved the relationship was over, having been a draining one
for her young, emotionally intense daughter. Tearfully, the daughter anticipated how difficult it would be to see this boy the next day.

"I wish I were Cinderella," she cried. The mom, a bit taken aback, asked the daughter what she meant. "I wish I could just be a character on a page. Cinderella doesn't have to make any decisions. Everything's done for her by someone else. All you do is turn the page, and she ends up happily ever after."

The mom, who had feminist leanings, was disturbed that her daughter would be drawn to Cinderella, for she was not the role model the mom had in mind for her daughter. Moreover, what did it mean that she wanted to be a dimensionless "character on a page"? The responsibilities of having a self seemed very high for this aching thirteen-year-old. Decisions have to be made; opinions have to be formed; stands have to be taken; and people get hurt and hurt others along the way. The mother interpreted her daughter's musings as a wish to relinquish selfhood.

Because her daughter was a confident, resilient kid, the mom let the dust settle on the episode. Concerned nonetheless, she made herself available to her daughter, talking with her about lots of other little things (school, vacation plans, her own work), noticing her daughter's mood, looking for behavioral changes. A couple of days later, when the mom casually checked in on the Cinderella comment, the daughter sent her mother a quizzical, "what-are-you-talking-about" facial expression. Laughingly, she brushed aside her mother's concern, "Oh, yeah, well, you know 'happily ever after' isn't real, Mom."

Though a wish to be Cinderella might be symptomatic of deep depression, this particular girl's fleeting desire to enter into a fairy tale meant only that she is an adolescent. The episode illustrates one of the truisms of teenagers: their reality moves fast. Wait two days, and with most adolescents, the problem that once seemed insurmountable sometimes ceases to exist. Likewise, who they are from day to day can change. Some days parents feel simpatico with the person who is their child, while other days that person seems like a stranger.

Adolescence: The Launching Pad for Space Shuttle Identity

"Identity" is a word we use to comfort ourselves when we've lost count of the number of holes in our adolescent's jeans and ear lobes. While it's a word we toss around a lot, we often underestimate what an incredibly abstract, multidimensional concept it is. Identity includes dimensions internal and external — feelings, ideas, values, ethnicity, personality, spirituality, appearance, jobs, lifestyle. Strong identity people possess a core of self. They know who they are, and they operate according to an internal blueprint that guides their decisions and actions. But, identity also involves a rich, ongoing process. A healthy self is not so much fixed as it is open, evolving, and adapting to life's changes. Throughout our lifetime, we arrive at various critical stages in our identity journeys, and foremost among them is adolescence.

Exploration of identity is the main agenda in adolescents' lives that parents don't have complete access to — nor are we supposed to. More so than parents realize, teenagers are actively redefining and revising their identities.

Although the adolescent years usher in significant changes, an identity starts to evolve from the moment of birth. A child's particular temperament, personality, and biology interact with the nurturing and socializing he receives at home, school, and elsewhere. Thus, what happens with identity during adolescence can be explained by some combination of nature/nurture factors. A booming, high-energy extrovert who has been encouraged by his parents to take risks may run for student-body president one day and sign up for Outward Bound the next, while an adolescent with a quiet, introspective temperament who has had little parental prodding may struggle more internally with the who-am-I question.

During adolescence, the stage is set for rapid propulsion in new identity directions. *The launching pad for identity formation is the point where physical maturation, increased cognitive capacity, and changing social expectations come together to ignite the process.* Adolescents enter puberty, become more critical thinkers, and feel less tied to their parents, and so the journey to become an individual reaches a highly stimulated threshold. These remarkable changes enable the adolescent to move into complex corners of identity. The trip covers vast territory and explores many intricate areas: who they are, what they think and believe, who they agree and disagree with, who their friends are, how they're different from their parents and friends, how they choose to use their time, where they want to go to school, and what they understand about the way the world works.

Such self-analysis and values analysis is the direct product of an adolescent's shift from concrete thinking to formal operations. Concrete thinking hems kids into the literal and the actual, but formal operations opens up the world of abstract and hypothetical thought, prediction, conjecture, interpretation, and higher symbolic logic.

We may think our adolescents are upstairs in their rooms listening to their CD's for hours on end with numb minds. It can certainly seem that way. But not only the music entrances them; they're astonished by their new ability to contemplate endlessly. If A, then B, then maybe C, and maybe D; if I make the eighth-grade basketball team, I'll have it in me to be a high school star, then I'll go to college on a basketball scholarship, and then maybe the NBA! Younger kids have the imagination to pretend they're a ballerina, superman, or the president of the United States, but they're still bound to the concrete; they put on the fur-tail hat and they *are*, magically, Daniel Boone. There's imagination and then there's formal operations, which can really take you places and help you plan and analyze the steps along the way. Though they can't always articulate it, teenagers can get scared by what's happening to their minds.

One way to visualize what it feels like to be an adolescent experiencing all the synapse connections is to consider a warp-speed analogy. As in a sci-fi space movie, they're moving along at the normal speed of light when suddenly with a jolt they're rocketed into warp speed. Accelerating so fast, so far, adolescents travel to lands they've never before known. They can write an incredible literature paper, ace their math final, or come downstairs from their room and announce whole new plans for their life: "I'm dropping piano and scouts and devoting myself exclusively to basketball."

An added implication of formal operations concerns an adolescent's burgeoning ability to compare the real to the possible. Before analytic thinking clicks in, parents are heroic, our flaws detected only during specific moments when we disappoint our young children. The "dethroning" of parents begins during the grade-school years, but adolescents have the powers to critique parents — our inconsistencies, our shortcomings, our deviations from abstract ideals — in more analytic terms. We can come up wanting in whole new ways. "My mother prides herself as a good churchgoing type," thinks one adolescent, "but she gossips about half the congregation." "My dad is always hassling me about homework and chores," thinks another, "but he sits around every night watching TV." Likewise, some adolescents become hypercritical of their own "real" self in contrast to a "possible" better self, which may contribute to plummeting self-esteem. ("If only I had a thinner body, could breeze through my classes, and could get some blue ribbons on the swim team.") As desirable as they are, adolescents' warp-speed thinking and increased cognitive capacity go hand in hand with self-absorption and a more skeptical attitude toward parents.

Identity's Incredible Journey and Its Necessary Detours

Traditionally, psychologists studying identity development have examined adolescents' shifting values around four large areas: sexuality, religion, politics, and vocation. There has also been significant interest in gender differences. Some studies, for example, have suggested that girls tend to have "relational" identities, which means they form ideas about who they are based on their obligations and feelings about their relationships with others.[1]

James Marcia devised an interview format used to study how adolescents' identities change from middle school through college.[2] Researchers have documented adolescents' shifts in values and commitments, observing how young people sift through parental and peer influences in order to arrive at their own unique, integrated set of values by the time they reach adulthood in their twenties. Four stages of identity exploration have been depicted:

Foreclosure: An identity is based on parents' values rather than one's own self-discovered path. Although committed, the identity is not self-chosen.

Identity diffusion: This is a stage of uncertainty, indecision, and lack of direction. It's a kind of limbo, without real struggle or conflict.

Moratorium: This is a period of turmoil, characterized by active questioning, exploring, decision making, and possibly even crisis.

Identity achievement: Only after going through the turmoil of Moratorium can one adopt an achieved self. In this stage, one feels committed. Having deliberated over and explored alternatives, one can then choose among them.

During early childhood, our offspring are pretty much foreclosed little clones of parents; this feels comfortable to us and adds to the reputed quiescence of the grade-school period. Grade-school kids might sometimes be moody and defiant, but they aren't in open and articulate warfare with us about our religious, political, and sexual mores. Middle schoolers are usually in the diffusion phase, shifting toward the trying on of different identities as they move into the moratorium stage, which characterizes high schoolers.

Much of an adolescent's identity journey takes the form of intensely felt, rushing decisions. To appreciate who a person is uniquely, we must trace not only the broad avenues of issues and values, but also the small detours and subtle forks in the road — all the things one has said yes to, considered in part, or declared an outright no to. Although parents are often able to track their adolescent's major life issues and crises, we are frequently unaware of the accumulating little decisions. In these minor forks in the road lie the nitty-gritty of the daily life of an adolescent: Should I go to the school dance or my soccer playoffs (am I a person who does the fun thing or someone who sacrifices an important personal event for the sake of my team)? Should I stand up to someone who is popular? Should I raise my hand and let myself be mouthy in class? Do I care whether my room is messy or not, even though my mother is on my back about it all the time? How should I react when a certain boy/girl looks at me? Do I try out for the school play? Do I want to quit basketball, since I'm mostly warming the bench?

For all the decisions adults make during a day, we would be confounded to take on so many, so rapidly. Although adults make similar judgment calls, we do so within the context of our established blueprint of values, which serves us well in choosing one option over another.

Identity formation is connected to what psychologists call individuation, that is, the process whereby a young person puts some distance between his own ideas and feelings and those of his parents. Adolescents necessarily wrestle with their identities vis-à-vis their parents, which is key to their achievement of a unique, differentiated self. As parents, we'd like to guide (if not control) our adolescents and support them in their angst and indecision. Importantly, privacy is the only way adolescents can be assured that the self they are forging is truly theirs. Sometimes our kids let us in, but not as often as they did when they were younger. Adolescents don't want to expose all of their anxieties to parents, for fear of having their questions ricochet back to them. They're in a fluid state, having jettisoned some of their old ideas but not yet committed to the new. Keeping parents at arm's length on some issues allows adolescents to question our values without too much parental reactivity or scrutiny. It enables a fragile exploration of new values and ideas (through formal operations and fantasy) that may not necessarily be acted on behaviorally. An adolescent's inability to individuate might indicate an underlying problem, for example, enmeshment with the parent. Individuation can also be a struggle for kids with great parents; working up the steam to distance and discover your own identity can be hard when your parents are nice, reasonable, and strong.

Without direct information from our teens confirming how necessary their who-am-I process is to healthy psychological development, we need to cultivate respect for the process of identity formation and be sympathetic to what it entails. It's relatively easy to respect something we can see or something of which we approve. Since we usually lack tangible evidence of our adolescent's identity turmoil, we have to sensitize ourselves to the highly private, mind-boggling work of identity exploration.

Good Parents Lose It Sometimes: Katherine, Rick, and Evan

Increasingly, parents are discovering the value of forming parent support groups through their schools, neighborhoods, or larger communities. On one occasion when I was facilitating such a group, a very telling story came up. This particular group contained a dozen or so well-acquainted moms and dads with seventh graders in the same school. One of the women, named Katherine, arrived at the meeting fuming. As will soon become clear, Katherine is a woman who ordinarily functions optimally, but under the circumstances retold below, her parenting seismograph recorded a significant tremor.

Katherine had come home about 6:00 that evening, groceries in arm, to hear the pounding of nails upstairs. Her thirteen-year-old son Evan had just completed a woodworking course, but why, she had wondered, wasn't he working in the basement? Unpacking the groceries, she had had the rising sensation that nails were coming right through the ceiling. Panicked, she had bounded up the stairs, rushed into Evan's room, and stood aghast at the sight. Using wood stockpiled in the back yard, Evan had built a bed loft with an attached desk underneath by nailing two-by-fours directly into the wall and the hardwood floor. The antique pineapple poster bedstead they had picked out together years before had been dismantled and was leaning against the hallway stairs saying to all, "I'm being turned out to pasture, and a new generation is replacing me."

Horrified, grieved, confused, and furious, Katherine had screamed at

Evan, "How dare you!" From there her tirade had escalated. She had accused him of damaging family property, of being insensitive to her feelings about the antique bed, and of deliberately planning the whole thing while she was away.

Relating her story to the support group, Katherine declared with aggression that turned out to be highly uncharacteristic, "I could have nailed *him* to the wall myself!" But then she added, "I guess I took it all very personally. I kept thinking, 'How could he do this to me?'"

A woman in the group responded, "They know just where to aim their blows. Obviously, you care about your house, so Evan is going to go for just the thing that gets to you. It's like Daniel [her son] practicing golf in our basement, making all those little chinks in the wallboard. He knows it's going to upset me."

Next, a thoughtful woman added, "That's the hard part, I mean, beside the destructiveness of it. You loved that bed because you'd bought it together. Evan's letting you know it's the end of an era." The group went on to reassure Katherine that Evan was still a "pretty conservative kid," and to talk about how kids' rooms are their personal space. During early adolescence, their need to create "territorial markings" and assert their independence becomes clear, as they plaster their walls with posters, throw the childhood toys in the back of the closet, and tack up Keep Out signs on their doors. Katherine explained to the group that she had allowed Evan to put up posters and transform his room in some ways, but this was going too far.

As we delved into the episode, Katherine, still smarting a little, commented that she and her husband, Rick, had had very different reactions to the desk-building project. "Rick actually encouraged this thing. Well, sort of. He and Evan had taken a woodworking class, and I guess they talked in a very general way about a bed as good project. Rick probably didn't imagine Evan was going to go through with it. He and I never knowingly undermine each other. But I had more than enough anger for him too. I guess I let everyone have it, and Rick was defensive and angry right back."

Another member of the group reminded Katherine that "everyone loses it sometimes" and that, on the whole, she wasn't a mother who was overreacting to her child's every move. "Remember just last month you were rhapsodizing about how Evan coming out of the shower with a towel around his waist looked like Michelangelo's David — youthful and vulnerable yet manly at the same time. But, even though so much of this stuff is temporary, it doesn't lessen the sting of watching the antique bed be replaced. It's a roller coaster ride. I can look back on my experience with my older son and see, in hindsight, that it was all pretty safe, but when you're on the roller coaster you can get scared and overreact to the lurch."

Two Perspectives on the Desk Debacle: Katherine's View and Evan's View

From comments made by support group members, I surmised that Katherine was a visually talented woman, who lavished tender care on her home and family. She enjoyed her domesticity, and part of her identity resided therein. From Katherine's point of view, Evan defaced not only his room but her identity as a maker of a warm, appealing family environment. By discarding the antique bed his mother values, Evan delivered a cross attack right between the eyes.

Because adolescents need to figure out how they differ from their parents, they test new ground strategically. In the process, they usually manage to tweak their parents' identities. What looks like a disaster to one family can be entirely acceptable to another. Some parents, whose values are not home and hearth, might laud their child's ingenuity for designing and building a desk and bed. ("No big deal. We can putty over the nail holes when he leaves home.") No one, however, is invulnerable; something that Katherine might accept with relative ease might devastate another parent. In the wake of Evan's identity binge, Katherine was grieving and sad for reasons other than the dismantling of the pineapple poster bed. She also suffered from the loss of the compliant little boy she tucked into the wonderful old bed every night. Her instincts were telling her to conserve the experiences she loves.

Evan, however, had a different spin on his carpentry experiment. Building the bed created a bumper crop of good feelings for him. First of all, he was heavily wrapped up in adaptive identity work. Having just completed a course in woodworking, he now possessed a new identity facet as a guy with a unique skill. Imagine the pleasure with which he eyed his prized creation and thought to himself, "I made this!"

Add to Evan's pleasure the anticipated thrill of showing his friends the bed. "Won't I be cool?" he would think to himself. By crafting a new and different bed, he likewise fashioned a new and different Evan, which became an admission ticket to his peer culture. It's similar with clothes:

you assume the new uniform of value among your peers in order to feel accepted.

Though Evan is a good kid who knows the household rules, he was high on himself. He felt empowered because the bed represented an independent choice; it was not his parents' in any way. An antique bed chosen six years ago with his mother couldn't possibly compete with the thrilling sense of autonomy he felt in making his own bed. His excitement in himself took precedence over considering the impact his behavior might have on others. *Developmentalists call this kind of behavior egocentric; early adolescents (ages twelve to fourteen) are often self-absorbed to the point that they do not separate their own thoughts from those others may have.*

If not an act of commission, like Evan's bed project, adolescents frequently commit acts of omission, like leaving dirty dishes or — the prime example — wet towels around, acts that may appear to be defiant. Many of the mistakes young adolescents make occur because they're wound up in themselves and their own thinking, musing about their science test, their complexion, their friendships, the big game this weekend. Because early adolescents' explorations of their new identities are so pervasive, it's safe to assume many of their passionate forays — making a fort in your prized pear tree, borrowing makeup — are often forms of self-preoccupation rather than flagrant rule breaking. Functionally selfish, they have a dozen items they've moved to higher priority than being a good citizen according to Mom and Dad.

Egocentric behavior peaks at about age thirteen and fourteen, during which time adolescents are preoccupied with their new bodies, thoughts, future fantasies, and daily experiences. At age thirteen, it may never have occurred to Evan that he didn't have permission to build his desk or that his mother would react vehemently. Had Evan been older — fifteen or sixteen — and pulled a similar stunt, he would most likely have proceeded with his project prepared to take the heat, knowing his mom would veto his plan. An older Evan would probably be acting deliberately, if not defiantly, based on his perceptions of his mother's inflexibility. But because Evan is younger, we need to interpret his transgression within the context of the egocentrism of a thirteen-year-old.

Katherine: The Good-Enough Parent

D. W. Winnicott introduced the term "good-enough mothering" into psychoanalytic theory to refer to the deep interplay between mother and child and the inevitable imperfections in the nurturing process. The good-enough mother — as opposed to the ideal or fairy-tale perfect mother — is human; try though she may, she cannot possibly provide her child with unconditional gratification of all of his needs. Sometimes the baby will experience pangs of hunger; sometimes he will feel wet and uncomfortable. And — some good news here — it is out of the parent's imperfections that the child develops a self capable of coping with the demands and frustrations of the external world. The child learns to soothe himself until the next meal, to pick himself up after he falls, and to survive the sting of a teacher's caustic remark on a paper.

How freeing it is to learn that "good enough" is the desired parenting state that enables a child to become more self-reliant! Owning up to imperfection means we can be more secure in our parenting and less anxious about damaging our child when we occasionally fail him, and it means we can say we're sorry when we slip up, without fearing that an apology will besmirch a fantasy identity of "perfect" parent. Proceed with caution, however: we each want to be the very best parent we can be and as intentional as possible in our actions.

Good enough means you're mostly good. Katherine exemplifies the good-enough parent because, even though she had a screaming match with her son, her overall interactional style with him remains healthy and positive. On another day or in another kind of crisis, Katherine (like Stella in chapter one and Dee in chapter two) would be capable of skillfully finessing the situation. Friends at the support group hinted that "losing it" is unusual for her, just as they described Evan as "pretty conservative." Katherine held her tongue when Evan put up acid rock posters; she gave an inch, but he took a mile. What finally prompted her to "lose it" was the way his more extreme transformation of his room occurred — without discussion or negotiation about what would be acceptable.

From a family systems perspective, of even greater concern than Katherine's fit of temper was the fact that Katherine and Rick split over the issue, Rick defending Evan to the hilt and Katherine vilifying both.

Family systems theorists refer to parents as the executive subsystem, which profoundly influences everything else going on in the family. *Professional observation corroborates what we know from common sense: parents in healthy families operate cohesively as a team.* Being part of a parental team does not preclude respectful disagreement or articulation of individual points of view; on the contrary, team players acknowledge the perspectives of others and work toward a mutually satisfying, unified solution. Sometimes, since each parent may have a biased view, converging the views — if the couple can do it — can lead to a better outcome anyway. Katherine commented that she and Rick "never knowingly undermine each other." They may occasionally express minor differences of opinion in front of Evan, but what matters ultimately is whether Rick and Katherine are "good-enough parents," standing together most of the time.

I offered Katherine some ideas that would help clear the air in her home. If possible, she, Rick, and Evan should reconvene to consider what prompted Evan to take a unilateral end-run with his woodworking. Katherine and Rick should decide whether they need to adjust their parenting to accommodate Evan's identity stirrings. A key goal of their interactions would be to encourage Evan to speak up in advance, make his case, and trust his parents to hear the part of him that is passionate about his needs (woodworking this time, something else next time). Katherine and Rick need to put a foot forward to reassure Evan that they will try their best to be open to his proposals, and, if his requests are reasonable, they will be willing to work toward a compromise with him.

Had Rick and Katherine had a chance to review a proposal from Evan to construct a bed (unattached to the hardwood floors), the family could potentially have reached an optimal outcome for all. By staying open — listening, validating, negotiating — Evan would have had the experience of expressing his needs and seeing them dealt with; Rick could have supported his son's woodworking achievement; and Katherine would have had the important nudge she needed to let go of her son a little more.

Their (Normal) Egocentrism and Our (Normal) Frustration with It

From moment to moment when parent-child caucuses are not an option, we have to respond on our feet. What's a parent to do about the unexpected identity binges, the infuriating wet towels, or the fact that she's upstairs in the morning changing clothes three times while you pack her sack lunch so she'll catch her bus? The good news is we don't need to muscle the force of our moral indignation because these behaviors are right in line with normal early adolescence. The bad news remains that these behaviors are the bane of our existence! ("She borrowed my best sweater, claiming she would value it with her life, but at the end of the day I found it crumpled in a corner of her room!")

Frustratingly enough, the standard advice given to parents on this matter is, "It's developmentally normal. This is what adolescents do. He'll grow out of it," which minimizes how parents suffer at the hands of their adolescents' egocentric behavior. Few of us have the patience to wait around until they do grow out of it (usually, by the time they're sixteen, they're more tuned in to others' needs), plus part of our role is to socialize them, that is, to help them be fit for companionship with others and/or help them see beyond their individual wishes and desires and appreciate those of others. Just because an action is normal or understandable does not mean we ignore it.

What matters is the kind of dialogue we have around actions (or nonactions) parents naturally find exasperating. Instead of thrashing around and lecturing, we can keep it precise. "Pick up the towel." Period. "Stop lipping and please come make your lunch." Period. "I'm angry that my best sweater is on the floor in your room. I expect you to pay to have it dry cleaned." We want to keep it simple, clean, and to the point, without recapping all their moves that made our life more difficult this week — even though we could easily do so. And, if we lose it or get nasty only sometimes, it means, like Katherine, we're human after all.

In nonjudgmental terms, we can inform them of the impact of their behavior: "I'm fuming. You forgot to put in the lasagna at 5:00, so we're going to be late for the meeting at 7:00. Think about it." It's a good idea to limit our responses to two lines, three maximum. If we let loose with the twenty-five-line enraged version, we're likely to find ourselves shaming and blaming ("How could you be so thoughtless and inconsiderate? You used to be such a good kid, and now I can't count on you to do anything around here!").

A succinct, focused response keeps the heat on the teenager. When we blast away at our kids, we steal our own thunder and actually undermine our goal of helping them learn the consequences and effects of their behavior on others. What the adolescent will register is how mean and out of control we are. Our message about their behavior gets lost in the mayhem of our griping, and they home in on our behavior instead of theirs.

Developmental psychologists studying adolescent egocentrism believe that peers may be the most powerful force in moving adolescents away from their self-focus. All day long, in countless interactions, teenagers are socializing others and being socialized: "You jerk, you forgot to call me back." "How selfish can you get. Can't you ever be on time?" "Stop hogging the ball." "You were really showing off." "What an obnoxious thing to say." "How immature!" Or, the number one piece of feedback among girls, "All you do is talk about yourself." Challenges like these help adolescents see how they're experienced by others.

Though it can get vicious, some of the comments peers make to one another are worth their weight in gold. In addition to parents, peers are primary socializing agents, promoting the "anti-egocentrism" cause, but we hardly ever credit them. Sometimes we get so distracted by "peer influence" as a negative — especially as we find ourselves competing for time, rapport, and influence — we forget we're not the only member of the socializing team.

The Primal Question: Is It Normal?

When I speak about identity to parent groups, someone invariably poses a question such as, "How do I know whether my daughter's wearing black is normal for her age or a sign that something is wrong?" In other words, When should I worry? Are changing tastes in hair, clothes, and music always harmless? The concerned parent faces a quandary. Garbs of black can mean many things — and we don't have a crystal ball to tell us whether next week she's going to add chains, shave her head, and pierce her nose or switch to forest green sweaters and plaid skirts. How do we separate out the red herrings and the relatively benign detours of identity exploration from changes that are cause for alarm?

Typically, parents confront their adolescent's identity exploration in four areas:

- Tastes, styles, and customs related to appearance, language, and room decor;
- Policy issues resulting in greater freedom and thereby a more autonomous self, such as car, money, phone use, and curfew;
- Low-level, infrequent risk-taking behaviors, like a class cut;
- More questionable risk-taking behaviors, like dicey friendship choices, regular substance use, and poor school performance.

It's important to distinguish among the normal desires adolescents have to participate in the customs of their peer groups; the negotiations necessary for policy arbitration; the decisive behavioral interventions for low-level risk behaviors; and the stringent intervention usually necessary for higher risk behaviors, which signal something more pressing than pure identity exploration.

If we can recognize which behavior is in which arena, we can keep our responses in context. Too often, we are pulled into battle over what's in our visual field. What we're usually debating is our tastes and customs versus theirs, and as any cultural anthropologist will say, we are deeply attached to our particular customs, though they vary widely from culture to culture. But, these are our children (or at least they were), so we struggle when they declare membership in their own new adolescent culture by adopting its ways. If we vehemently jump and tackle every taste, policy, or low-level risk-taking adventure, we run the risk of failing an important parental goal — to support and accept our adolescent's development of a unique and healthy identity.

Recall the story about the blind men who touch single parts of an elephant (the ear, the trunk, the leg) and describe different beasts. The point is to look at the whole elephant before you judge. Aside from the thing that upsets you — like the black clothes — are there troubling behaviors accompanying it? Is she disruptive or inattentive in school, lying or deceiving you, sleeping all day, showing little initiative, hanging out with a group you consider deadbeats, or spending a great deal of unaccounted for time in secret activities? Look at the big picture. How is she "managing" all the things that are going on in her life? *While there is no formula to judge "normalcy" in identity development, it does involve putting on a wide-angle lens to get a view of the child's overall psychosocial adjustment.* Remove yourself from the immediate struggle and find out how your adolescent is functioning in other places, from other people's perspective.

It is often difficult to accept a taste or style that, from an adult's cultural perspective, is outrageous. For the most part, parents should save their "nonnegotiables" for issues that are central to their adolescent's health and safety, but sometimes we feel compelled to exercise a veto. Let's say, for example, your otherwise very "normal" ninth-grade daughter approaches you and asks permission to get a rosebud tattoo on her ankle, and you're dead set against the idea. (Let's also say she's done some research and knows a safe place to undergo this procedure.) If this is a battle you're willing to choose, what's your best strategy? First of all, consider not reacting immediately, especially if she seems determined and you feel panicked. Although some adolescents will accept a direct "absolutely not" and the problem is solved, a forceful negative risks polarization: you say, "No"; she says, "Yes"; you say, "Don't you dare!"; she says, "How are you going to stop me? It's my body." Conversations like this are to be avoided because they'll lock her into a position.

The quick refusal eliminates the option of letting her explore her suggestion mentally, which is exactly what you want her to do. Continue a dialogue about it, help her expand her perspective on what this decision means, and let her ruminate. Perhaps if she mulls it over long enough, the excitement will subside. If her suggestion is outside the peer-acceptability zone, one of her friends may talk her out of it. Nevertheless, make sure your daughter knows where you stand. You can say, "By the way, don't do anything until we can work this out. I'm trying to stay open to your suggestion, but I definitely have a negative reaction."

Much depends on how easily your daughter lets go of her idea and on your rapport with her. She may actually be looking for you to guide her or act as an inhibiting force. ("My mom/dad wouldn't let me get a tattoo!") But, if she continues to press the issue, you'll need to do your own exploring. What's behind your daughter's request? Maybe she needs a change so she can feel unique. Could there be another way to help her achieve this same feeling? Can you compromise? (No tattoo, but O.K. to something else.) The important point is to use your parental power wisely. Even though you feel strongly about her suggestion and you're going to work hard to keep that tattoo off her ankle, take care not to attack her overall competence or her worth as a person.

To a large extent, where parents draw the line depends on our ideologies and identities as parents and our family history. In other words, how we view our adolescent's identity exploration is a function of our own values and our self-image (tolerant, strict, open-minded, idealistic, feminist, conservative, socially conscious, and so on). Our identities — and our hot buttons — often dictate how we will respond to a request to discontinue church attendance, dye hair, date a boy three years older, or take up modeling instead of soccer.

By looking back at our own adolescence, we can gain insight into our biases. Parents who had a wild adolescence tend to either minimize their child's actions ("Hey, I survived driving a car ninety miles per hour stinking drunk!") or overanticipate ("I'm watching out to make sure my kid doesn't do what I did!"). Parents who were as pure as the driven snow sometimes think anything looks bad because they lack the experience to recognize normal experimentation. Or they may be naïve and therefore miss the clues. Ironically, the judgments of parents from dysfunctional families have something in common with parents who grew up squeaky clean. Their notion of "good" is often idealized or too good, so when their child starts talking back they don't know what it means. Those with significant dysfunction in their childhoods may react to benign identity stretches as signs of impending disaster — "like I always feared, like me."

While many parents are concerned about "too much" identity exploration, others worry about "too little," particularly if they have a shy child who seems dependent on the family. What if we have a child who contentedly wears the clothes of our choosing? What about a teenager who isn't kicking up his heels? If a teen isn't aggressive in his identity search, is he stuck in his identity process? Not necessarily. We might label the teen "goody-goody," when he or she may simply have a quieter, more congenial temperament and parents who have gently been encouraging independence.

To determine whether an adolescent is progressing along his identity path in a healthy manner, we look at particular individuals and families. By observing the way parents interact with their child, we notice whether there is flexibility, humor, respect, and openness. We can tell whether parents feel threatened by differences of opinion or whether they're encouraging their child to grow and question.

Emotional Distancing: Am I Losing My Child?

Although others may make light of changes in appearance and behavior as simply part of adolescence, we aren't always able to dismiss our own child's metamorphosis with ease and maintain trust that it's all benign. We worry that we're losing them.

Adolescents necessarily assume some emotional distance (often accompanied by negativity) from their parents. Distancing is a harbinger of a new developmental period that says, "I need to be farther from you, parent, so I can figure out my feelings, identity, and heavy personal stuff." We ask our adolescents to talk to us, but some parts of their journey are too precious and private. Sometimes what is happening to them is so abstract and confusing they're unable to articulate what is going on.

Startling new appearances, more frequent conflict, and distancing can cause parents to worry their child is no longer theirs, even if they have a history of a good relationship with their child. A closer look usually reveals that most children have not cast their parents off. A few decades ago, parents were told to prepare during adolescence for a severing of the relationship, that separation was the prerequisite for healthy identity formation. More recent research, however, demonstrates that children in healthy families stay connected to their parents in many important ways, though it may sometimes look and feel otherwise. In fact, a distinguishing characteristic of truly troubled youth is their lack of attachment to their parents.

Problems with adolescents and privacy crop up at two extremes: when parents are underaccepting of normal distancing or when they're overaccepting of problematic distancing. Giving adolescents some privacy and respecting what they're going through does not mean we should overlook signs of true withdrawal from the family. If your adolescent is in his room all the time, never talks to you, and never joins the family for dinner, there's good reason to be concerned. If your teenager is obviously avoiding you, and you feel extremely removed from his world, consider a consult with a therapist to determine whether there's cause for action.

As adolescents create a unique self, they shift away from pure orientation to their parents. However, the experiences of early upbringing and many basic parental values remain within an adolescent. Sometimes, determining an adolescent's "closeness" to parents versus peers depends on how we pose the question. Daniel Offer and his colleagues conducted two large studies with a random sampling of thousands of adolescents. When asked whose company they prefer, 80 percent of adolescents chose peers over parents. Nonetheless, when asked whose disapproval they most dreaded, 80 percent were more concerned about their parents' disapproval than that of their peers.[3]

Just how much our child needs to distance in order to individuate depends in large part on our individual family's existing mode of operating: how close we've been, in what way, and whether our child perceives that closeness as intrusive. Do we have a relationship that is enmeshed? Or are we disengaged? What kind of boundaries have we maintained? If we've been trespassing too much on their mental and physical space, we're likely to get shut off during adolescence. But the opposite isn't true. Disengaged parents have sent their child so many "go away" messages that the teenager will probably stay detached.

If boundaries between children and parents have been relatively clear, adoles-

cents will know that it is acceptable to have differences of opinion and feel ambivalent about parents, without threatening the basic security of their family relationships. With appropriate boundaries, adolescents and parents can disagree and get angry at one another and realize that there will be no grudges, resentment, or loss of love. Adolescents can speak their minds, explore their own ideas, and figure out who they are without cutting off from parents.

Barring depression, enmeshment, or a family context of parent-child breakdown, adolescents will often come to their parents — but usually on an adolescent's own terms. Even in healthy families with clear boundaries, adolescents may not open up at parents' attempts to knock on the door. We have to enter on their opens. By staying alert, we can catch a fleeting moment when they're less guarded. Perhaps it's a moment in a carpool when we log in and talk freely without an agenda with them, a pause during a commercial while watching one of their TV shows together, or a question they pose while we're in the middle of cooking dinner. The more supportive and relaxed we are when they let us in, the more likely we are to be invited back. While there will be times when we do indeed have to crash into their lives ("You need to do X" or, "We have to talk about X"), intimacy comes when both parties feel open to it.

An Issue with Emma: Unified Parenting When Divorced

Some of the biggest "wars" between parents occur over adolescent identity exploration and policy milestones associated with identity: When can they ride the bus alone? When do they get a car? When can they stay home alone at night or over the weekend? When can they babysit? When can they start going out? Or, as in the next family story, when can Emma get her ears pierced? Bear in mind that this is not just a story about piercing ears, which may seem innocuous to parents struggling with tougher calls. It's about the hard decision one mother faced over an identity issue of real significance to her family.

As difficult as it sometimes is for parents who are married to stick together in their decisions, divorced parents can have a tougher time hanging up their gloves to coparent effectively. To help with the writing of this book, my coauthor and I conducted an informal survey, posing the question: "What is one of the hardest parenting experiences you've faced so far?" Here is the response of Josephine, a divorced mother of three children, her oldest being Emma.

An ongoing challenge is respecting the parenting decisions of and continuing to coparent with an ex-spouse whom I truly dislike. The most dramatic situation to date occurred when Emma, then twelve, asked if she could get her ears pierced the summer before entering seventh grade.

The parental policy, which my ex-husband and I had agreed upon, had been that Emma could get her ears pierced when she started menstruating or turned thirteen, whichever came first. As it turned out, entering seventh grade was going to be a significant transition for Emma. That fall, she would be bused to a new school and would be attending classes with a whole new group of kids. She felt that going to the new school was a rite of passage, which she wanted to celebrate by piercing her ears. I thought that her request was very reasonable and forthright so I said I would talk to her father, Ed.

Ed vehemently disagreed with me. He felt Emma should wait and that I was shaking family values to suggest we yield to Emma's request. Ed could find no way to support a change in the original parent policy. Although it was extremely hard for me to uphold what I felt to be an arbitrary and rigid line, I felt that a unified parenting message was more important than endorsing Emma's desire.

I was in the difficult position of explaining to Emma that her request was a respectable one, that her father and I disagreed in our response, but that it was important to come to a decision her father and I could both live with.

In April of her seventh-grade year, Emma turned thirteen. We made an appointment with a jeweler, and a caravan of well-wishers (two close friends, her younger brother and sister, and I) accompanied her to her ceremonial rite of passage. She chose pretty green stones for her first studs and stood bravely while they were injected through her ear lobes. Her father gave her a pair of sterling earrings to wear when the studs could be removed.

The next month, her first period arrived, and our eldest girl had become a young woman. It amazes me how immediately and absolutely her status was confirmed by those two small green stones twinkling in her ear lobes!

Creating Rituals

There are two important points to make about this incident. First of all, Josephine represents a mom who, rather than dreading adolescence, devised with her child a rite of passage to celebrate an important step into adulthood. Specialists in adolescent health have observed how our culture, unlike many others, lacks obvious, external markers signaling the status transition from childhood to adulthood. The implied threat is that kids may turn to maladaptive behaviors (like alcohol or too much makeup) to initiate themselves. Receiving a driver's license, participating in a school "moving up" ceremony, or reaching drinking age are inadequate rites of passage. Some religions, Judaism for example, have special rituals. To counteract our dearth of cultural ritual, some families, like Josephine's, have created their own rites to acknowledge the crossover in a meaningful way.

Weighing the Price of a Split Decision

The second issue: parental division. For all of its excellent intentions, the timing of the ear piercing rite of passage was creating problems for Emma. Josephine became tuned in to the fact that her daughter was having to wait too long, and she needed a perk to mark the change to a new school. In her heart, this mom could have killed her ex-spouse when he lashed out against her for considering Emma's valid request. Holding his ground, Ed insisted they stick to the bargain: thirteen or her menstrual period. How difficult it is to stand by someone you detest, and how easy it would have been for Josephine to use her intellect to justify an enormous row. Smart people can get bollixed up in a divorce situation out of a desire to go after their ex. It took enormous strength for her to concede her point of view, realizing it was more dangerous to inflame the parenting system than to ask her daughter to wait eight months to pierce her ears. In the end, this difficult decision was her best move.

Polarizing over an adolescent issue is always a risk in conflictual marriages or divorces. Right when an issue (body piercing, quitting honors math, selecting a college) requires expert negotiation skills, the process can break down if parents split. Long-standing and unresolved parenting differences seem to become charged by identity issues that emerge during adolescence. Parents (married or divorced) who are fortunate enough not to possess a pattern of divisiveness, yet still find themselves disagreeing, often resolve the issue by halving the difference: each parent moves to a middle position between the two poles. (Mom says twelve but Dad says fourteen, so they settle on thirteen.) Why not save the energy and spare your child from falling into the chasm that divisiveness creates by going fifty-fifty?

Every parent must make individual decisions about how to resolve an impasse. Sometimes intervention is the answer. Both compromising and the refusal to compromise carry consequences for parents and the family.

Leigh's Identity Challenge: Leanne, Bob, and Leigh Palmer

As parents of adolescents, watching our children grow up and become who they will be, we have to ask ourselves how graciously we might accept a destiny for our son or daughter that we would not choose. Not that parents should acquiesce to all paths their child takes, but what if it looks relatively safe and it looks true to who they are?

The dilemma is compounded when a particular identity makes the child part of a minority group. The road tends to be easier for those who are pretty much like everyone else. Whether a child's uniqueness is being academically gifted in an inflexible classroom, being Jewish on December 25th, or being physically disabled in an ambulatory society, if you don't fall within the norm, you're going to face obstacles of one type or another. Often these differences build character, especially if the parents and child are able to make the most of overcoming obstacles.

For many parents, having a child who is gay or lesbian becomes an extreme test of what parents are capable of accepting and supporting. In our heterosexually biased society, gays and lesbians can fall prey to discrimination, and adolescents who think this might be part of their identity have a heightened awareness of societal prejudices against gays and lesbians. They are truly frightened and confused. Different studies indicate that anywhere from one in ten to one in twenty people are gay or lesbian, which means, if not our own child, odds are high that a friend of our child's may turn out to have this identity. As things currently stand, adolescents who think they might be gay or lesbian always see it as painful news. Understanding the trauma that many of these kids go through can help us react in a more educated, compassionate way.

Leigh's Secret

Depressed and suicidal, sixteen-year-old Leigh came with her parents to the Adolescent Clinic at the University of Washington in Seattle for an evaluation. I have worked for seventeen years as a supervising faculty psychologist in this federally funded multidisciplinary program (one of seven training programs of its type in the country), which brings together psychologists, social workers, nutritionists, nurses, and physicians. Like many families, the Palmers, who lived in a small town, came to the university to get the services they perceived as lacking in their community. The family consisted of a father, Bob Palmer, a lumber mill worker; a mother, Leanne Palmer, a homemaker and part-time grocery store clerk; Leigh, their oldest child; a daughter, age eleven; and a son, age eight. As is customary at our clinic, on her first visit Leigh had a physical exam; she was interviewed individually; and the family was interviewed as a group.

About a year prior to their visit, at age fifteen, Leigh had ingested fifteen to twenty aspirin, and the family turned for help to their community mental health clinic. Expressing the belief that most problems can be solved by clean living, Mr. Palmer was uncomfortable seeking consultation. The Palmers also felt that the therapy they received at their community clinic had been worthless because Leigh had recently attempted suicide again with aspirin.

"Leigh wouldn't open up," Bob Palmer explained irritably. "We weren't getting anywhere." His rigid, controlling tone seemed to cause Leigh discomfort and hamper her ability to speak freely.

Perhaps through therapy already received, the Palmers were aware that ingesting fifteen to twenty aspirin is more of a "call for help" than a true effort to end life. Aspirin overdose is low in lethality, especially compared to guns or hanging. Nonetheless, people who are desperate can make mistakes, so the suicidal message of an aspirin overdose cannot be minimized. My least favorite term for a low-lethality suicide attempt is suicide "gesture" or "attention-getting suicide attempt" because we focus on "attention-getting," that is, manipulation, rather than the message of intolerable pain that the adolescent feels.

Frustrated but very sincere, Leanne Palmer asked, "Why did she have to go and do it again since her cry was heard?" By focusing some of their disappointment on earlier psychological services, the Palmers could be less angry with their daughter for actions that make any parent feel powerless, frightened, and overwhelmed.

When the interdisciplinary medical team huddled after the interviews and examinations, we reached a consensus: Leigh was not clinically depressed, but she was hiding some kind of secret, which warranted further investigation. We asked to see her back for a few sessions.

Coming Out

What Leigh finally disclosed in her fourth individual session was that she felt tormented by a sense that she was gay. ("Gay" is generally reserved to describe males, while "lesbian" is the correct term for females, but adolescent girls often have a more difficult time using the word "lesbian" than they do the word "gay.") Agonizing over this possibility, Leigh said she would rather die than have this suspicion about herself be true.

Most people think of coming out as the process wherein people who already know they are gay or lesbian inform others of their sexual identity. Actually, there are two processes: coming out to one's self, which takes place privately, followed by coming out to others. Both stages are accompanied by severe stress. The first process often occurs during adolescence because the various leaps in cognitive, social, and physical development unleash sexual feelings, thoughts about their implications, and ultimately the consolidation of a sexual identity. Many teenagers who will eventually identify themselves as gays or lesbians spend their whole adolescence trying to prove to themselves and others that they're heterosexual. This may be abetted by heavy use of alcohol or drugs. It's more common for girls who dread they might be lesbian to put their sexuality in a box and hide it, so statistically girls tend to come out later than boys.

Over the next several sessions, Leigh explained that she was constantly preoccupied with thoughts about being gay, what it meant, whether it might change, and how she would deal with it if it turned out to be true. "My parents would die," she lamented. "My life would be over."

One of Leigh's more heart-rending and significant stories concerned an incident with her mother. While Leigh and her mom were cleaning out a closet, her mom remarked they should save certain nice old wooden toys so that they could someday be given to Leigh's own children. Leigh described the split-second wave of remorse washing over her. "It was like an instinct telling me no way. There's nothing I would like more than to have a husband and children, but I just know it's not going to happen."

Eloquently, Leigh related how thoughts of being gay constantly came up — when her parents made remarks about her future ("It's not going to be like they think"), when she watched TV commercials ("Nobody's gay in advertising"), when she talked with her friends ("All of their concerns seem so trivial compared to this"), and when she flirted with boys ("I'm just faking it to prove to everybody and myself that I like guys, but it's such a charade").

When I asked Leigh about her sexual fantasies, she replied sheepishly that she always started a romantic fantasy the "right" way — with a guy — but once she got into it, the partner always turned into a girl. That she could not stay aroused with an image of boy indicated that she had a high probability of being lesbian. Another classic pattern is what I call the "yo-yo" response, swinging from grudging acceptance to denial to despair. Leigh would open up, ask questions about being gay, and want to talk about it. Then she would do an about-face, say something critical of herself, comment on how impossible and intolerable it would be if she were gay, and wish desperately that she were straight. Eventually, she would loop in another direction, grimly declaring, "I'm never going to be straight."

A couple of months later, Leigh still described being miserable most of the time, but her intense feelings of despair had lifted once she began talking about her real concerns in counseling. More and more, as Leigh meandered around the issue of her sexual identity, she repeated a phrase that calmed her as she began anticipating challenges ahead: "It just is."

Is Leigh Lesbian? Coping with the Question

Over the years of running an adolescent clinic, we've developed an approach we've found most helpful for kids who are questioning the nature of their sexual identity. Our clinic, like others across the country that specialize in adolescent health, recognizes that the paramount goal is to keep these adolescents as safe and healthy as possible. They need reassurance of a positive outcome, a secure environment to explore their feelings, and a process for examining their identity that keeps unmanageable pain and hopelessness at bay. We encourage adolescents to stay in the questioning mode as long as they need to in order to reduce their panic and chances of impulsive actions or suicide.

In many ways, Leigh was typical of adolescents going through the difficult process of coming to terms with a lesbian sexual identity.

- She was depressed and, in fact, suicidal at the idea of being lesbian. Statistically, 30 percent to 50 percent of gays acknowledge suicidal thoughts and/or behavior during their initial period of coming out to themselves.[4]
- She loathed the possibility of being lesbian, while neither having any information about being gay/lesbian nor knowing any gay/lesbian person.
- She was convinced her parents would reject her for life.
- She felt that if she were lesbian, it would automatically rule out the possibility of being a well-adjusted individual with a career, relationships, children, and a fulfilling life.
- She had sensed these feelings about herself for years before the realization of their staying power pushed her to acute despair.

During their sexual awakening, 25 to 33 percent of adolescents (the higher range is for boys) have feelings of arousal or some type of sexual contact with a member of the same sex. For adolescents who are heterosexual, these experiences are fleeting and do not usually cause significant distress. When an adolescent expresses fears about being gay or lesbian to an adult or a doctor, a common reassurance is, "A lot of kids pass through this phase." This is entirely true of some adolescents: many heterosexuals explore their sexual identity with members of the same sex. Because identity is a self-discovery process, it is not judicious to make predictions or label the adolescent. We have observed, however, that adolescents who experience extreme stress and pervasive and enduring preoccupation with the issue most often do turn out to be gay/lesbian.

To provide a safety net of psychological support for adolescents as they ponder their sexual identities, counselors at our clinic emphasize these points:

1. These feelings are nobody's fault or choice.

2. To the question, "Why did this happen to me?" we let them know that there is no consensus among researchers about the factors that determine whether someone will be primarily gay, heterosexual, or bisexual. It is widely believed that we are each born with the capacity for all three response patterns. Somehow, probably the result of a

combination of genetic, hormonal, cultural, and environmental variables, we end up with the emotional, behavioral, and sexual responses that determine our sexual identity.

3. Therapy cannot change one's sexual orientation; in fact, efforts to do so are not only ineffective, they're also destructive and unethical.[5]

4. Parents, even the best-intentioned, least-homophobic ones, will need to go through their own grieving process. They need to seek information and find ways to support themselves. Parental support and acceptance of a child's sexual preference is a critical variable in whether the child makes a positive adjustment.

5. Adolescents with concerns about being gay or lesbian can benefit from a support group. Most importantly, they should not have to go through this process alone.

6. Gay or lesbian teens should not rush the process of coming out to others. Because of the discrimination in our culture, they can be victims of abuse at home or at school.

7. Gay or lesbian teens do not need to "act" on their sexual feelings, especially if they are disturbed by them; nevertheless, discussions about sexual experimentation should include safe sex information and the option of abstinence.

8. Adolescents with questions about their sexual identities need to find ways to continue exploring their whole identity, putting their energies into areas that can help them still feel competent, in control, and optimistic about their future.

9. Often, anxiety and depression can lead to alcohol or drug use, in an effort to numb or block out upsetting feelings. Coping and stress management techniques are important to learn.

What Happened to Leigh?

Leigh was an adolescent who responded positively to the approach described above. She was comforted by the idea that she could explore and address her concerns about her sexual identity without "doing anything about it" or without "deciding anything final." Once she saw that there was more to her identity than just sexual preference, she was able to think about other aspects of her who-am-I process and engage herself more fully in her whole life as an adolescent. She dedicated herself to girls' basketball and to her classwork, and began to see some of the fruits of her striving.

After her first crush on a girl fizzled, she put earnest effort into a relationship with a boy, but the relationship failed miserably. Two years after therapy had begun, Leigh went off to college, having determined that her sexual identity was lesbian. She had moved from being a suicidal sixteen-year-old to becoming a well-adjusted young woman ready to meet the challenges of her identity issues with courage, tenacity, and maturity.

And what about her parents? Six months into therapy, Leigh decided she wanted her parents to know about her feelings. She said, "I can't stand the deception anymore." The Palmers responded with shock, disbelief, resistance, grief, and shame. They went through a common phase called bargaining, asking "Isn't this a choice she has made?" "Can't we do something about it?"

By the time Leigh departed for college, they were resigned but not fully accepting of her identity as lesbian. They began to read on the topic and hinted they might attend a PFLAG (Parents and Friends of Lesbians and Gays) meeting.

Not every adolescent is as traumatized as Leigh was while coming out to herself, and not all parents take as long as the Palmers did to make peace with it. The Palmers' lack of education about gay and lesbian issues, their rigid attitudes, and their cultural/rural background fueled negative notions. It made their adjustment and their ability to support their daughter more difficult, just as it exacerbated Leigh's struggles with her lesbianism.

What I've related of Leigh and her parents is the mere beginning of a story about being gay or lesbian. Once one accepts a gay or lesbian sexual identity, many struggles lie ahead, not the least of which is coming out to one's peers and relatives. And then there's the difficult parallel process of parental grieving over a new, unexpected minority identity for their child, which should be handled independent of what's happening with the child. Even in the most informed of families, concerns abound. Parents who have or will have direct experience with a gay or lesbian child would do best to immerse themselves in some of the excellent resources on these topics, which will enable them to get on with the task of supporting their child for who he is.

Regardless of a child's sexual orientation, what all parents might take away from Leigh's story is how intensely parents and child alike struggled with an identity everyone was initially loath to acknowledge. In its broadest sense, this vignette is about accepting a child for who he authentically is. A great deal of our protest against an uncomfortable aspect of our child's identity ties back into our own egoism. We can't quite bring ourselves to believe this is happening to our child. When the self emerging is true to who our child is, then we need to come to terms with this reality. Our acceptance is critical: children who have supportive parents are better able to accept themselves, which can head off a lifetime of internal strife.

What Looks Good May Not Actually Be That Good: The Randolph Family

The distinct message I received from Adam and Claire Randolph during the family's first therapy session was that they were highly uncomfortable with their son's problem and hoped I could "fix it." The Randolph's only child, eighteen-year-old Chip, had been fainting without apparent cause. These syncopal episodes, as they're called, had occurred predominately during track practice. Prior to this spring — it was April when I became involved — Chip had never had so much as a single dizzy spell, let alone fainting spells. His health had been perfect. When a comprehensive medical workup revealed no physical explanation, the episodes were diagnosed as stress related and psychosomatic, and Chip's case was referred to me. Technically, "psychosomatic" indicates that a symptom is caused by an interaction of physiological and psychological factors. Many people, however, take this diagnosis very personally — some see it as an insult — because they believe it means the problem is in their head, when in fact the illness is very real.

Chip's parents were proud of him; he had achieved top marks in school, had excelled in soccer, basketball, and track, was popular and well liked among his peers, and would next fall attend his father's alma mater. Though on the surface everything in the family appeared to be fine, there were nonetheless significant problems. Because the parents maintained a high degree of control and put much energy into maintaining the status quo, the family functioned in the midrange and was on its way to dysfunction.

The Randolph family was well regarded in their community, Claire as an exemplary volunteer and Adam as a skilled litigator and partner in one of the city's largest law firms. When I first saw them, Adam was sixty, Claire was forty-eight, and they had been contentedly married for twenty-three years.

There was a lot of guardedness during the first few visits, with everyone, including Chip, describing how baffled he/she was over the fainting. "For heaven's sake, what could Chip possibly be stressed about, with college acceptance behind him?" asserted Adam, his brow furrowed and his jaw clenched. "The world is his oyster. He can drift through the rest of the school year, knowing he's headed off to one of the best schools in the country next year." I could tell Adam was feeling very ill at ease and that this referral threatened his personal pride in his family identity. When I intimated as much and explained the complexity of the psyche-soma (mind-body) connection among high-powered individuals, Adam loosened up a little and showed some of his more amiable side.

Chip appeared to be as dumbfounded as his parents, asserting that there were really no major stresses in his life. His rigid body language and constricted tone of voice pled otherwise. When I pressed a little further about expectations for next fall, Chip made some blurry statements about graduating, leaving everyone behind, starting a new chapter at college.

Although patients often have a difficult time identifying the stressors contributing to psychosomatic illness, experienced clinicians are less mystified. Sometimes people are so habituated to their own stresses and to repressing them, they are not so much withholding information as they are honestly reporting that they don't feel the pressures in their lives as pressures.

After the family interview, I saw Chip for several individual sessions, which initially focused on stress management and relaxation techniques. Stress management is a logical, first step intervention for people suffering from anxiety, but in Chip's case I viewed it more as a temporary aid than a cure. I scheduled a couple more family sessions, surmising that the tense, perfectionistic family environment was integral to Chip's symptoms. Sure enough, Claire was the first to express a different view of their family life, acknowledging that perhaps there was some additional tension in the house because of Adam's problem at work. Because his partners had voted to restructure the firm's pension pool, Adam's retirement benefits would be far less than what he had been anticipating. Mentioning strife at work raised Adam's hackles, though he fought valiantly to disclaim any problem:

"Yes, it has been an issue. But that's my affair, and I'll figure it out by myself. It certainly doesn't involve Chip."

Wearing Blinders to Avoid Seeing Differences

Psychologically naive, Adam vigorously denied the impact of a significant financial setback on him and his family. To be sure, Adam's upset was not "causing" Chip's fainting; rather, Adam was out of touch with his own major psychological issues. Observing Adam brush off an obviously painful situation as if it were a crumb on his sleeve, I realized it was very likely others in the family, who collaborated in this family norm, operated like him — without much astuteness or consciousness of their inner lives. Everyone's hands had been fast on the wheel, pursuing a narrow course, never allowing questions about direction or potential differences among family members to divert them.

Neither Chip nor his parents had been cognizant of the pressures on Chip, for denial had become a way of life. In therapy sessions (without parents), Chip very inhibitedly, slowly but surely, started talking about his misgivings about his direction. The competition in high school had troubled him, and he dreaded the thought of four intense years at a prestigious school, everyone checking out each other's grades, jockeying to get into a professional school from there. An easygoing and gentle person, he wasn't sure what he wanted to do, but he was terrified of disappointing his parents, especially now that his father was so distressed about work.

As we probed further, Chip realized he could not recall one time when he directly took on his parents, disagreeing with them about values, politics, social opinions. He thought of his parents as a unit and earnestly maintained, "Mom has lots of power in the family because Dad is gone so much. She controls everything in the house — well, almost. Dad does have to O.K. most of the purchases."

Until now, matters had gone smoothly for Chip. "I always felt that my parents' choices were my choices." But now, it just "felt wrong" to be heading off to Dad's school. And, come to think of it, he had had some tinges of regret the last few winters because he would have rather tried out for the school play instead of basketball. Basketball had been his dad's big sport, so drama wasn't really an option. And he hadn't really liked running for class office. Then there was the time that all his friends shaved their heads, but he hadn't dared because he knew his parents would "freak out." Chip wasn't exactly sure what he felt — maybe it had been O.K. — but then again, if all things were equal and his parents were in Siberia, he probably would have done some things differently. When I asked Chip what he thought would have happened if he had confessed some of his differences of opinion to his parents, he literally could not respond. He just shook his head. "No way," he said.

Chip's Foreclosure

A main cause of Chip's problem was family rigidity and control. Although Chip referred to his father as the family member who set the family standard, it was clear that Claire also endorsed the pursuit of excellence. Family closeness was equated with looking, acting, and thinking identically. From very early childhood, Chip was subjected to a larger-than-life father who brooked no opposition and a mother who enjoyed this pedestal by proxy. Although Claire was a different person, she had by association taken on many of Adam's qualities in Chip's eyes. Because he never felt safe to question, disagree, or set his own course, mild-mannered Chip made the necessary mental accommodations to his mother and father. So sensitive was he to disappointing his parents that he ultimately adopted his parents' every hope, wish, or desire.

Depending on their temperament, children react differently to parents who expect family conformity and stellar performance in competitive areas. Unlike Chip, some strong-willed kids will act out to get their own space. Control system backfiring, the teenager spins out of control (drugs, alcohol, cults), rebelling against what they perceive to be parental tyranny. Other kids might truly enjoy being as high-powered as a parent, but Chip was not his father's genetic twin. His difficulties with his family protocol had gone underground to the extent that he initially had no dissonance with his problem. Instead of acting "out," he had acted "in." He experienced everything as "just fine, no problem," while his fainting spells indicated that it was not.

"Foreclosure" refers to a type of arrest in identity development. Foreclosed, Chip had neither progressed through the necessary stages of exploring who he is, nor had he differentiated himself, his values, his choices from those of his parents. We might go so far as to say he was paying the toll for having been set up to rely entirely on conformity and authority. Contemplating college and his future during spring of his senior year, Chip had started to know himself a little better and was beginning to separate his leanings from those of his parents. Maybe Dad's college wasn't the way to go after all. His reaction to this discrepancy of opinion: panic.

Families at Developmental Crossroads

Parents with adolescents are almost always moving through their own developmental identity crossroads. Couples with intact marriages are becoming a twosome again (gladly or sadly, or ideally a little of each); they're facing the second half or last part of their career path; and they may be dealing with aging parents. Knowing they've reached a chronological half-life, they may be asking, "What else?"

The Randolphs' family story brings home this idea. Adam, in particular, had formidable tensions in his life. We sometimes make light of the notion of a midlife crisis, as if it were a passing phase for adults to simply get over. A midlife crisis, which has everything to do with continued identity development, is a deep personal reflection that may yield a decision to change. It's a threshold where we consider the past in order to determine a possible new direction.

No matter his assertive demeanor, Adam was depressed and beginning to show it. At sixty, he was on a downward slope, distressed about retirement at age sixty-five. Changes in the legal profession had brought about an unexpected redistribution of his partnership pension monies. Adam had never had to deal with the emotions of personal vulnerability. With his self-esteem tied to his net worth and status as a lawyer, he suffered deeply, wondering if his career had been a farce. In therapy, he agonized over whether to sue his law firm or let it go and put his energy into private consulting. His work ethic driving him, Adam defined himself as important and successful only as long as he was in control — of his firm, of his marriage, and of his relationship with his son. When these three spheres began resisting him, he was in a serious bind, wondering "Who am I if I am not this?" Clearly, Adam faced a developmental challenge as daunting as his son's.

When Chip informed his parents during a family therapy session of his indecision about attending Adam's alma mater, Adam was incredulous. "He's shooting himself in the foot, handicapping his whole future. This is a once-in-a-lifetime opportunity, and he's thinking about turning it down. He'll regret it!" As his own life options were closing down, he could not bear to see his son make a decision he considered limiting. Little could

Adam see that Chip needed to figure out what would be best for him, instead of following unquestioningly in his father's tracks.

Claire cooperated with therapy, initially "just for Chip," though she sensed that the whole family had issues to address. Claire was devoted to her husband, busy with volunteer activities. She had, however, been musing about the career in early childhood education that she passed up. In spite of her wistfulness, she neither regretted the path she had chosen, nor did she really mind her subservient role in the marriage. From the start, she recognized Adam as a strong man who needed to control. His firm, powerful nature was part of what attracted her to him.

What she didn't expect was for Adam to go on tilt like this. Claire's particular developmental crossroad was more of a questioning juncture. She knew she couldn't change Adam, but he had become difficult to live with; he was withdrawn, moody, and irritable. "Where did you put my book!" "Why isn't dinner ready?" "Can't you see how incompetently these cleaners pressed my shirt?" At first her heart went out to him as he struggled with his firm's new phase-out plan. But, in therapy she said, "Now that I'm on the receiving end of his moods, my marriage isn't much fun for me." Her friends advised her to take care of herself and get out of the house more, but her reduced attention on him made him even more temperamental. Claire was tired of his judgments, and her patience was diminishing.

A common family situation is a confluence of identity crises: Chip was trying to find his own bearings; Adam, an aging man, was experiencing loss of power; and Claire felt devalued and uncertain about the man in whom she invested her life.

Each family member had work to do. Adam needed to rebuild his identity as a successful retired attorney, even though he wouldn't have the pension to prove it. His challenge was to figure out ways to involve himself in life and still feel productive, creative, and powerful — without being the kingpin. Ultimately, he learned to do this. He became active in professional organizations and developed a passion for golfing.

Claire explained how difficult it was to be treated "more like a housekeeper than a valued wife." Like many women of her generation, Claire had put her developmental needs in the back seat. She needed to become more invested in her own friendships, hobbies, and community work, so that less of her world would be determined by Adam's unreliable moods. Humbled, Adam began to listen to her, and he recognized how much he needed her — as a true partner.

Shortly after he began therapy, Chip's fainting spells disappeared. Once they realized the stakes, Claire and Adam reassured Chip they would support whatever choice he made . . . to go to Dad's college? No, the question remained in the air. Chip decided to defer college for a year and headed off to art school in France.

The Rewards of a Little Adolescent Rebellion

I have talked with many patients at midlife who once resembled Chip, but did not run into his kind of brick wall at age eighteen. (Arrested identity development is only one type of midlife crisis.) In their forties, these patients suffer deeply, staring vacantly at the ceiling during therapy, asking, "Why didn't I follow my gut?" More often than not, they were subjected in their youth to some kind of "identity molding." A parent's role in the adolescent identity-formation process is to look for the spark and help ignite the fire within the child. We want to enhance a child's belief in himself and to encourage him to explore his own path.

During adolescence, our children change physically, emotionally, and socially. How difficult it is to trust that although we may indeed have lost the child, the young adult remains connected to us. And it sometimes takes enormous patience to socialize and interact with adolescents in respectful ways. The ability to distinguish between behaviors we should tolerate because they're part of healthy identity formation and those on our "nonnegotiable" list is a demanding parental task.

As parents, we may deplore the loud music and slovenly attire. We may abhor the way our adolescents become so self-consumed as to forget to take out the trash, or the way they push our buttons, showing up at the dinner table with a radical new look. But if we judge our adolescents only by the veneer of appearances, we risk being unsupportive of behaviors that are healthy to identity formation. Surely, we want certain kinds of change more than we want unquestioned allegiance to our ways. Research clearly indicates that young people who have struggled, differentiated themselves from their parents, and committed to a unique positive self are more ethical, empathetic, and well adjusted than those youths who are low in identity achievement.[6] They are willing to assume more personal responsibility for themselves and their world, and for this outcome, a share of parental aggravation is a small cost to exact.

4

Navigating Character

*Goal: Take an active role in fostering your
adolescent's character development and sense
of purpose.*

 Ｃ HARACTER is about being a good
person, having decent values, and doing the true thing. All encompassing,
character includes everything from simple gestures like please and thank
you to idealistic decisions about sticking out one's neck for a noble
though losing cause. It pertains to caring and responsibility on a personal
level, as well as justice and individual rights on a more abstract level.[1]

 Good character is something we hope to instill in our children. Ask a
group of parents whether they care about character development and all
hands will rise in the affirmative. During adolescence, however, when our
hold on our kids seems more tenuous than it did during the early years,
we sometimes ease off on our efforts to shape character. Academics get top
billing as our focus shifts from raising "good" kids to raising "smart" kids.
Thrown by identity changes and made increasingly anxious by threats of
AIDS, date rape, and drug addiction, we locate character in the side aisles
when we should be giving it an orchestra seat.

 To some extent it's true that our children's characters are relatively
established by the time they reach adolescence. All the influences of our
nurturing and rearing from birth to twelve culminate in a person with
budding values, habits, patterns of responding, and repertoires of behavior.
Moreover, we don't spend nearly as many hours with them as we once did.
They're headed across the lake at the tiller of their own boat, sailing in the

winds of their culture and time. But because they're not yet completely on their own, parents still have ways to guide their course. It's well within our capacity to stay connected and provide meaningful direction for character development.

Generating a list of agreed-upon character virtues is a relatively simple matter. As parents, we nod our heads in favor of qualities like respect, responsibility, compassion, honesty, decency, integrity, tolerance, resilience, fairness, courage, self-control, humility, empathy, loyalty, and forgiveness. But how do we reap the desired behavior?

On one level, we promote character by arranging or accommodating activities for our children that (if well chosen) have a character-building function built into them, such as church/synagogue attendance, athletic team participation, and extracurricular activities like scouts or choir. We make sure they're contributing to the family through regular chores and responsibilities for example, and to society, perhaps through volunteer work. We talk to our kids about moral issues, help them to see others' points of view, and encourage them to be thoughtful and considerate. We raise their consciousness about tactless, insensitive remarks and actions. We discuss what's going on in the world and our reactions to these events. As difficult and time-consuming as these important, overt actions are, they're still only step one in navigating the waters of character development.

We pass character values to our children in the way we (parents and role models) carry ourselves. Whether we realize it or not, we are constantly educating our children about character, even when we are not directly addressing it. They're observing what we say, what we do, and how we do it. They're noticing all the decisions we make about running our lives, gathering data on the values and behavior that constitute our personal character. The apple doesn't fall far from the tree. If the example set has been negative, children may react against behaviors from which they've most likely suffered. How do we treat our spouses and other people? How do we deal with our problems and errors? How do we cope with stress and time crunches? What kind of language do we use to express anger or upset? Have we made an effort to balance our lives? Are we actively dedicated to the good of the greater community and society? What examples have we set about meeting commitments, delaying gratification, and taking a stand? What decisions do we make about TV, alcohol consumption, our bodies and looks, material goods, money, competition, sharing power with others, and showing love?

Small gestures speak volumes. Before we get busy building our children's character, we want to make sure our own acts are relatively clean and we've integrated what we say with what we do. Differences exist among knowing the right thing to do, caring about it, and behaving according to one's moral principles.[2] Do we talk to our kids about personal responsibility, but in our haste neglect to rewind the videotape before returning it? Do we lecture on honesty, then fudge our kid's age at the ski lift to get a cheaper ticket? Do we espouse the value of authenticity, then hang up the phone and ridicule the person with whom we so happily conversed?

Let's say we've worked with our kids to cultivate and reinforce good habits and positive behaviors. So far, so good, but there's more. Character development also occurs from the negative underside of experience. Ironically, wrestling honestly and forthrightly with mistakes, problems, and imperfect behavior — ours and theirs — may be the best way to develop the healthy qualities we all want to see in our children. When the sailing is smooth and we've yet to be tempted or tried, who's to say whether we possess virtues like fortitude or commitment?

The often-missed opportunities for character building rise out of the three D's of experience: disappointments, difficulties, and dilemmas. Certainly, we feel pleased when our particular child shows the initiative to try out for the lead in the school play, or bravely sticks up for a friend, or performs an unnecessary act of generosity, and we want to cheer our kids on so they'll feel motivated to do more of the same. But we also want to be there to provide guidance when our children hit a shoal or are forced off course by gale force winds. Too often, when there's a lapse into lying, cheating, or stealing, we rescue our children outright or react explosively, commandeering their ship and depriving them of valuable experience.

The vignettes that follow illustrate some of the nuances of character and show how direct action to build character, parental modeling, and struggling with the three D's form the high seas of character development. With a goal as elusive as character, however, we must guard against global prescriptions. Life yields many surprise turns. Even though the situations and ideas about character described in this chapter generally hold up, there will always be the unique story of how a person developed or failed to develop character.

Gary and Jessica Wu: A "Too Precious" Child Gets on Course

There are many reasons why parents come up short in their character-building efforts. Perhaps it's out of neglect or perhaps it's out of the opposite — a syndrome known as the too precious child.[3] A precious child is one who has had copious amounts of attention paid to him. Parents of these children care intensely about doing everything right and not making mistakes. Usually, circumstances play a part. A precious child might come from older parents who, in their years of waiting, formulated many ideas about child rearing in the abstract. They might be parents who have suffered some type of loss or have struggled with fertility issues. Or, there might be family-of-origin issues, such as parents raised in poverty who want to give their child all. Whatever the particular pathway to creating a too precious child, the parents are often so busy making their child's life wonderful and free from adversity that they don't invest in the arduous effort of refusing a child's demands or letting the child struggle with his own issues.

Once a child becomes a teenager, we can no longer start from "go." If we see significant shortcomings in our adolescents, we must ask what natural or unnatural predators interfered with our efforts to develop character. If the precious-child syndrome is a factor, parents can ask, "Why did I indulge so many of my child's whims?" "How did my child come to think so much of herself and not enough of others?" Before addressing their child's character, parents must put other issues in order — specifically, parental authority.

Gary Wu is a self-effacing, soft-spoken, forty-eight-year-old single parent. He came to my office for a consultation because, as he put it, "I want to learn how to be a better parent." Seated on the couch opposite me, he reflected calmly, "During the whole marriage breakup and divorce, my wife and I were so busy giving our daughter Jessica everything she wanted that we didn't think about what she needed. We never made her do chores. Neither of us could say 'no' convincingly to her. She'd throw a tizzy, and we'd let her have her way. Now that the dust has settled on my divorce, I can see more clearly how permissive I was with Jessie."

Guilt over marital strife and divorce had been a roadblock to Jessica's character development. When he first entered therapy, Gary was limping along as a parent. Coping with a turbulent divorce and dealing with a backwash of issues as well, Gary would, according to Beavers's continuum, be viewed as functioning adequately because he had problems establishing control with his daughter. But, family functioning is not fixed, and because Gary and Jessica both adapted to circumstances, they eventually rebounded to a state of health.

Before we could focus on Jessica's character, we had to repair some of the damage of the divorce. Gary, whose parents were Chinese immigrants, told me his story with clarity and composure, walking the fine line between self-accusation and defensiveness; he knew that over the years he hadn't done things exactly right with his twelve-year-old daughter, of whom he had sole custody since his divorce a year ago. For years, Gary had struggled to keep his stormy marriage intact for the sake of Jessica, who was conceived shortly after he and Linda exchanged vows. "The marriage was a disaster from the start," Gary recalled forlornly.

Gary described Linda, whom he had met in high school, as someone "who almost didn't graduate because she spent so much time surfing." As an impressionable Chinese male growing up in Los Angeles in the '60s, he had fallen hard for the spontaneous blonde whose zest for life seemed the antithesis to the Chinese traditions he saw as stodgy and was reacting against in forging his American identity. Unable to read the subtleties of American culture, Gary hadn't known what he was getting into, and he now realized his efforts to homogenize his cultural distinctions had been an overreaction. Linda turned out to be a woman who drank heavily, slept long hours, and abandoned the home for weeks at a time. Behind closed doors, they had argued incessantly, Gary criticizing Linda's "inability to be a proper mother" and Linda demeaning the "stinking old Chinese garbage" he was always throwing at her.

Currently Linda was following a guru in Oregon though staying in touch with Jessica. Gary and I spent some time in therapy discussing his failed marriage and his recent appreciation of his Chinese heritage and its more traditional family-centered lifestyle. We also explored how his excesses grew out of his situation; however, our primary focus was Jessica's well-being.

To be sure, not all children of divorce become overindulged like Jessica — neglect is another extreme possibility. The impact of divorce on children is variable and highly dependent on the individual personalities of the parents and the marital situation prior to divorce. Research has shown that when children go into a divorce psychologically well adjusted, they usually come through the divorce that way too. It is the bad marriage and the negative circumstances the child experiences before and after the divorce that cause most of the psychological harm often associated with divorce per se.[4]

The prognosis for successful outcome for children of divorce depends heavily on three factors. First of all, are both parents still present and involved in the child's life in a way that maintains secure attachment? Secondly, have the parents resumed all the roles of responsible parenting? And lastly, are parents able to set aside their differences and animosity and coparent in an effective manner?

Gary's problem resided in the second factor, though there were also concerns about Linda's absenteeism. My job as therapist was to help Gary resume the role of a responsible, authoritative parent — one who could be both loving and stern when necessary. Linda's chaotic lifestyle, heavy alcohol use, and unexplained departures left Jessica with an anxious attachment to her mother. Reacting to Linda's instability and Jessica's anxiety, Gary compensated by trying to be an absolute, loving presence for his daughter, which created two parental excesses — Linda's abandonment and Gary's indulgence. Because he hadn't offered Jessica some of the limits she needed for the last twelve years, Gary now encountered a strong-willed, self-centered young lady who whined and pouted vainly until her father gave in to her demands. She was expert at wearing her father down — and it didn't take much for him to capitulate. Although Jessica had been exposed to numerous three D's (difficulties, dilemmas, and disappointments) related to her mother's problems and her parents' divorce, she lacked experience in coping with those of everyday living. Gary's reaction to his daughter was classic. Intensely aware of the ways in which Jessica struggled, he tried to make up for this hardship by bailing Jessie out of tough situations that might have been opportunities for growing and learning.

Gary was unsure of his parenting skills; he hadn't as a child paid much attention to his mother's parenting techniques, since he never would have imagined that one day he'd be the sole guiding force in a child's life. His parents were hard-working immigrants, and their focus was on acculturation, good behavior, and success in school, rather than the inner conflicts of an adolescent. But Gary had received as a child the important ingredient of a secure attachment; his parents had been reliable, responsive to his basic needs, and had provided a stable home life.

Though he started from a difficult place, Gary achieved great heights. Because he had no deeply embedded emotional blocks or scars from his own upbringing, Gary took my coaching suggestions as his marching orders and began to correct past parenting excesses. To Jessica's demands, he responded with limits, respect, and clear communication about what he felt, what he expected from her, and what he needed her to work on with him. He established immediate consequences for her outbursts. One instance of her tantruming occurred when they were out in the car, and she began screaming at him to stop at a store to get the exact shampoo she needed. He made two respectful requests for her to leave off this behavior. When she continued screaming, he simply got out of the car and let her carry on until she ran out of steam. Verbal abuse in the car, which had once been her trademark, began to taper.

Parents, like Gary, can impose a lot of firmness because they have the sensitivity, thoughtfulness, and nurturing skills to balance out the strictness. Gary was concerned not only about tantrums but also about the total picture of who Jessica was at age twelve. Gary had to assert basic control before he could initiate efforts to build Jessica's character. Until she could subdue her anxiety, frustration, and anger more effectively, she couldn't move on to higher-level goals: compassion, empathy, the resolution of moral dilemmas. Virtues such as tolerance, fairness, and generosity of spirit are built on a foundation of self-control and a willingness to defer immediate gratification. Over time, I worked in therapy with Jessica on loss issues related to her mother and with Gary on his need to increase his authoritativeness. Jessica's behavior followed a pattern that research tells us is typical of most children whose parents divorce: within a couple of years of the divorce, initial disturbances, which included sleep problems, school problems, and minor depression, subsided, and Jessica accepted the breakup of her family and adjusted to her new way of living.[5]

A Dilemma About Honesty and Loyalty:
Should Gary Make Jessica Do the "Right" Thing?

The following episode came up about a year and a half into therapy, after Gary and Jessica had made significant headway toward their major goals. The family was beginning to blossom, and we were able to navigate problems more directly hinged to character. As a therapist, I often pause to reflect on my values, principles, and parenting inclinations versus those of the people I see in my practice. Differences in values surface around issues of character, and a case in point was a dilemma Gary discussed with me during a couple of our sessions.

Socially, Jessica was shuffling the fringes, jockeying for position among various cliques of girls in her class. Whom to stand with in the hall, whom to call for the homework assignment, whom to share a locker with were urgent matters. Highly sensitive to the social implications of each move, Jessica faced a difficult decision. She had accepted an invitation to attend a special play with Betsy, a friend she'd known since kindergarten. Though she looked forward to the play, she now considered this old friend "dead wood," setting her sights on a more sophisticated, popular group. A couple of days before the play, Jessica received a coveted invitation — same evening and time as the play — to a coed party at the home of one of the class's most popular girls. Impulsively, she accepted. Double-booked, Jessica now had to decide whether to go to the play or the party. Gary described his initial exchange with his daughter on the matter, which went something like this:

"I know I got an invitation at the last minute because one of the girls couldn't go," Jessie had said to him. "She wants an even number of girls and boys at the party. I definitely want to go."

"Does it bother you to be asked so late?" asked Gary.

"Heck, no. At least I get to go," replied Jessica.

"What about Betsy and the play?"

"Oh, she won't know. I'll think of something."

"What will that 'something' be?"

"I don't know, Dad. Leave me alone. I'll figure it out."

At the time of our next session, Gary had, indeed, left Jessica alone to "figure it out," and he was quite comfortable with his suspension of judgment. Many parents in this type of situation — and I count myself among them — would have mounted a high moral horse, or exposed a bias, dropping a few pearls of wisdom about friendship, loyalty, and commitment. Though I refrained from saying so, my own vote was that Jessica needed some direction with her predicament, but I've also learned from parents in my practice that there's more than one way to do things. I decided to see what would develop. In therapy, I will assert an opinion when I'm absolutely convinced it's what a child needs — for instance, earlier I had said that Jessica needed more limits and a stronger parent-child boundary.

In this instance, however, Jessica could learn by getting guidance, following through on her commitment, and doing the right thing because Gary insisted she do so, or she could learn by breaking her commitment, going to the party, being stung by her own conscience, or suffering other natural consequences. As a therapist, I watch for hubristic assumptions that I always know what's best; parents often have an intuitive feel for what they are ready to try, what they believe will work, and what solution they see as most advantageous to their child. As Gary and I talked about the problem, I became convinced that Jessica would receive a valuable lesson because of the way Gary intended to handle the problem.

In situations like these, parents can subject their adolescent to the Socratic method, a nonjudgmental inquiry process that allows for free exploration of a moral dilemma. Gary asked Jessica a series of neutral questions, designed to help her see the different sides of her dilemma. With Gary as her guide, she ran through all the pros and cons of the play versus the party, as well as the risks and benefits of each potential decision. He was able to engage in this practice without inserting his own answers because he truly felt it was her decision and didn't want to influence her. As long as she reflected, made a conscious decision, and was aware of consequences, she would reap the benefit of some type of life experience. If Gary were to force her to go to the play, she'd learn something about her father; if she had to make up her own mind, she'd learn something about herself.

Gary approached the topic with Jessica one step at a time, saying that he might be willing to let her make her own decision, if he was sure she had thought it through. This provided a basis for evaluating whether Jessica was making a decision with her eyes open. He let her know he had serious reservations about her lying to Betsy. Though Jessica tried to obscure the situation and convince him she really wouldn't be lying, he made her face up to what she would be doing and call a lie a lie. Throughout the dialogue, Gary remained supportive. He said, "I can see you're in a bind with this. You must feel pretty torn." And then he handed her the decision. "It's yours," he said.

The morning of the play/party — she had procrastinated at length — Jessica called Betsy to tell her she wasn't feeling well and didn't think she could go to the play. Like so many teenagers today, Betsy had her ear to the ground. To Jessica's explanation, Betsy swiftly rejoined, "You're not trying to get out of this and go to that party, are you? Did you get invited?" which took the wind out of Jessica's sails. Jessica haltingly replied, "I have a headache. I don't know. I'll call you back."

Deflated by Betsy's quick deduction, Jessica determined she had no choice other than to attend the play with Betsy. Though she had been willing to maneuver covertly to get out of going, she couldn't bring herself to confront Betsy directly, especially since Betsy saw through her ruse. Pulling out of the party at the last minute set Jessica back a notch with the popular girls and of course, she had to decide whether she would lie or explain to them about her prior obligation. "Either way, I'm burned," she told her father. "I might as well just tell the truth."

When our kids are neck-deep in the swamp of a moral dilemma, it's all too tempting to help extricate them from their problem with grace and integrity. This is a very defensible parenting position; it's our job to help them navigate their moral course. And we suffer along with our children when they make mistakes, for their mistakes affect us to the degree we are identified with them. We think, "Not my child! How could she do something like this, and how could I stand by and let it happen?" Gary was willing to take a calculated risk; he understood that there would be a lesson for Jessica either way. He took the time to go through a decision-making process with her. Had he cared intensely whether she went to the party or the play, the Socratic process would have been a charade, because he would have been invested in a decision.

Gary was convinced that after her experience, Jessica would think twice before trying to lie, and she would not commit herself so casually to something she felt lukewarm about from the outset. Jessica realized she had set her own trap through her deceitfulness and eagerness to belong to the popular group — a valuable character lesson.

Putting Adolescents to Work: Chores, Paying Jobs, and Volunteerism

In household matters, Gary had assumed the role of a "superdad," making dinners three nights a week, doing the laundry, tidying the house, and herding after Jessica like a devoted sheltie, picking up her clothes, dirty dishes, and magazines. As I do with many parents in my practice — I encouraged Gary to enlist Jessica's participation in household responsibilities and establish regular chores for her.

Especially during the '90s, with many dual-career families, we may not want to spend the precious little time we have with our children insisting on chores. Researchers have found that children in busy single-parent or two-career homes do fewer chores than children in traditional homes.[6] This phenomenon may be related to the fact that it often takes more energy and effort to get a child to do a chore than for us to do it ourselves. We become the proverbial broken record: "Please take out the trash." "Please fold this load of laundry." "Please pick up your books." Moreover, having our kids do chores might not seem like a priority; we'd rather they were cracking their books to make A's or practicing ballet. "When," we ask ourselves, "will they find the time in their busy schedule to wash the car?"

Parenting is a process whereby we slowly and steadily prepare our children for the real world. Adulthood involves taking responsibility for oneself, which necessarily includes a certain amount of "schlock" — laundry, dishes, cleaning, and walking the dog. If we don't incorporate some of these duties into our children's lives, will they be fully prepared for what life entails?

What about the issue of regular paying jobs for adolescents? Does employment inherently build character? Yes and no. Promoting a work ethic, we often glorify individual enterprise and the climb up the ladder of success, and automatically equate employment with doing something useful and good.

Ellen Greenberger's and Laurence Steinberg's research raised some red flags about adolescent employment.[7] Here are three of their key findings. Most types of work that adolescents are able to get have few redeeming qualities to them. The work tends to involve rote, nonthinking kinds of tasks, like flipping hamburgers, which deaden the mind and fail to teach anything worthwhile. Secondly, their study suggests that adolescents who work over twelve hours a week are taking valuable time away from school, friends, and family. Lastly, adolescents tend not to use the money they earn wisely. Most kids end up spending it on more clothes, records, and entertainment, which means that having a paying job may actually be abetting materialism instead of building character. Before we encourage an adolescent to enter the work force, we need to know the extent of the time commitment, what he will be doing, what he will be learning from the experience, and how he plans to use the money.

On the other hand, there are compelling reasons for kids to have jobs, especially summer or weekend jobs when they're saving for a trip, for school expenses, or to help out the family. Job hunting requires initiative, and those who are earning their own way may have an enhanced sense of self-worth. Moreover, some kids who have been unsuccessful at school and home find their strengths when placed in a new work setting and receive unprecedented amounts of positive feedback.

A less-than-optimal job in the right dose can teach any adolescent some valuable lessons — if it's not taking away from something that might be more important to learn. For adolescents working during the school year, we always have to ask: What are the motives for making money? What will the benefits be? Are there more productive ways to show initiative and feel good about oneself? Parents should make sure the experience of being employed isn't merely feeding an adolescent's consumer appetite.

For some families, volunteer work becomes a viable alternative to paid work. I recently observed a family — parents and two teenagers together — picking up trash in a park one Sunday morning. Many families who choose not to attend church substitute a volunteer activity. My guess is that the adolescents I saw did not cheerfully rise from their warm beds on a weekend morning to perform community service, but the parents (who might have preferred a morning with the Sunday paper themselves) recognized the value of giving one's self and one's time to a cause. Unless parents are sanctimonious — a major turnoff for adolescents — the volunteerism that parents model combined with work performed together for others will go a long way in loosening the chains of self-absorption.

Volunteerism, like a paying job, exacts initiative and follow-through, but, unlike most paying jobs for adolescents, it often puts kids in positions of true responsibility. Volunteer work can immerse adolescents in real-world problems and send them searching for solutions. Kids know the difference between passing time on a task for some spare cash and making a meaningful contribution. Work on a political campaign or in a retirement home, soup kitchen, thrift shop, or daycare center teaches lessons on giving back to the community. By volunteer working, our teenagers won't end up with extra money for the clothes or CDs they crave, which in itself might contribute to character development.

A Tale of Two Families: Terry, Donna, and Steve Rowe; Sam, Carol, and Scott DeSanto

What follows is a view inside two different families, illustrating how critical family dynamics are to parents' efforts to cultivate character. This scenario is a composite of boys and situations on which I've counseled. Two ninth-grade boys, Terry and Sam, pulled a serious prank and their respective families handled the episode differently. Temperamentally, both boys are high energy, impetuous, wild-side leaders of their pack. Popular, athletic, and smart enough, they specialize in petty mischief — stomping on ketchup packets in the school cafeteria, coating doorknobs with Vaseline, prying open lockers and filling them with blown-up condoms. Though both boys suffered as a result of the crisis described below, Terry, whose family is midrange to dysfunctional, realized no gains, while Sam, whose family drew on their significant strengths, grew in the wake of the mishap. I see a lot of Terrys and Sams in my practice, and skilled parenting makes all the difference.

Terry and Sam's prank occurred on a Thursday night, the evening before a big basketball game — Eagles versus the Mustangs in the state playoffs. Both boys were first-string players. Egged on by a group of guys who remained outside the school, Terry and Sam slid through a gym window and spray-painted slurs against the Mustangs on gym walls. Predictably, one slur read "Mustangs Suck!" but it was a second graphic that caused pandemonium in the school. A work of graffiti depicted a swooping eagle in the act of castrating a rearing, defenseless mustang, and beneath it the caption read, "Eagles Castrate Mustangs!" The next morning hundreds of students crowded into the gym to see the drawing before it was removed. The mob scene delayed classes and tests had to be postponed. Late in the day, Mrs. Freeman, the principal, having determined who the graffiti artists were, called Terry and Sam into her office and suspended them from school for a week. An irritated Mrs. Freeman telephoned the boys' homes and, in each case, the mothers were informed of the incident and the disciplinary action.

When Terry arrived home, his mother, Donna, was at her wit's end. "How do you think I feel being the mom with the kid who always gets in trouble? Your behavior is thoroughly humiliating me! I can't go anywhere without someone asking me about your shenanigans, and this mess is the ultimate. This is vandalism! You've defaced school property!"

Terry responded by making light of what happened. "Don't get hysterical, Mom. It was only spray paint. It's not like it's permanent. Graffiti is all over the place." Donna was outraged at Terry's attitude. She thought to herself, "Doesn't he get it?"

A common parental reaction to an adolescent who minimizes his actions is to intensify the emotion. We want to convince them they need to mend their erring ways. Often matters escalate into a power struggle, with the parent criticizing the behavior and the child becoming more and more defensive and less and less willing to assume responsibility.

Terry had watched his mother spin out of control many times. So instead of arguing directly with his mom, he cleverly redirected her attention. "I get all the heat from Mrs. Freeman. She's after me, Ma, you know that. She calls you all the time about stupid stuff. Sam was the major player in this, and I'm getting the heat. Other guys were hanging around too. I may have been the artist, but you know I'd never use a word like 'castrate' on my own."

Donna began to think about how her son was always the one in trouble. Because it diverted her own shame and offered her some relief, Donna decided that her son was being scapegoated by the principal. In a huff, she called Mrs. Freeman back and demanded to know which other boys had been present and why they had escaped punishment. She became engaged in a screaming match with the principal, defending her son and accusing Mrs. Freeman of having it in for her kid. Then she called the mothers of two boys who observed the graffiti prank. Donna was so worked up, however, that the women rushed to their sons' defenses. Donna wanted the other boys to take some of the blame, which would have made her son "less bad," but the other moms were taken aback. "This was Terry's and Sam's thing," they told her. "My kid just watched." Meanwhile, as Donna quibbled on the phone, Terry slipped out of the room.

Instead of dealing directly with her son, Donna triangulated two times, first to Mrs. Freeman and then to the other two mothers. *Triangulation occurs when anxiety and conflict between two people become so intense that they seek temporary relief by offloading it to a third party.* Instead of keeping the conflict between her son and herself, Donna's flooding feelings were directed at Mrs. Freeman and other parents. In its least sophisticated form, triangulation is a version of kick the cat. The process is also called displacement: when we don't know how to direct our feelings toward one party, we displace or direct them to someone else. By triangulating — or displacing — Donna not only stirred up unnecessary trouble with others, she avoided dealing with Terry's wrongdoings. And what, we might ask, happened to the working alliance between parent and school, each playing a role in the development of the child?

Though he lacked details, Steve Rowe knew that things were again hot at home because of an urgent voice-mail message he had received from Donna. In the past, Steve had gotten into a lot of trouble with his wife by trying to defend Terry. As he entered the house, he reminded himself to wear kid gloves with his wife and show his anger at Terry right along with Donna.

Donna summoned Terry back into the room and described the incident play-by-play. Worked up, she dragged Terry through the coals again, while Terry continued to downplay his culpability. Steve made an effort to match her vehemence so she wouldn't blast him too. He declared Terry grounded for a month, but Terry started to negotiate: "O.K., Dad, but you gotta at least let me go to the game tomorrow night. These are the playoffs. It would be a real torture to miss the whole thing. I mean, it's bad enough that I can't play." Steve winced, thinking how tough it was that Terry had been suspended and couldn't play.

"No way," said Donna, who was on a roll: "This has to stop. Today he's spraying gym walls; tomorrow he'll be planting bomb scares."

Ultimately, Steve couldn't tolerate Donna's fire. He said the poison words, "Now Donna, aren't you getting a little carried away? He's not a criminal."

"How dare you 'Now Donna' me! What audacity! You never get the phone calls. You never have to deal with this. I'm constantly humiliated, while you're safely hidden in your office. These pranks are so male. You encourage Terry by telling your stories about the good ol' days and the panty raids." Hurling insults at each other, they told Terry to leave the room; they wanted to argue in private. "Just get out. You're grounded," said Donna.

What did Terry take away from the experience? "I got in trouble at school again." "Mrs. Freeman is always on my case." "Mom is frightening because she gets so hysterical." "Dad would be much cooler about this,

but I know he has to get heavy with me or Mom will lose it with him."
"My parents are out of control." Brooding over his parents, Terry felt little
anguish over his prank.

Sam DeSanto's Character-Building Experience

Carol DeSanto, Sam's mother, received the phone call from Mrs. Freeman
informing her of her son's vandalism and suspension. Carol was discour-
aged and angry because it was the third time this year she had received a
dreaded message from the principal. When Sam came home, Carol expressed her disappointment, in less inflammatory terms than Donna. *Paradoxically, a calm parental approach can sometimes enhance seriousness and put
more pressure on the child.* Though Donna's emotions were more intense
than Carol's, emotionality was not the critical difference in the incident.
Rather, Donna's mistakes were more like the wrong moves in a chess
game instead of the temperament she brought to the table.

"Obviously, I'm disturbed that you've acted with such poor judgment," said Carol gravely. "This is a really big one, Sam."

Sam tried to minimize what happened. "It was only spray paint. It's
not like it's permanent. Graffiti is all over the place." Carol said nothing.
She looked at him and shook her head. She remained tight-lipped and
stern. For Sam, there was no friction; he was unable to create a fiery
diversion. Sam boisterously complained about Mrs. Freeman, telling Carol
how she was always picking on him and how the other boys hadn't been
suspended.

Carol validated Sam's feeling about Mrs. Freeman. "I'm sure it must
feel like she's after you a lot. She's got her job to do, and this was seriously
disruptive to the school."

Searching for an escape hatch, Sam told his mom that Terry was the
one who bought the paint and did most of the spraying. "The other guys
were right in there with us," he claimed.

Carol responded with a word teenagers find so useful: "Whatever."
After a pause, she continued, "I'm not going to deal with Terry and the
other boys. We need to talk about your actions." Unlike Donna, Carol
kept the episode contained; she did not become sidetracked by discussions
about Mrs. Freeman or the other mothers. Nonetheless, Carol was not
afraid to face whatever facts about Sam and his impetuous actions she
needed to face. Incidents like this were horrendous but they galvanized

Carol to deal directly with her son. She took the necessary measures to see that he gained insights into his mistakes. Recognizing how difficult it is to deal with a child of Sam's temperament, she has steeled herself to be patient with the process.

Sam wanted to know where he stood, so he said that he assumed he would be grounded. "That's a start," Carol responded. "Yes, you're grounded. But, you know, we're going to have to review this whole thing with Dad when he gets home. I want you to go to your room until he gets here. No phone. I want you to think about what you need to do to make amends. Think about how disruptive this incident has been and about the things it's taken away from everyone. What about the kids who studied for their tests and couldn't take them? What about the classwork the kids missed? Think about the janitors. What else might they have been able to do for the school today if they hadn't had to clean this up before the game? Were the janitors able to put up the special banners for the playoffs?"

Carol's technique was to send Sam off with an assignment that would make him reflect on what he had done. Although a serious transgression in a child often triggers the parent-lecture reflex, Carol wanted to let Sam sit in his stew. She also knew that she didn't need to rush to judgment or make a hasty decision. Waiting for her husband, Scott, to come home did not mean she intended to hand control and a decision regarding a punishment over to her husband. On the contrary, she views their parenting dynamic as a joint partnership, so she wanted to consult with her partner and then decide on a course of action with him.

When Scott DeSanto came home, he and Carol met to determine what to do. This gave them an opportunity to express their grief, anger, and frustration without Sam in the room and prepare a plan of action. Carol and Scott knew why Sam spray-painted the gym: Sam is an impetuous young man who readily gives way to what is cool and compelling in the moment. The DeSantos' goal was to teach Sam to resist these impulses and develop greater foresight into his behaviors. They want him to be more responsible and respectful of others — two important building blocks of character.

When Carol, Scott, and Sam gathered, Carol insisted her son tell his own story. Sam's punishment incorporated a time component that would allow him to ponder over what he had done before facing his parents. He was grounded for two weeks, including the next night's playoff game. His parents took advantage of the natural negative consequences of Sam's disappointment in missing the game.

Sam's punishment was designed to repair damage — physically and psychically. Sam was directed to make arrangements with Mrs. Freeman to do service for the school to compensate for the cost of painting the gym. Moreover, Carol and Scott capitalized on Sam's assignment to assess the impact of his behavior on the school. He had to write a letter of apology to Mrs. Freeman explaining his understanding of the ripple effects of his actions. Knowing that their son became wrapped up in the excitement of the moment, Carol and Scott wanted Sam to think hard about his behavior from the perspective of Mrs. Freeman, the teachers, the custodians, and the students who lost out on learning that day. In writing the letter, Sam had to imagine what it would be like to deal with someone like himself.

Instead of shaming Sam, the DeSantos engaged their son in a practice called role taking. *The goal of role taking is to recognize and appreciate multiple points of view and integrate them into your own so that these perspectives will be present in subsequent thinking and behavior.* Adolescents' advanced cognitive skills allow them to be sensitive to others' perspectives, a key component of empathy and character development. Carol and Scott are working toward the day when Sam can put on his brakes and be aware of the negative impacts of actions that might seem harmless or fun at the time.

Parents, too, can avoid battles with each other if they engage in more role taking and develop greater empathy for the other's situation. Even if he was well intended when saying "Now, Donna," Steve Rowe failed to respect the pain she suffered in dealing with the principal. Moreover, Steve formed a coalition with his son. Instead of hammering away at a spouse in a bad situation, we might put ourselves in their shoes. Steve could have acknowledged all that Donna had been through. He might have established a coparenting situation by saying something like, "Donna, I see you've been dealing with this situation all afternoon. Let's take a break together so you can get me up to speed, and we can figure out how we can handle this." Donna had a valid point: she always receives the phone call about Terry. Clearly, these parents need a plan to shoulder the burdens equally.

By arguing over this crisis, the Rowes put themselves in the eye of the storm, shifting the focus onto themselves. The DeSantos, however, guided

Sam's punishment without becoming too distracted from their goals. The DeSantos extended some trust that Sam would receive the lessons he needed as he worked through the writing of his letter and reflected privately. The important distinctions between the two families had little to do with the temperaments of Carol versus Donna; indeed, many of us would not be able to remain as calm and rational as Carol. The critical difference is that the Rowes engaged in a number of classic dysfunctional patterns: triangulation, a parent-child coalition, parental splitting, and unfocused shaming, blaming, and punishment. Even if Carol had been more hot-tempered like Donna, the flaw in the Rowes' handling of the episode was that Terry received no guidance to help him turn his unruly behavior around.

The issue of character may not have entered into Carol's and Scott's deliberations, but consider the courage it took for Sam to face his misdeed in an honorable way. Making the most of a difficult situation, Sam's parents put him in a position of responsibility. And for him, the negative experience of going too far, followed by the challenge of correcting the mistake, constituted a truly important character lesson.

The Inner Workings of Morality

In the preceding vignette, Terry represents a boy who has been shamed throughout his childhood. Such children internalize the shame and loathing. Because they are not encouraged to overcome their impulses and act out of high self-regard, they often wrestle with their demons by repression, suppression, denial, and avoidance.

Object relations theory recognizes that we each have within us the potential for good and bad. *Under the best of circumstances children bond to their loved ones (called love objects), who socialize them to do other than that which they most selfishly crave.* Children want those whom they love to love back, so they do good "for them." During the preschool years, children do the right thing (wait turns, share, don't hit) not because they reason through it morally, but because their loved ones expect it of them and support them in learning values of human decency. Though children initially perform good actions with an external love object in mind, by the time they reach adolescence they've internalized this process. They have become their "others," and it's themselves they want to please. They choose to wait turns, share, and not hit.

Described in terms of ego development, the id tells us to do what we want; the superego, or conscience, tells us what we should do to be good; and the ego mediates between the two, operating like a manager, deciding what makes the best sense for the business of the day. Grappling with our good and bad impulses, our "observing ego" makes choices, processing them through a value system. Even when no one's looking, we want to do the right thing because that's who we are.

If shaming is the only act in a parental repertoire, the child is not given a sense of security and is not able to think of himself as a "good" kid who acts out of self-worth to solve his problems honorably. Shaming reinforces a self-image of "bad kid." Consider, for example, the issue of deception. Some parents are surprised to learn that a certain amount of lying is normal for adolescents. It is counterintuitive for us not to be shocked and outraged by our adolescent's lying. Horrified, we hold up the dunce cap. Nonetheless, we want to avoid a pernicious cycle of child lying and parent shaming, because it harms self-worth.

When a teenager lies, we want to address it objectively. We might talk about the temptation to lie and how we all have to struggle not to do so, letting them know we appreciate their dilemma. We might talk about how lying can temporarily get us out of a jam, but then we have to pay the cost of our conscience afterward. We might point out how lying contaminates trust between people and how a code of honesty benefits everyone. We can let our children know we'll support their efforts to value truth, even it means they end up in a jam of another kind. While this kind of exchange borders on the kind of moralizing that teenagers inherently reject, our acknowledgment of and appreciation for their grappling with universal impulses usually will keep their attention focused on the conversation.

Don't mince words. We can say, "You did a terrible thing by lying. We've got to think about where this lying is coming from and how you're going to manage to overcome this impulse next time." Keep in mind that well-adjusted teenagers do not usually lie out of maliciousness; they lie to avoid getting in trouble. The point we want to convey is that lying injures honor and credibility, but they can restore these character strengths by prioritizing honesty in the future. As parents, we're like cheerleaders, encouraging our children on, letting them know they have a chance to exercise their good. The message we want to send is, "I believe in you! You can do it!"

A Character Conundrum: Janisse, Brooke, Kendra, and Paul Beller, and Sugargram

A troubled family with a teenager came to my office, suffering from the pain of their malfunctioning family system. "I simply don't understand why a girl who has money in her pocket would stuff fifty dollars' worth of clothes in her backpack," complained an incredulous Janisse, rubbing her darkly circled, reddened eyes.

Seventeen-year-old Kendra slouched in one of my office chairs opposite her mother and father and retorted sharply, "God, Mom, give it a break. You've been repeating this same line for weeks. Everybody shoplifts. I just had the bad luck of getting caught."

Paul, Kendra's father, who appeared indifferent to the family's situation, impatiently interrupted his daughter and bluntly said, "I've got to make a phone call in a few minutes. How long is this meeting, Jan?" He shifted his weight, crossed his legs, and folded his arms.

"Dr. Kastner," said Janisse, turning away from Paul, whom she did not answer, "Kendra doesn't seem to be willing to accept any responsibility for what she's done. I refuse to believe 'everybody does it.'"

Then Kendra demonstrated the irreverent attitude her mother had told me about when she made the appointment. "Mom, what do you want from me? You act as if I just murdered the pope. You want me to lay prostrate on an altar and whip myself for five years before you'll be satisfied with my penance. I paid the fine and did my service time with the store, and now you drag me into therapy like I'm a psych case."

"It's not just this incident, Dr. Kastner," pleaded Janisse, looking to me for sympathy and avoiding speaking to her daughter directly. "She taunts me and snaps rude wisecracks at me all the time, especially in front of her friends. She tells me to shut up and mind my own business whenever I show an interest in her, and she literally never shows any interest in us. She'd just as soon spend all her time with her friends or in her room."

Paul leaned forward and laced his fingers together as he prepared for what looked to be a major statement. "Janisse is too sensitive and too cautious. She is forever fretting about Kendra." Abruptly he moved the conversation to himself. "You see, I'm a risk taker. When I had a chance to go out and build houses on my own, I took it. Now I'm a player. If you don't gamble sometimes, you don't get anywhere."

Again, Janisse directed the conversation to concerns closer to home. "Kendra does not lift one finger around the house to help. We can't even get her to empty the dishwasher. It's all take and no give. She gets a generous allowance and wastes it. We've probably brought this on ourselves."

"She's lazy," interjected Paul.

Though Janisse tried to keep the conversation centered on responsibility, Paul's focus repeatedly shifted back to himself. He was making every effort to discount Kendra's shoplifting incident, even as he skewered her as "lazy." At this point in the consultation, I wanted to learn how much responsibility Paul and Janisse were willing to take for their daughter's irresponsibility.

"Janisse," I asked, "how have you and Paul brought this on yourselves exactly?"

"Well," she responded, shaking her head and staring at her lap, "it's practically a cliché. We've spoiled both our daughters. Paul and I each put in long hours at our jobs, so I guess we've always suffered from the guilty working-parent syndrome. When we'd come home at night and on the weekends, we'd want to enjoy Kendra and Brooke, our nineteen-year-old, who is at college. Paul and I were both brought up in the postwar school of hard knocks. We've worked our ways to a good living, and we wanted our children to have what we never had — ski lessons, soccer camp, nice clothes. So we didn't nag them, and we avoided big hassles over making them do chores."

"You call this a problem, with all the kids using drugs and getting pregnant?" Paul balked. "This is ridiculous — a mountain out of a molehill. When I was a kid it would have taken robbing a bank to warrant a trip to the shrink."

The best therapy strategy at this point was for me to agree with Paul, who was clearly not willing to cooperate, and then later take back control. "You're right, Paul. Parents do seek consultation on problems of less severity than criminal behavior these days. I'm impressed by parents who are willing to work on issues that might relate to responsibility and respect."

I decided to engage Paul for a while and establish a rapport. I heard about his plans to expand his small building business; he thoroughly enjoyed the telling. Then I turned to Janisse and asked, "A while ago, you said 'they' in reference to your daughters. Do you see the same spoiling process with both Kendra and Brooke?" Kendra stopped picking the Styrofoam wrapping off the side of her Coke bottle and became interested all of a sudden, which typically happens in therapy when the focus shifts onto another family member. She looked her mother straight in the eye for her response.

"I'm not sure. Brooke, as the firstborn, seemed to be more driven, but last summer we started to see a more indulgent side. She came home from college and felt perfectly entitled to treat our house like a hotel. I don't know." Janisse's voice trailed off.

Not wanting to spend too much time on Janisse's compendium of complaints about her spoiled daughters, I tried a different angle. I wanted to continue probing the quality of this family's relationships to determine whether anyone could identify a possible oasis in their family desert.

"Kendra," I asked, "when do you enjoy being with your parents these days? I mean before the shoplifting fiasco. I understand it's been red hot since then."

Kendra pensively replied, "Oh, I guess when we're on vacation. But we're not really enjoying one another. Basically, I'm with my friends and they're with theirs."

Janisse interrupted plaintively, "This is precisely the problem. We try to provide pleasant family times, but even then her attitude is cold and rejecting. It's as if she'd really prefer we were never with her."

"Why would I want to be around you two?" said Kendra. "I'm rude, I'm cold, I'm spoiled. There you have it."

"Look, where is all this going?" said Paul. "She pinched some clothes. She got her wrists slapped. I know guys who have done a lot worse and never paid it back like we did with Kendra. I can't hang around here much longer, listening to the same complaints I hear at home."

I told Paul that I appreciated his commitment to parenting Kendra by persisting through the evaluation process, and then I pursued a different angle. I asked Kendra, "Who do you feel most accepts you for who you are? Not the 'rude, cold' person you just described, but for the person you believe yourself to be?"

Kendra sensed my earnest attempt to understand her situation, so she obliged me with another reflective response. "Well, I might say my friends, but they can run hot and cold. I guess my grandmother."

Kendra's answer hit Janisse's hot button. "Yes, she thinks you can do no wrong. That's convenient. But she doesn't have to deal with the store manager or the neighbors when you have a party when we're out of town. She gets to be the Sugargram, as she loves to call herself."

This response presented an intergenerational dimension to their family problems. I chose to examine this lead, for it was bound to be part of the picture.

"So, Janisse, what is your relationship with your mother like?"

Janisse became noticeably uncomfortable in her chair, but seemed relieved to have an opportunity to explain her outburst. "It's a difficult relationship. We have to work at getting along."

"What an understatement!" interrupted Kendra. "She drives you nuts. You can't stand it that she's nice to me when you're mad at me."

"That's not it. Of course, it annoys me that she enjoys the Sugargram role so much. It's as if she's glad you're giving me a hard time out of revenge. No matter what I achieved or did for her, I could never gain her approval. No matter how much I include her, it's never enough. She has always been so critical of me and has never shown any insight into her own unbelievably demanding and difficult personality. She's a classic self-absorbed, meddling grandmother."

As our evaluation session continued and I gathered more information about their situation, I saw how deeply this family suffered. Here was a father preoccupied with himself who had very little interest in therapy; an exhausted, overwhelmed mother who felt guilty about working and was entangled in a problematic relationship with her own mother; and an adolescent who was morally adrift.

Three Faces of Shoplifting

After many years of treating different adolescents brought in for consultation following a shoplifting incident, I've come to categorize their actions according to three types. On the most benign end of the spectrum, shoplifting can represent a fluky, risk-taking impulse. Kendra said, "Everybody does it," which may not be much of an exaggeration.

When I interview a family that seems to be functioning well despite a shoplifting incident — the teenager is not excessively mouthy and disruptive, is not failing in school, is not involved with a deviant peer group, and everyone in the family seems to be pretty much on-task developmentally — I'm ready to assume that the shoplifting was a one-time impulse. These mistakes usually occur during early adolescence, and, handled properly, can ultimately be positive learning experiences. Parents should approach this type of shoplifting as a severe transgression. Instead of either attacking the child's character or minimizing the situation, they should help their child find ways to restrain from impetuously taking risks. Following this type of shoplift, some teenagers become immunized for life, never to commit another crime so long as they live.

On the opposite end of the spectrum are shoplifting incidents that occur as symptoms of a conduct disorder. When a family history reveals a host of deviant behaviors, which might include truancy, other lawbreaking episodes, and behavioral problems dating back to earlier childhood, there is a good chance the shoplifting is part of a more destructive pattern. Diagnosis and treatment is long-term, and a deeper understanding would entail a study of conduct disorder and antisocial personality.

Between these two categories are adolescents who suffer from a character deficit that I call failure-to-thrive. "Failure-to-thrive" is often used to describe children who are insufficiently nourished; as with food, some children are malnourished in values. Kendra belonged in this group. To call her a thief would be to miss the point: she is angry and confused, limping along rather than flourishing. On her current course, she is unlikely to be either a thriving and successful adult with a one-time shoplift behind her, or a destructive member of society, advancing from shoplifting to greater crimes. As matters now stand, she's likely to enter the ranks of the marginal performers in life. Without a moral compass, such people lack passion for anything meaningful. They get by without finely tuned values, steady bearings, and direction that makes for a vital life.

Character Problems En Masse

Although there are other ways to describe the Beller family, one lens through which to view them would be that of character. Families that struggle with character often have a family-wide phenomenon at work. While Paul was the easiest to identify as a person with a character problem, each member of the family had a particular challenge. Both parents fulfilled the basics of life — they worked; they paid the bills (usually very late, as I can attest); they provided materially for their children, even struggling to do so; they were thought of in the community as decent citizens, parishioners, and neighbors. Kendra and Brooke went to school and performed adequately, earning mostly C's. But, beyond the basics, this family was flagging.

Members of this family lacked what Robert Coles calls moral purpose.[8] *They lacked strength and confidence to set a sure course. Their efforts were directed at "passing" with their jobs, school, and family. They fended off criticism from others rather than thriving with higher goals.*

Although Janisse described Kendra's shoplifting as a riddle — "I simply don't understand why a girl who has money in her pocket would stuff fifty dollars' worth of clothes in her backpack" — her action is explicable. Therapists often refer to this type of behavior as a ticket of admission or a calling card that says "help." Though Kendra was what we call an identified patient or a symptom bearer, clearly the entire family needed to be examined in order to find the origins of their family-wide failure-to-thrive. Although on some level Kendra enjoyed her parents' permissiveness, their material indulgences, and her excessive amount of freedom, we know that all children need structure, clear rules, predictable consequences, and relief from the malleable family environment that earns them labels like "spoiled brat."

Parallels between father and daughter were more apparent than those between mother and daughter, for it turned out that Kendra was cutting corners in her adolescent life in the same way Paul was in his small business. From numerous comments dropped during therapy, I deduced that Paul was comfortable with illegal bookkeeping practices, and Kendra's shoplifting was fairly unimportant to him. Paul showed many of the characteristics of narcissism because he was grandiose, lacked empathy, and was hypersensitive to what others thought of them. Paul conversed almost in non sequiturs, directing all roads back to himself. My responses to Paul, which bordered on obsequiousness, spoke to his need to be acknowledged and calmed him down so he could cooperate with the session.

Narcissism is a clinically defined disorder with wide-ranging implications. Issues such as depression, anxiety, and behavioral problems can be treated through therapy, but narcissism can be pervasive and chronic — practically impervious to character-building efforts. In the heat of marital discord, people are sometimes tempted to write their spouse off as untreatable or unchangeable. Simply because someone experiences a spouse as arrogant, selfish, or insensitive does not mean that person is a textbook narcissist, since perceptions can be biased. A marriage is a complicated arrangement, with *both* members contributing to the existing dynamic. Making these types of diagnoses is a precarious business and should not be done without professional consultation.

With his business floundering, Paul was scrambling to keep his loans paid and remained unwilling to address the family's difficulties. Early on, he dropped out of therapy because he was "too busy." When all members of the family system participate, there's a higher probability of working toward a satisfactory outcome. A parallel situation would be treating a chemically dependent teen who has an actively alcoholic father; we're better off if we can mobilize the father as well. In some families, though, it's not possible to involve everyone, and so we had to deal with what we had. Those available to work with were Kendra, Janisse, and Sugargram.

Unfinished Business: Enlisting the Dissenter

Janisse's relationship with her mother had infected Janisse's relationship with her own daughter. Technically called a cross-generational grand-mother-granddaughter coalition, this pattern is not uncommon in adolescent therapy. As the snippet from the evaluation session suggests, Sugargram was using her granddaughter to fight an unresolved battle with her daughter.

In subsequent sessions, Janisse revealed the emotional toll of her difficult relationship with her mother. In spite of her mother's critical, demanding ways, while growing up Janisse had sought her mother's approval relentlessly. Harboring intense resentment, Janisse remained involved with her mother out of guilt-ridden loyalty, but her feelings were transparent, and Sugargram felt unappreciated and rejected. Oblivious to her own ability to be nasty and dismissive, Sugargram constantly complained about Janisse's ingratitude — fueling a cycle of mutual hostility.

In therapy, Sugargram sobbed that her life had been extremely difficult as a single mother and that Janisse had never shown an understanding of her many sacrifices. Her husband had abandoned the family when Janisse was two years old. Sugargram was a staunch Catholic who had done everything she could to maintain high behavioral standards and raise Janisse properly. For Janisse, these standards translated into a view of her mother as oppressive, demanding, and critical.

A classic child-rearing pattern is that of a parent who steers away from a parenting practice that made her miserable as a child but unwittingly recapitulates it. Janisse had resented her mother's autocratic, controlling ways, so the pendulum swung and Janisse became permissive. Because Kendra was not getting the parenting structure she needed, she had become a surly young woman who inspired the very criticism and negativity that Janisse experienced with her own mother. Janisse ended up in the same kind of relationship with Kendra she had so hoped to avoid — resentful and bitter.

Another intergenerational pattern Janisse repeated was that she married a man who was in some way unavailable. Janisse's father had physically abandoned the family, while Paul was functionally absent. Initially, Janisse described Sugargram as a martyr, by which she meant an angry person who felt sorry for herself. As Janisse looked back on her mother's life and on her own during therapy, her perspective began to shift. She saw that Paul had abandoned the family, much as her father had, and that she had taken up a role similar to her mother's. Seeing the connection was a breakthrough for her, and she was willing to do anything to keep from repeating the pattern.

Although Janisse's solution to her difficult relationship with her mother had been to create a distance, I recommended the opposite tactic. Because she realized she was "becoming her mother," Janisse was open to a move as previously unthinkable and paradoxical as the one I suggested: to acknowledge her mother's contribution to her life and ask for her help with her daughter.

Janisse enlisted Sugargram's support to sprinkle her "sugar" in ways that would enhance Kendra's character rather than sabotage it. Janisse needed her mother's support in this difficult situation, and Sugargram could appreciate the effort to modify Kendra's ways especially if we removed the incentive to dissent, that is, to punish Janisse for underappreciating her.

Sugargram was actually desperate for a role in the family that would be valued by Janisse. She agreed to stop winking at Kendra's infractions and to stop giving her cash. Janisse and her mother made a pact to focus on appreciating each other (past, present, and future) and to refrain from criticizing each other. Janisse realized that this was the same pivot she needed to improve her relationship with her own daughter.

Sugargram helped out in one particularly memorable endeavor. She had planned to pay Kendra's fees for camp in California during the following summer, but Janisse proposed a different plan. She arranged for Kendra to volunteer in a summer preschool program for abused children, and Sugargram offered to pay Kendra a small stipend for her work there. Though Kendra put up a fuss, she eventually conceded and learned that she had a gift for dealing with difficult kids. Kendra also discovered that her friends were much more interested in her stories from her volunteer experience than they would have been in tales from camp.

Although Janisse, Kendra, and Sugargram did some good work in therapy and were certainly better off for it, many unresolved issues remained, and I felt uncertain of where they would go with their lives. Before she came to therapy, Kendra had had seventeen years of dismal habits, and her father would remain problematic. Her experience working in the preschool helped engender a new respect for herself, but would this experience be enough? Would Janisse be able to hold firm in the face of Paul's cynicism and self-absorption? Would Janisse and Sugargram maintain their pact? Would this family revert to their old behavior patterns, losing sight of their higher purpose and direction?

In the 1970s and '80s, child psychologists observed a swing of the pendulum away from the values placed on authority and "proper" behavior in the '50s. Reacting to those values, many families over the past twenty years have focused on enriching the lives of their children and on developing more supportive, less authoritarian disciplinary styles. Recently, however, we've seen an increased societal awareness of the need for some of the emphasis on moral development that was prevalent in the '50s. As we try to blend the best of both worlds — maintaining authority without becoming authoritarian, remaining supportive without becoming permissive, providing opportunities for our children without simply handing them over — we set our sights on character.

In much of today's parenting literature and in parenting skills seminars, character remains less a tidily defined concept than a broad, multifaceted quality that encompasses everything from pursuits as mundane as manners to virtues as lofty as altruism, integrity, and moral purpose. Though no exact recipe for cultivating it in our children exists, we are usually able to identify character (or the appalling lack of it) in action. With that in mind, the most basic lesson of character building is to *support* character virtues when we see them, and, likewise, to counter behaviors lacking virtue. Parenting with a value on character involves conscious prioritizing, being aware of who we are as role models, and making an effort to seize opportunities to help our children learn through the three D's. It takes a willingness to let our children know that there are few pat answers, that there is usually a certain amount of tension and struggle in making the right decision, and that taking others' views into consideration may run against the grain of one's own self-interest.

5

The Social Kaleidoscope

Goal: Maintain a mostly positive, close relationship with your adolescent while also fostering his or her prosocial friendships and interpersonal skills.

Picture yourself standing alone, center stage, half-prepared, disoriented and distracted, about to give a talk. Welling up within is an uneasy mix of self-confidence and creeping self-doubt, as the peering eyes of a thousand potential critics bear down. It is this sense of someone watching and someone critiquing, ever present in the adolescent sensibility, that David Elkind called the phenomenon of the "imaginary audience."[1]

Why are adolescents fixated on being "cool"? Why do they travel in packs? relate minute details of their day to one another? exchange banter with weird affectation? High on the list of reasons is their inordinate self-consciousness; they feel at center stage, and their audience — real and of their own making — isn't altogether friendly. Taking their awkward, growing selves into increasingly complex social situations — thinking about the implications of what others are thinking about them — slips them into knots only a Houdini could untie.

Because adolescents' minds are working overtime, most feel a lot of social pressure. If we could get inside their heads and live through the uncertainties and assaults of their day, we'd come to see how the patterns of their experience shift from teachers to friends to parents, and we'd see how lacking parents sometimes are in grasping the nuances of their world view. Adolescent boys in my practice have revealed to me some of the pockets of their internal lives. Henry, below, is a composite of those many teenage boys who have shared the ups and downs of their days with me. I've spliced together Henry's internal life with an incident that came to my attention while consulting with a school.

Dealing with "Stuff": An Internal Monologue of Fourteen-Year-Old Henry

A groggy Henry sinks into the song playing on his clock radio, figuring he has plenty of time to throw on his clothes and get ready for school, when he hears his mom screaming up the stairs, "Henry, get up or you'll miss your carpool and have to bike to school again!"

That screeching voice. Why did I stay up so late last night?

"HENRY! I'M WARNING YOU!"

God, I've got a math test first period. Mr. Spinelli puts stuff on it that's not in the book, and we're supposed to be able to figure it out. I shouldn't have copied Eric's homework two days ago. This really sucks. I don't know where my calculator is.

Shuffling into the hallway, Henry responds, "I'm up, Ma. I'm waiting for the bathroom."

That bitch Kristen is still in the bathroom.

Henry bangs on the door, yelling "bathroom hog." Kristen, his older sister, frostily informs him from the other side of the closed door that this was his week to be first in the bathroom, but since he missed his chance, he'll just have to cool his jets until she's finished. As they argue, Mom hurries by, reminding Henry he should have picked himself out of bed a half-hour ago. "Remember the sibling conflict rule," she adds. "Anything longer than five minutes and your allowances will be docked again."

Abruptly, the bathroom door swings open. "Watch it in there," says Kristen. "I'm tired of cleaning up your piss on the toilet seat." Henry flips her the bird.

Everybody is against me around here. How does Kristen manage to get Mom on her side every time? Oh, God, four new zits.

Henry gently flicks at the pimples on his fair skin with a fingernail, but his face becomes a patchwork of red, swollen blotches. With a wet washcloth he tries to flatten his hair, sticking out like a bristle brush. Time passing, Mom (back down in the kitchen again) yells up the stairs, citing a research report that says kids who skip breakfast perform worse on tests than those who start off their day with a good breakfast. "Get down here!"

she shouts. Henry psychs himself up about his math test, but worries he has studied the wrong parts of the chapter. Lunging down the stairs, he discovers his carpool has left without him. Kristen, however, made the ride.

That bitch could have asked them to wait. Thirty seconds. So now I have to "suffer the natural consequences" of not being ready on time. Spare me that line. I'm going to flunk the test for sure.

Henry pedals furiously all the way to school, locks his bike, and sprints to class, arriving out of breath, gasping for air, his body heaving and shaking. Mr. Spinelli hands him the test and a detention slip. He struggles through the test, but he's stuck on the part that requires a calculator. Mr. Spinelli says, "That's very unfortunate for you. You need to come prepared for class." Later, in the corridor while changing classes, Henry sees Brandeth.

I feel like shit. I know I blew that test, and now Mom and Dad will be on me even more. God, there's Brandeth. I can't believe the way she tosses her hair back like that. She's looking at me. Maybe she's not. She's trying to look like she's not looking at me. I don't know whether that note was for real. It said Brandeth thought I was cute. If that note was a setup, I'll look really lame if I start paying attention and talking to her. Christ, what's that!

Henry steps on one of his untied shoelaces and jerks forward, books falling out of his backpack. Flushed with heat, he feels sweat beads breaking out on his upper lip. Brandeth and the three girls with her giggle coyly. Two of Henry's good friends whack him on the back and tease him all the way to Spanish class about being head over heels over Brandeth. "Hey, dude," taunts one of the guys as Henry takes his seat in class, "what are you trying to hide with that book in your lap?"

I can't let them know they're getting to me. I want to die. I want to go back to yesterday and start over again. If only I could transport myself. I'd get up earlier and hog the bathroom so Kristen would have to go to school with smashed hair and feel as shitty as I do now. I could kill that test. I'd walk smoothly and coolly by Brandeth while she pushed her long hair back with her fingers. Maybe Willie would bother her, and I'd move in and shove him off. And Brandeth would sorta be crying and look at me gratefully and reach out to me.

Henry notices Ms. Santiago standing over him. "I have told you repeatedly that I will call your parents in for a conference if you do not stop daydreaming in class," she says sternly. "Where is your homework? We're all waiting for you!" He finds his homework fast, heads to the blackboard to write one of the homework sentences, but there's a careless mistake in it.

Later, outside at lunch recess, the guys are still razzing him about his smooth move in the hall in front of Brandeth. They accuse him of tripping over his hard-on. Although Henry tries to ignore them and shoot some hoops, he is playing poorly. "Glad you're on the other team, man," Willie snarls.

I hate these guys. No one is on my side. God, I'd do anything for a couple of good baskets, but the harder I try, the more I miss, and the more shit they sling me. I'm choking. I've got to get a hold of myself or, oh Jesus, don't let me bawl in front of everyone.

Henry body checks Willie. Willie pushes him, and they start knocking each other around. The track coach, Mr. Chu, breaks up the scuffle. He talks to the boys about thinking before acting and the need to inhibit impulses by coming up with alternative problem-solving strategies to violence.

What bullshit. Why doesn't this guy just make a tape and play it over and over. He's getting off on his anti-violence lecture. But, Jesus, of all the people who had to come along . . . when I'm trying to make the track team. Willie is doing his suck-up thing with Mr. Chu so he'll think I started the whole thing. I don't care if I do get blamed. I'm fast. They need me on that team. I'm not going to lower myself.

On the way home in his carpool, Kristen scolds Henry for fighting at school. Henry sneers at her, and the carpool parent comments on his bad attitude. At home, Henry retreats to his room to listen to his Walkman. He worries about what his parents are going to do when they see his math grade. He wonders whether the Spanish teacher or the coach are going to call his parents and whether he'll get cut from track because of the fight. He thinks about ways to find out who sent that note and whether it's true that Brandeth thinks he's cute. He fantasizes about sex with Brandeth, about Mr. Chu having a heart attack, about Kristen flunking a class, about Willie getting caught stealing something from the school and getting expelled, and about taking the track team to the state championship. Then his mom catches him in bed when he has promised to mow the lawn after school. "How could you break your promise after what happened this morning! Henry, is there something wrong?"

She is on my case every minute. She's always begging me to talk to her about my feelings, and then I get this creepy feeling all over, like I'm getting suffocated.

She's looking really sad because I won't talk to her. I feel lousy, but I just want to be left alone, no demands on me.

"Henry," yells Kristen. "Phone! It's a girrrrl! It's Brandeth." Henry smiles.

The Agony and the Ecstasy

Sensitive and self-conscious, Henry feels a tremendous amount of pressure. For starters, rousing himself from the warmth of bed to the tune of a shrill parental reprimand assaults his senses. He knows he looks cold and detached to his sister and mother, but he can't do anything about it because he's flooded with anxiety about his math test. He has to deal with his sister in the bathroom, unruly hair, pimples, screaming voices, the time crunch, and the agitation of a high-speed bike ride to school. Lost calculator aside, he is not set up to perform well on his test.

Henry has incredible yearnings for Brandeth, and like most boys his age, he doesn't know how to handle these emotions. He is a blur of unfocused desire. Walking down the hall between classes is exciting and exhilarating, as he dissects Brandeth's every move and imagines everyone scrutinizing his reaction to Brandeth. But what if Brandeth snubs him?

Young adolescents are sophisticated enough to flirt and emit attracting body language, but they rarely talk directly to the person they like. Typically, they first deal through "agent" friends, who scope out interest levels. Notes travel back and forth like business faxes in this far-from-private process. Because pubescent teenagers are bewildered by their own consuming fascination over the opposite sex, there is great incentive to get involved in someone else's courtship dance. Friends can help each other out, but they can also spread gossip and tease.

Perplexed and distracted by the anonymous note he has received, Henry trips, an utterly humiliating experience. Already feeling highly vulnerable because of his excitement over Brandeth, he feels unglued by his friends' relentless taunting. Though we often associate adolescent social cruelty with girls, boys can be kings of the putdown, bullying each other in unbelievably gauche ways. Many young adolescent boys, for example, accuse one other of having hard-ons, in part because they're so self-conscious about their own dismayingly random erections.

Overloaded emotionally, Henry needs to work off his fixation on Brandeth, the taunting, and the degrading experiences he has had in math and Spanish by shooting hoops. However, he's so wound up that this also goes badly. On the basketball court, Henry performs miserably, adding more insult and frustration to his day. Tears are not an option for him, so his feelings erupt physically. *More so than we realize, boys' aggressiveness happens out of feelings of vulnerability and frustration.*

What about the coach's response to the fight, which Henry privately labels "bullshit"? For that matter, did the mom, the math teacher, or the Spanish teacher do or say anything wrong? Not really. From an adult perspective, they responded appropriately, according to their targeted objectives. Henry's mother wants to shepherd him out the door on time and minimize sibling conflict; Mr. Spinelli hopes to teach Henry to be more responsible about remembering his calculator; Ms. Santiago is trying to keep his attention focused; and Mr. Chu is making an effort to reason with the boys about violence.

Henry is on another page. By gaining access to his internal processing of events, we realize how affronted he feels by each of these adult's well-intended responses. Though the mom, the teachers, and the coach have valid points of view, Henry is too wrapped up in his own feelings to find meaning in what's being said to him. He defends himself by dismissing their efforts. What's illustrated here is an instance of colliding social worlds, with adolescent and adults approaching from different directions, preoccupied by different concerns.

At best, in these situations, our adult role is that of a social anthropologist, trying to make sense of the behavior that's puzzling us. Henry's trials are not a "what-to-do" story for parents; rather, they're about understanding and appreciating the shifting, kaleidoscopic patterns of our kid's internal world, which are outside of our line of vision. Our kids have a lot more on their social platter than our particular objectives: for example, as Henry's mom focuses on fair bathroom policy, he's coping with test anxiety.

If we develop empathy for our teenager's multifaceted world, we are less likely to simply respond to the troubling picture facing us, overreact, judge, and proceed with our singular view and rational protocol, which adolescents often reject. While knowing what a typical teenage boy like Henry goes through can help us become more empathetic and patient, we do not have it within our means to forestall the social turmoil that adolescents experience. And, importantly, Henry's situation is typical of adolescence, and not a crisis that calls for intervention.

Henry's caring mom wants to talk with him so she can figure out why he's not mowing the lawn, but he's unreceptive. Sometimes we're able to offer advice or problem-solve with our teenagers, but other times — as Henry's story illustrates — we're not able to get through to them. Though we can encourage our children to verbalize their thoughts and their needs, early adolescents are experiencing a great deal — cognitively, emotionally, and socially. They are often so befuddled they can't articulate what they are feeling, though increasingly, as they mature, they can. In the meantime, a commiserating glance, a shoulder touch, a musing comment like "Looks like you're working some things out," or any gesture that conveys understanding is an amazing gift to an adolescent who feels overwhelmed but suffocated by a direct inquiry at the wrong time.

If we're more or less confident about the job we've been doing as parents, who our adolescent is, and the relative safety of his or her situation, during those moments when our kids are aching and we can't soothe them, we can reassure ourselves. Keep in mind that your child is going out into the world with a part of you, which can help carry them along. Though Henry is cold to his mother, he's more connected to her than he shows. We want to be a strong presence for our children and provide a secure base from which they can operate, but we run into trouble when we try to provide hands-on help with all their social slings and arrows. Henry's mother probably won't be able to extricate him from his woes, but when he finishes his phone call, things might seem brighter to him, and if she's a mature mom, she will be able to accept the situation.

Parental Involvement in an Adolescent's Social Life: Not an Either/Or Question

A question parents often ask me is, "When should I intervene in my child's life, and when should I back out altogether?" *The solution is to be neither completely "in" nor "out" of an adolescent's social world, but to assume a middle posture whereby we observe, remain available and supportive, and stay generally apprised of their social interactions.* Avoid the two extremes — constantly inquiring and investigating or consistently ignoring and overlooking. Our role is to oversee, not to be an omnipresence. Then you can make judgments as to whether your adolescent would benefit from more direct parent facilitating or more space to negotiate their own course.

In making judgment calls about whether to move closer or maintain a respectful watch, we use three information systems, each of which by itself could be flawed. First, we use our personal sensors and intuition — what we know and feel about our child combined with what we know about the world. It is, however, dangerous to plunge into a child's life if your gut feel is your only cue. Some parents are rendered anxious by their biological nature, family background, or social history, while other parents can be naive, blasé, and indifferent to prompts in their adolescents' lives that call for intervention. Because temperamental and family-of-origin issues can distort our sensors, parents need to draw on additional information sources when sizing up any given situation.

Secondly, we stay attuned to what we hear from voices around us, from other parents, teachers, friends, people in the neighborhood. Is someone whose views we generally respect raising a particular concern? As we listen to others, we want to remain alert to their potential biases or misinterpretation.

Thirdly, we take heed of the feedback we're receiving from our child. Some kids are thin-skinned, while others are downright callous. Some like to mull over advice from others, while others want to fly on their own. Look at the signals your child is sending and tailor your responses thusly. How comfortable is the child with parental inquiries? Do you detect problem behaviors that might suggest he needs more parent involvement? Or do behaviors say you're hovering too closely? Does the child withdraw dramatically or respond angrily and indignantly when approached? If withdrawals or protest are extreme or if they become predominant ways of responding, it could suggest something is amiss, and a professional consultation would be advised. If by using these three methods you sense a true social problem, increase your involvement as a parent.

Another type of parent social assessment is the technique of spot checking. In our observing/supporting role, we don't need to stay on top of our child on an ongoing basis; but perhaps it's been a couple of months since we've verified whether they actually went where they told us they would be going or we've tracked whether they're with their usual group of friends. In an unobtrusive way, we do some follow-up at random intervals. Sometimes spot checking simply involves focusing our attention in a more intentional way; this technique can be particularly valuable during those periods when we feel like we're losing the general frequency of their world. With a good listening ear, we catch their signal when it's coming our way and tune in carefully to make sure nothing is amiss.

Adolescent Social Bruises: Advantages of Staying in an Apprising, Supportive Mode

Certain social bruisings are as typical for an adolescent as skinned knees are for preschoolers. Learning about the kinds of social wounds most kids will suffer can help us know when it may be appropriate to shift from an ongoing observing and supportive role to an intervening role. If an adolescent has occasional and varied social mishaps similar to those listed below, the parent can usually consider the experience within the normative range. Knowing what's normal can keep us from overreacting to our adolescents' hurt even as we continue to support them. Although some teenagers go unscathed, most will:

- Have a significant fight (physical or verbal) with a friend. Sometimes they will start it; sometimes the friend will.
- Get dumped by a member of the opposite sex, and most of them will dump someone else.
- Be on the receiving end of a mean or nasty comment or action (for example, a prank phone call) and most will say or do something hurtful to someone else.
- Be the object of gossip, and most will gossip about others.
- Be excluded in some way from a group they want to belong to or a party they want to attend, and most will conspire to do the same to another.
- Lose an important friend, either by getting dropped by that person or dropping that person.
- Feel social pressure to do something they normally wouldn't do (for example, lie about where they're going), and most will pressure another to do the same.
- Be unable to share a grievance or point of view openly with a friend or in a group, and most will be blind to an aspect of their own behavior that a friend should but doesn't tell them about.
- Be overly critical of a friend, and most will be defensive about or hurt by receiving criticism that is unfairly harsh.

What catches most parents' attention about a list like this is, "Aha — my teenager isn't only receiving insult and injury; she's also dishing it out." We hear more about the sins of others than we do about our own child's social crimes. Moreover, this list should assure parents that their child isn't the only one to have had feelings hurt by a best friend.

While suffering from any of the above social stings, adolescents might benefit from some type of parental action — a sanction, for example, if there's been a fight or they've been pressured into inappropriate behavior; a discussion if they've been excluded or have lost a friend; or strategic questioning if gossip is wreaking havoc in their life.

Nevertheless, there are potential gains for our kids if we don't immediately step into the middle of these situations. *As long as we are able to oversee what is happening and provide support as needed, it is almost always preferable to let adolescents be the acting agent in solving their social difficulties. The process of thinking through their problems and acting independently helps build social competence and self-esteem.* How tempting it is to call another child's parent or teacher when our child's stings are smarting. However, it's usually *our* anxiety about their anxiety that prompts us to rush to the rescue. The reality is, adolescents will wrong and hurt others socially, and be wronged and hurt by others, and this is their platform for social learning.

If we solve our children's dilemmas for them, we can be party to a type of triangulation. It's common for two children who can't handle their conflict to reach out (triangulate) to a third person to resolve the issue and thereby reduce whatever negative emotion they're harboring. Children who consistently look for someone else to jump in on their side may grow up lacking the ability to manage the inevitable stresses of human interaction, rendering them less able to deal directly with conflicts in their mature relationships and marriages.

Unnecessary intervention also reinforces a "victim" role. By rescuing and overprotecting, we send the implicit message, "You can't do it." Thus, children learn they are helpless or incompetent. Over time, some "victims" find power by letting others do for them, and they become comfortable in that role. A typical chain of events can play out as innocently as this: a child feels someone has wronged her; upset and unhappy, she complains to her parents; the parents are unable to maintain a boundary between their child's pain and their pain, so they're incapable of working with her on solutions that may take time and involve continued hurt for her; to resolve the problem, they intervene directly with the offender (or her parents). The child has discovered how powerful she is because she can call in someone bigger to wage war on her behalf. No matter how expedient this solution, a problem remains because the locus of power is external rather than from within as she determines to call on others to solve her problems rather than to rely on herself.

As dysfunctional as the rescuer/victim trap is, we also want to be on the alert for kids who believe they can handle all their problems on their own — kids who clam up and won't call for help, no matter how much they ache. Gender becomes a factor here, for parents are more likely to rescue girls while leaving boys to be strong and pull themselves up by their bootstraps. In fact, we might never learn of our boys' acute social injuries because by adolescence they are often sufficiently gender-typed to neither complain about nor disclose their hurt and anger.

Ideally, parents should encourage their children to salve their own minor social bruises, while also looking to others for support. The adolescent's temperament, experience, and situation will determine the extent to which parents need to emphasize the value of self-reliance and/or the value of accepting help. The parent's job is not to eliminate all suffering or difficulty in a child's life. If our adolescent has been hurt, sometimes our role is to validate and empathize and let them feel the sting and grow from it. Nevertheless, it's critical to remain watchful, so that if a social scratch becomes a deep hurt we can shift into the intervening mode and get our kids the help they need.

Adolescent Social Problems: Active Intervention

If a social dilemma is persistent, intensifying, or not being resolved with an adolescent's own efforts (often accompanied by parental support) then it is likely it has blossomed into a problem needing either more overt parental intervention or clinical/school intervention. We might make a judgment call that what is going on has crossed a line, and there has been real cruelty, not typical teenage effrontery. Or, we might see a normal behavior compounding to the extent that it has simply gone too far. Perhaps you hear your teen is making a habit of prank phone calling, of kissing openly in an exhibitionistic way on the school grounds, or of routinely showing off and disrupting her classes. When a troublesome pattern arises, parents need to initiate home, school, or counselor meetings. Though these infractions need attention, they should be addressed delicately. Adolescents are often threatened and resentful of adult intervention, which they may perceive as coercive and meddling.

How can you intervene if, for example, your thirteen-year-old son has become the object of a vicious social attack — perhaps he is receiving scathing notes day after day at school? In today's world, how we respond has everything to do with sociocultural context; we're all painfully aware that a honk of a car horn on an L.A. freeway can lead to gunfire. Provoking a stranger is dangerous business: anything can happen. In a high-violence school with unpredictable kids, an adolescent's only sane response to harassment would be to button his mouth and get help from responsible adults. In a really rough situation, an outright rescue of the child — changing schools or removing him from the predicament — may be appropriate.

But what if your child is being teased by known culprits who are just trying to get his goat? Given a relatively benign context, the parent's first move is to help the adolescent confront them himself. Though parents often advise their children to ignore bullies (and some we should!), unhappily, this usually does not make them disappear. Because the adolescent's effort to ignore is often anxious and shaky, the perpetrators enjoy their impact — they know they're getting through — even as the victim tries to act as if it's not bothering him. Ignoring becomes part of the power struggle. Only if the response is true indifference with no revealing "vibes" will it work.

Bullies know they have power, so the countermove must be strong enough to take it away. Counsel your adolescent to make his retort a short, cutting, one-liner delivered with disdain: "You're disgusting." "Kids say that in fourth grade. You're lame." "You are so immature." Since "immature" is the very thing young adolescents are trying hard not to be, this can be a particularly pithy putdown. Potent words labeling their behavior carry more weight than profanity or direct name calling. The adolescent should be prepared for a comeback, but he should not become engaged in an exchange. The point is to keep it short, simple, and acidic. We want to teach our adolescents that if the situation appears controllable and safe, the first order of business is not to report automatically to someone for rescue. Our kids need to learn to be good at countering bullies. Then, if they are still unsuccessful despite efforts to stave off their harassers, they can call in sources of authority to help evaluate their dilemma and form a plan.

Social Rules That Bind

In many ways, Henry's monologue typifies the internal life of a fourteen-year-old boy: he feels hassled and put down, worries about school, feels vulnerable about girls, and reacts to "stuff" physically and inarticulately. While some of Henry's reactions are byproducts of the moment, others are representative of adolescent boyhood. Sometimes girls will experience the same emotions, though common observation tells us they are less likely to haul off and hit another person. A daughter of one of my friends, fourteen-year-old Carrie is as endearingly normal a girl as Henry is such a boy. On the day we had the following conversation, her particular dilemma was that she — an eighth-grade girl — liked a seventh-grade boy.

Carrie: I'm just so tired of all the rules.

LK: Rules? What do you mean?

Carrie: Well, you can only like and be nice to certain girls. If you are too nice to the wrong girl, that's not good. And, you've got to be really nice to certain girls, or you'll get it from them. And, you can only like certain boys or else you're a nerd to like them too.

LK: Any more rules?

Carrie: Oh, yeah. An eighth-grade girl can't like a seventh-grade boy. Forget it! But a seventh-grade girl might like an eighth-grade boy, but she can't do anything about it unless he likes her too, but then the eighth-grade girls will hate her and be really mean to her since she took one of *their* boys. But, after a while, maybe she'll be accepted . . . if she's really nice and sucks up to the eighth-grade girls. But she'll get screwed if she doesn't.

LK: Boy, it's really rigid, huh?

Carrie: Oh, that's nothing. Everything has rules. If you wear something like a Mickey Mouse sweatshirt, you can get teased. If you don't give enough attention to certain people, they'll think you're snobby. If you don't return phone calls because you might have too much homework, they might think you're too goody-goody. Every time you do something, you wonder who's going to criticize you.

LK: These are tough rules, aren't they?

Carrie: Rules are everywhere. It's depressing. Every step you take, you might be crossing somebody's rule.

LK: Does that keep you from saying and doing things, for fear of breaking a rule?

Carrie: Of course, all the time.

LK: Do you think it's the same for boys?

Carrie: No way! They do what they want.

This is a script only a girl could speak, but before venturing into the complex terrain of gender, there are a couple of quick generalities about rules and conformity to mull over. As is true of all societies, the social world of adolescence is intricate, complex, and saturated with rules, perceived and actual. Just as young children figure out the rules of game playing (don't cheat; take turns; be generous if you win; don't toss the board if you lose), adolescents — girls and boys alike — form strategies to stay in their social game. An adolescent who is hypersensitive to rules, as one could argue Carrie is, can feel constricted, but a teenager who is oblivious to the implied rules of her subculture is likely to spend a lot of time wondering why she feels shunned. And then again, there will always be the rebels, who thrive on their overt scorn for the rules.

Though adolescents have the fluidity to try on new identities and experiment with dress, hairstyles, music, leisure activities, and behaviors in ways adults cannot, it's as awkward for a teenager to shift from the preps to the skaters as it would be for an adult to finesse the transition from investment banker to folksinger. To belong, Carrie feels pressure to conform to the rules, codes, and expectations of her peer group, but some of her feelings can be attributed to the fact that she is fourteen.

From a developmental perspective, conformity typically peaks at ages twelve to fourteen, decreases some by fifteen to seventeen, then decreases further by nineteen to twenty-one. Once she vaults the hurdle of middle adolescence, Carrie will probably feel freer of the rules now preoccupying her. Parents may feel they've lost their young adolescent to peers and peer influence, but most teenagers lose their clonelike ways by the beginning of high school and take pride in individuality.

The Gender Question

Researchers, notably Carol Gilligan and her colleagues, have sought explanations for the long-recognized plummet of girls' self-esteem, which can occur around ages twelve or thirteen.[2] Once clear, candid, and sure of themselves, some girls, upon reaching puberty, become increasingly tentative, guarded, and hesitant in word and deed. What happens? Researchers have suggested that girls tune in to the value the culture places on their being sweet and amiable, and thus suffer from what has been called "the tyranny of niceness."[3]

Girls begin to restrict themselves psychically, out of fear of "crossing somebody's rule," to use Carrie's phrase. Because girls put a priority on attachment, connection, and being liked, they lose their voices and over-accommodate themselves to others for the sake of the relationship. The closing down of a girl's world does not come solely from peers. Some researchers have demonstrated that in classrooms across the United States, girls are encouraged to speak quietly, avoid math and science courses, and defer to the more dominating presence of boys.[4]

In a sense, Carrie's remarks are a classic "feminine" gender script. Rule-bound, she is intensely worried about relationships, about making the right move socially, about being accepted by others, and about who is "nice" or "mean" to whom. If this were the only snapshot in the album of who Carrie is, we'd have cause for concern, for the outlook she expresses is deeply disconcerting. But because I know her well, as she expressed her frustration to me I realized her sentiments were more her swerve for the day than a despairing loss of voice. Though in the moment she felt boxed-in by rules, she has at other times shown a healthy gutsiness and a willingness to abandon convention. Later in our conversation she told me about trying out for a talent show, and I was struck by her self-confidence.

As our children's views of their relationships and predicaments modify and readjust, as in a kaleidoscope, parents will want to broaden their vision to see the pattern of the whole. Were we to scrutinize only Carrie's script or, for that matter, only Henry's stiff-arming of his mother, we would have a misleadingly bleak perspective on their lives. What would be truly concerning for a parent and clinically significant to an evaluating psychologist would be if

Carrie's and Henry's social experiences were chronic and not interspersed with other positive patterns.

My conversation with Carrie touched on a provocative question parents frequently raise: Why are girls so mean to each other? When responding to this question, the first point I make is that boys are plenty mean to one another too, but we might have to stand in a ski lift line or hang around a gym to overhear their cruelty because boys are not likely to verbalize their anguish. We know more about what goes on among girls because they are usually more open with their parents (their moms in particular) about their peer hardships.

Parents then might wonder why girls have the propensity to be so expressive about their grievances. That some mothers are a receptive audience or that some girls tend to be naturally more communicative can facilitate this openness. *Compared to boys, girls tend to have more self-esteem invested in their relationships, and thus they are often described as having "relational identities."* By and large, they rank themselves by how their relationships are going, whereas boys are more likely to experience feelings of status from task-oriented realms (sports, school achievement) or by their talents. When girls fall prey to meanness, more of their self-worth and identity is on the line. Because they hurt more, they're more likely to be expressive. Girls tend to put their aggressive, competitive impulses into relationship-juggling and jockeying. Stakes being as high as they are on relationships, it gets intense. Boys are more apt to funnel their aggressiveness into sports, hobbies, and external achievement, which can be no less cutthroat than girls' reputed "meanness."

Many mothers thirst for their daughters to be strong and resilient without heeding their own duty to act as role models or considering work they might need to do personally. Recently, a mother of a twelve-year-old girl came to my office articulating fears about female voicelessness and the adolescent girl slump. Her daughter was worrying too much about what her friends thought; she was criticizing her body; her grades were slipping.

The mother then related an incident between her daughter and her husband, in which he had ripped into the daughter because she had accidentally taped over some family vacation footage in the video camera. When the dad forbade her from ever using the camera again, the daughter pouted for a week. The mother wanted her daughter to stand up to her father and use her "voice" to explain what happened. She wanted her daughter to convince her father that she'd made an honest error and should have another opportunity to prove her competence with the camera. I later learned that the father also tended to step on Mom's toes in an offensive manner, but, ironically, she explained to me, "I've learned to tolerate it since it keeps our marriage freer of conflict." She identified with her daughter's silencing, but the only agenda she felt compelled to push was for her daughter to develop a strong voice. My question to her was, "Are you expecting something of your twelve-year-old that you haven't done at age forty-two?"

Another woman who saw me for a consultation was the mother of three adolescent sons. She noticed that they, like their father, exhibited qualities we associate with male stereotypes. Specifically, her sons had picked up her husband's tendency to dismiss her ideas with disparaging remarks — to treat her as a "she," less important than "he." Observing young women her sons' ages, she saw a cohort of strong girls involved in competitive sports and reared by mothers who came of age with a heightened consciousness of power and gender inequities. She believed these girls would not tolerate in a relationship the kind of discounting, disrespectful behaviors she saw in her sons, and thus she feared she was raising sons who would be "dinosaurs" in the next generation.

It's noteworthy that in both these cases the women truly disliked the way their husbands had treated them over the years, but they came to see me less for their own sakes than for their children's sakes. What's implied is, "My pain can be tolerated, but the pain I feel for my child can't be." While they did not feel enough for themselves, they felt so strongly about the imprint of gender-stereotyped behavior on their children, they initiated consultations. An interesting note: mothers do put more consultations into gear, for theirs is the territory of "worrying about the children." Over the past fifteen years, however, I've experienced a steady increase in calls from fathers, perhaps a heartening sign of gender balance.

In talks with healthy young girls, I hear comments that remind me of the perils of living in a world offering specific challenges for those born female, whether they be psychic vulnerabilities related to attachment, safety, fair opportunities, or problematic family dynamics. In extreme cases, pressures on girls can lead to phenomena like restrictive dieting, depression, and dependence on male acceptance for self-esteem.

If it's sounding pretty tough to be a girl, consider the perils for boys, which are no less extreme than those for girls. Many parents of boys come into my office agonizing over pressures on boys to be macho — drive fast, binge drink, test their mettle, be a rock. These types of gender-based concerns are valid. Parental worries about boys' troubles versus girls' troubles reflect research findings: boys are more likely to act out their emotional difficulties behaviorally (drugs, conduct problems), while girls are more likely to "act in," causing their problems to manifest themselves in the forms of depression and anxiety.

The challenges of being born male or female can become stumbling blocks for many adolescents. Nevertheless, alongside the significant problems that come to my attention, I hear a lot of adolescents articulating healthy strategies for coping and overcoming life's obstacles, gender-related and otherwise.

Whenever I'm asked to assess the vulnerability of any particular girl or boy, I consider gender issues. I consider many other things too, for the teenagers who are most at-risk for various problems are not vulnerable solely because of their gender. Poverty, racism, educational impasses, family dysfunction, biological makeup, and other hardships of their childhood weigh heavily.

We want our kids to be as healthy, evolved, and as free from gender limitations as possible. Attending to our adolescents' vulnerabilities, gender-related and otherwise, parents can take steps to promote more adaptive patterns and address whatever excesses or deficits we see. Because girls tend to care more deeply about where they stand with others than they do about realizing their own ambitions, the parent's job can be to instill in them a healthy resistance. Girls need strong boundaries so they can consider themselves and their own needs as well as those of others. We want to empower our daughters to challenge gender-stereotyped expectations and to maintain a strong individual presence as they enter into relationships and go out in the world.

Since a risk for boys is shutting off, isolating, and becoming an island, the parent's job can be to help boys be more expressive of their feelings and sensitive to those of others. We can discourage physical aggression and encourage problem solving. Boys tend not to ask each other for help, and rarely do they give one another productive emotional feedback. If fathers or significant male figures can be the ones to role-model and encourage the various counters to male stereotypes, all the better.

Very few of today's parents would hope to raise a child whose attributes are exclusively gender-typed, that is, a girl who is only sweet, attractive, and accommodating, or a boy who is only tough, dominant, and stoic. Most of us see the advantage in a hybrid role model, whereby individuals have strengths traditionally associated with both genders. A young adult male who, while maintaining his masculinity, can grasp interpersonal dynamics, accept an egalitarian relationship with a female, and collaborate with others is likely to be more successful in the next millennium than one who lacks these strengths. A young adult female who, while valuing her feminine nature, comfortably asserts herself, is unruffled by having a body size that may not befit a current *Cosmopolitan* magazine cover, and who accounts for her own needs and ambitions in tandem with those of others will have advantages unavailable to women in the past.

"Those Friends"

A challenge for parents is to accept our children's need for relationships that do not involve us. As their friendships deepen and peer-group activities absorb more of their time, our adolescents need our attention in different ways. When our children are young, we get used to being at the center of their social orbit. When our kids start spinning off in their own directions during adolescence, our gravity seeks to pull them back into our safer sphere, so they won't be pulled into a black hole "out there."

When they're not around us, then who will they be around? Since the norm is for adolescents to prefer the companionship of peers over parents, do we have any say about exactly who these friends are? Knowing, as most parents do, about the lure of peer conformity, how enticing it is to think that we might have a shot at selecting the very peers with whom our adolescents could conform. *The sobering truth is that we do not have it in our power to choose our adolescent's friends.* Gone are the days when we could call up and arrange a play-date for our young child, for these moves are no longer appropriate or possible. Moreover, since friendship choices are largely a function of identity, personality, background, and shared interests, the friends we might choose for our children probably say more about us than they do our kids. By the time they reach adolescence, our children truly are themselves, and it is within their means to try out various types of friendships.

Much of our anxiety about the world (increasing violence, drug use, sex offenses) is heightened as we scrutinize our adolescent's friendship choices and speculate whether these particular friends enhance our child's vulnerability. Likewise, our anxiety about who our child is becoming is often galvanized as an issue about "those friends." Granted, peers influence one another, sometimes negatively. Moreover, almost all of our most feared adolescent experiences, such as drugs, sex, or violence, take place within a peer context. Nevertheless, screening out bad friends as a means of protecting our kids is only a limited solution.

"Bad" friends often receive undue emphasis and focus, when we should instead be posing broader developmental questions. Key among these questions is "Why did our child choose a particular peer group?" Friendship choices occur as part of an overarching social developmental process. As adolescents explore their identity and pursue popularity as a (seeming) pathway to greater self-esteem, they try on all sorts of behaviors, such as school underachievement, swearing, or acting defiant, which we might attribute to bad peer influence. It is usually more appropriate to target the entire adolescent *growth process* rather than the peer, who is just one piece of the process. As with all learning processes — walking, talking, reading — we don't get to skip the undesirable aspects en route to mastery.

I'll give you an example. Let's say you have a thirteen-year-old daughter who has struck up a friendship with a girl you consider "fast." When this friend spends the night, the girls arrange a sneak visit from a group of boys, until of course you catch them at it and spoil their fun. After the friend leaves the following morning, you notice that your daughter has acquired a little swagger in her hips from this friend. The all-too-common parental reaction would be to blame the peer as a contaminating influence on the daughter. We indulge ourselves in the illusion that the scheme with boys and the swagger were rooted in an association with "the fast friend," which means we don't have to deal with our own daughter's budding sexuality. Our discomfort causes us to triangulate and focus our anxiety on the peer as "a bad kid." We jump in and restrict the friendship, when we should be seeking insight into who our child is becoming and the kinds of social choices and preferences she is inclined to make. Why did she invite this friend over, and in what way did it bring something out in her she might have needed to explore or express? Is there something we need to address in our own methods of parenting (for example, our ability to accept adolescent development)? Does zeroing in on the friend obscure a problem with our own child's behavior?

If we take a random cross-section of parents — diverse in values and interests though they may be — they are likely to find common ground in complaining about the annoying behaviors of other kids: they're messy and loud; they help themselves to food from our refrigerators; they exchange drivel on the teen-chat line, running up the bill; they're bossy and they exert undue influence over our adolescent's decisions. Instead of grousing about our children's friends, we need to keep in mind that, in most cases, these behaviors are usually no better or no worse than our own teenagers'. If we attack or blame these friends in our adolescent's presence, we risk alienating our child because we are likewise attacking a decision to spend time with this person.

While it is only too easy to pick apart our children's friends, we rarely reflect on how much growth and development occurs through "those friends." We seldom appreciate the good things they're doing for our child — even during their seemingly endless hours on the phone. Friendship experiences can foster emotional sensitivity to others. Through friendships, our children learn to see points of view outside their own and to understand the why's and wherefore's of that perspective. They learn to develop caring behavior; they learn ways to support another person; they learn how to share, how to be responsible in a relationship, how to stay loyal, and how much they should reasonably expect from others. Imagine, for example, overhearing a snippet of a phone call when a daughter is acting as counsel and intermediary to a peer: "You see, she's mad at you because she thinks you're mad at her." We may judge this interaction to be pretty convoluted, but consider how many adults become engaged in the very dynamic these adolescent girls are working out! Through friendships, adolescents acquire interpersonal tools they will desperately need for the maze of future romantic and collegial relationships. Most of this valuable peer interaction and influence occurs when parents are elsewhere, so we usually chalk up credit for positive behaviors like growing empathy, for example, to our adolescent's own maturation. But could our children ever mature in the ways we admire outside of a peer culture of friendships?

Although our children place an increasing value on peer relationships in early to middle adolescence, research on the normal population has not revealed that this overshadows the importance of supportive parents. It's a mistake to pit parental influence against peer influence, for there are functions that parents uniquely fulfill. Though we're more in the background, adolescents rarely blossom without the irreplaceable parent system. We're the secure, caring, trusting attachment figures, which explains why they're free to be moody, detached, rude, and irritable with us. As secure fixtures, parents are not as high-maintenance as friends. Friendships must be earned and maintained, which is hard work. Adolescents continue to look to their parents for guidance, even while they are tuning in to their peers. By late adolescence, both parent and peer influences diminish in favor of increasingly independent thinking. They listen, but as emerging adults, they prefer to chart their own course.

"My Father's a Dork"

The clues are there all along: our grade-school kids begin acting more arrogant toward us in their friends' presence; they don't want us volunteering in their fifth-grade classroom. It can feel like a slap in the face when our young adolescent makes it apparent we're something of an embarrassment to him or her. They now want us to drop them off a block from school, and they back away from our enthusiastic rush into their circle to congratulate them after a stellar athletic performance.

In private moments, our kids might be back in our laps, but when their friends are around, we're under close scrutiny. Our behaviors become a sore spot if we violate their rules of coolness. Consider the following example, related to me in excruciating detail by a twelve-year-old.

During a carpool, her dad dialed the radio to a country music station and began singing along with twangy sentimentalism. The daughter switched the channel and asked him to stop, but thinking he was being funny, he returned to the country station and continued crooning. Her friends laughed, but she was humiliated. Her dad retorted defensively, "Where's your sense of humor?"

An issue central to this situation is the adolescent's boundaries. *More so than during later adolescence, most young adolescents are still identified and merged with their parents.* They want us to conform to the perfect reflection of who they want us to be, as well as who they, themselves, want to be. The father is, in effect, besmirching his daughter's image by behaving in ways that she wouldn't dare.

In a sense, the daughter is projecting onto her father. *Projection, the transposing of our thoughts and emotions onto another person, is a classic defense mechanism that assumes a variety of forms.* In this example, the daughter is preoccupied by her own worries about being cool around her friends. Unable to put a boundary around her own distress and contain her own conflict, she diverts the problem to her father: he's the nerd; he's ruining my chances at being liked, and accepted, and "cool." By projecting her internal turmoil onto her father, she receives the dual benefits of relieving herself of conflict ("I'm not the problem here — he is"), and of being able to unload her rage on him. The daughter also projects her feelings onto her friends, assuming that they will judge her dad the same way she does or, worse yet, judge her for her dad's uncoolness. If her father seems like a jerk to her, she's egocentric enough to assume everyone else thinks the same. While projection can be a sign of pathology in extreme instances, people often project in their relationships in relatively benign ways, and parents of adolescents typically become their children's prime targets.

A related issue is that our adolescents can feel uneasy when we outshine them. This may seem a bit paradoxical, since the daughter would hardly consider the dad's singing "outshining," but his action is one-upmanship, especially if her friends actually think her dad is funny. Even our most well-intentioned gestures can simply be too much. During our children's early years we could bring cupcakes into their classroom and strike up a chorus of "Happy Birthday," but once our kids become middle schoolers, we'd best reconsider. Disappearing into the background and not talking too much when, say, we're driving a carpool, becomes an advantage; it's remarkable how much we can learn.

"My Child Is a Loner"

Although many of us experience moments when we wish for closer companionships, loneliness can be acutely felt by adolescents who are home on Friday and Saturday nights, when everyone else seems to be out and involved in social activities. Parents of socially withdrawn grade schoolers certainly feel their child's pain, but they're often able to take up a fair amount of slack through their own supportive relationships with their child.

In the middle-school years, however, a lack of peer relationships becomes a greater problem because adolescents depend on peer interaction for their identity and social development. It is through social transactions that people learn about themselves and the world.

There's a circular phenomenon at work: children with social aptitude tend to be well liked, so they're invited and included, which creates more opportunities for being around people, which, in turn, helps them develop their social skills. Some kids ease into the loop automatically, if not with a large group of peers and schoolwide visibility, with a small group of like companions who share similar interests. Although research indicates that looks (more important for girls) and athletic ability (more important for boys) are high on the list of what makes for popularity, well-liked kids have certain other characteristics. Pleasant, helpful, and relaxed, they're good at conversation, at cooperating, and at recognizing other's feelings. They're skilled at resolving arguments and are capable of giving and receiving negative feedback. Able to judge the impression they're making, they can adjust to the feedback they're receiving about their behavior.

Parents of children who sit on the social sidelines often wonder whether they should wait it out or push their child to become more involved. How far should parents go to help their child develop friendships? Parents of grade schoolers can often get away with engineering play-dates for a shy child. Since most parents realize this will flop during adolescence, they might be tempted to plan a party or gathering for their child. This, too, can be dicey because shy people usually want to fade into the walls in large groups, especially if they're the object or center of attention.

In actuality, there's not a lot parents can do to change a shy child, but they can actually hurt their child and their relationship with him by treating temperament as if it were something to be fixed. Parents need to accept their child's temperament as a biological given, like blue eyes or curly hair. *Shy children should neither be pushed nor let be; they should be nudged in a way that encourages social experience but does not send a message that something is wrong with them.*

Nudging is usually more successful when parents scope out existing resources and build on props already present. What works best is to find situations that will bring about natural interaction with others. Parents can create a family policy of being social and insist that their child participate in two activities, one related to school and the other extracurricular. A possible technique is to work with a child to generate a list of ten activities he would consider joining. The negotiable part of the deal is that the child can choose among any of them, and the nonnegotiable part is that he must do something. Shy kids often prefer an activity in which they're competing mostly with themselves; this frees them from the evaluating glances of others and allows them to excel without calling attention to themselves.

Sometimes children are able to grow in new ways under the guidance of an adult mentor who isn't their parent because that adult can tap into potential that parents either can't identify or can't access. Because they don't elicit a "parent worry factor," teachers, coaches, and scout leaders are often able to garner strengths and bring about greater participation from a withdrawn child.

Another technique that may work is to develop contacts with families who have kids the same age and plan multifamily outings. Caution is advised, however, for teenagers are adept at detecting parental agendas.

Children who are shy often have at least one parent with a similar temperament who can recall feelings of social embarrassment. Typically, the alike parent has a unique understanding of that child, sometimes to the point of identifying with the child. *To whatever degree various conditions (anxiety, depression, obesity, attention deficit, alcoholism, or shyness) are hereditary, there is a possibility of "specialness" in the relationship of the child and the similar parent.* The link can range from guilt, denial, and distancing to advocacy and empathy. However, this type of link can reinforce a parent-child coalition, which interferes with the marital boundary. When this type of dynamic develops, a professional consultation is appropriate.

Parents with shy children can also take heart in the distinction between being lonely and being shy. Lonely means there's a yearned-for intimacy one lacks; shy people, on the other hand, don't necessarily crave greater intimacy or closer contact. And, as they reach young adulthood, many natural loners come more out of their shell.

Mother and Daughter Tornadoes: Sheri and Rachel

Screaming matches between mothers and teenage daughters can be as commonplace as rain on a spring day. Sometimes, fathers, bemused by the emotional downpouring, wonder what brought on this seasonal shift. Arguments between high-strung mothers and high-strung, pubescent daughters can look so crazy that I have had many healthy, well-adjusted families seek consultation to determine if they have a clinical problem. Just as fathers and sons often need to work out their masculinity and power issues, mothers and daughters struggle in ways that differ significantly from cross-gender or male-male conflicts.

More so than fathers, mothers tend to be sympathetic to their daughter's problems, which increases the likelihood of a daughter's laying open her upsets and frustrations to her mom. But why are some mothers and daughters especially vulnerable to the kinds of arguments that spin out of control? Factors that determine the level of volatility include: parent and child temperament (withdrawn/calm, all the way along a contin-

uum to high-strung/reactive); existence of social circumstances or specific stressors (boyfriend blues, financial problems, state of marriage, poor
health); availability of support (friends to vent to as an alternative to letting
it all fly at each other); biological factors (puberty, menopause); boundary
issues (strong or weak); and family-of-origin baggage (presence or absence of a parent's emotional triggers).

At one end of the spectrum is the combination at lowest risk for
blowups: calm mother temperament, calm daughter temperament, few
social stressors, social support, strong boundaries, and lack of family-of-
origin triggers. On the other end are those most likely to engage in
mighty battle: a reactive mother, a reactive daughter, hormonal mood
instability in daughter or mother, social stressors, lack of support, weak
boundaries, and unresolved family-of-origin issues.

A mother-daughter duo I saw for a consultation was Rachel, a high-
strung mother, and Sheri, her thirteen-year-old daughter of similar temperament. This pair serves as a clear example because the only risk variable
was two reactive temperaments clashing against each other in a moment
of upset. Although they were two healthy individuals with no problematic
stressors in their lives, they would time and again lose control of themselves during arguments. They related one of their rows to me. Thoughts
and feelings related to their dialogue are added in parentheses, which will
help explain why their argument became so intense.

Rachel: Here's your blue sweater. I picked it up at the cleaners on my way
home so you can wear it for your school picture tomorrow. (Last year
was such a scene when she got her pictures back. I really didn't have
time to go to the cleaners, but I was glad to go out of my way because
she's so self-conscious about her looks and her body.)

Sheri [sneering]: I'm not wearing that. (I'll feel like a pig in that sweater. I
don't know what to wear. I'm so frustrated. I want my pictures to be
really good.)

Rachel [surprised]: What do you mean you're "not wearing that"? We talked
about this. We decided. It'll look good. (I can't believe she's changing
her mind like this again!)

Sheri [pitch rising]: I don't want to wear it. Why are you shoving it at me like
that? (I'm going to look bad no matter what! I hate everything I own.
Allison has everything she wants. Her pictures always turn out great.

She's thin and beautiful. I hate the way I look. My haircut looks dorky. If I smile with my mouth closed, my lips pooch out over my braces. If I smile naturally, my braces take over the whole picture.)

Rachel [*outraged*]: I'm not shoving it at you. I went out of my way to pick this up for you. Is this the kind of thank you I get? Look, last year, you were hysterical because the plaid on your blouse clashed with the criss-crossing of your braces. This is a plain sweater. It's a dark color. We went through this. (I can't reason with this child! Her hysterics are driving me crazy.)

Sheri [*whining*]: Come on, Mom. Take me to Allison's. Please? I talked to her today in school, and she said she has a great idea for something I could borrow. (Why won't she help me out here. I'm really desperate. I don't know what to wear. I hate that stupid sweater. Doesn't she understand how important this is?)

Rachel [*anger mounting*]: You've got to be kidding me. I am not going to drive you over to Allison's tonight! And besides, Allison is not your size, and her clothes are just not your colors. You need a dark color for the white background in the picture. (Why won't she wear the damn sweater! This is too much. I can't believe she's going into one of her tizzies. We had a plan. This wasn't supposed to happen.)

Sheri [*sounding panicky*]: Another ugly picture. You don't care. You just want me to wear that sweater because you don't want to take me to Allison's. I have to go to Allison's, Mom! (I can't stand how she won't listen. She thinks this is some stupid, petty thing. What do I have to do to show her how important this is to me, and how awful I feel.)

Rachel [*becoming hysterical*]: How dare you say I don't care, just because I don't want to be your chauffeur. I already went to the dry cleaners for you, and now you want me to take you halfway across town to Allison's, when we already decided on the blue sweater! (I feel used. Totally used.)

Sheri [*tears welling in eyes*]: Mom, it'll look terrible. I've got it figured out with Allison. I just need a ride. Won't you take me? Where are you going? Mom, don't be that way. (She's not listening to me. She's just walking out of the room.)

Rachel [*shouting from outside the room*]: Fine, then don't wear it. Find something else in your closet. I've got to make dinner. (I don't know what to do. Should I take her to Allison's? She's following me into the kitchen. Oh, no, we're going to have another one of our scenes!)

In this exchange, Rachel's points are very reasonable: last year's picture didn't work; the blue sweater will look better; we decided on this sweater; it's unnecessary for me to drive you to Allison's; Allison's clothes aren't your best colors.

Nonetheless, Rachel is ambivalent, poised on a fence unable to decide whether she should rescue her suffering daughter and drive her to Allison's or stand firm in the face of her daughter's hysteria.

Chances are slim that Rachel's rational points could ever solve Sheri's problem of what to wear, for that is actually not what Sheri wants or, for that matter, needs. The more dogged Rachel remains about the merits of the blue sweater, the more outraged Sheri becomes. In Sheri's state of anxiety over her picture, she's looking to offload her emotions on her mom so she won't have to manage them herself. Anxiety circles from mother to daughter and then back again. The child is agitated and upset; the parent becomes agitated and upset; child and parent are both pulled into a whirlwind that spins away, from room to room, as Sheri chases after her mother, and they continue to quarrel about the blue sweater.

By comparing what Rachel and Sheri say with what they think and feel (in parentheses), we get a better sense of what this argument is about — and it's not only the blue sweater. *Like so many arguments, this one is not just about apparent "content" (the sweater) — it's about the interpersonal process of escalating anxiety, perceived betrayals, and frustrated goals.* The issues here relate to Sheri's feelings of frustration over her looks, her anxiety about the picture, and her need for her mother to share her misery. Though this scenario involved volatility and irrationality, it was clear of any other family or social stressors. Had Sheri or her mother been experiencing other difficulties, these too would have been pitched into the fray, adding more whirling debris to the argument.

Moving Out Gracefully

Time and again, loving mothers will, in their compassion, be pulled into their daughter's tornadoes. These conflicts are especially painful because each party feels the loser: the parent because the adolescent is angry, resentful, and rejecting of her wise counsel, and the child because she feels abandoned, not heard, and unresolved in an extremely distressing situation. As she considers whether to drive Sheri to Allison's, Rachel reflects that she feels used by her daughter. Chauffeuring demands aside, Sheri is, in a sense, using her mother. Instead of dealing with her anxiety about her appearance, her feelings of inferiority to Allison, and her anguish over lack of control on an important occasion, Sheri blames her mother, focusing on how she is not coming through for her.

What's a mother to do? *Although we want to be supportive of our children, we need to seek a balance. We don't want to let them use us as their emotional dumping ground (displacement), yet we don't want to abandon or rescue them. Be empathetic and supportive, but extricate yourself from the eye of the storm so you don't lose perspective.*

The guidelines I describe below are specific to a situation when your child is cranked for a fight; she's in some kind of upset state or mood. It might be the day before school starts, before or after a big test, or during a major social shake-up. Whatever the specifics, the whirlwind is about her anxiety and her need for her mom to feel as bad as she does; she wants to involve her mom in her upset because she is seeking comfort and support.

If we see our child becoming more and more hysterical, our job is to remove ourselves from the immediacy of the situation but still remain affirmative. Our task is to shift the paradigm because nothing productive is happening, and we don't want to reinforce the behavior. Adolescents are adept at keeping arguments alive, and to maneuver deftly, parents need a certain kind of boundary — one that keeps us from getting completely drawn in, but one that also allows us to be sensitive to what's going on (that is, neither enmeshment nor shut-off). With this type of boundary, we're able to shield ourselves from the harsh, personal content of the dialogue ("Mom, you don't care!"), so we can think, decipher, and decide what to say without being reactive or devastated by their words. Without the boundary, we take in the attack and are more likely to attack back, and the whole process becomes more aggressive and regressive, like two fighting kids. Managing our role in this type of situation means mind over matter; it takes not responding to everything they say. In a whirlwind, we want to proceed in the general direction of these seven guidelines, which are more of a loose process than a step-by-step procedure:

1. Confirm their feelings
2. Let them know of your concern for their problem
3. Admit you can't solve their problem
4. Express your faith in their ability to figure it out
5. Move away from the central spin without abandoning or rejecting
6. Check back in to prove you care and are not abandoning them
7. Offer some kind of nurturance

Notice the child-centeredness of these guidelines, which requires that the parent subordinate her agenda (wear the blue sweater) and her feelings (not being appreciated) during the crisis. Also critical are the parent's tone, inflection, and validation of feeling, for it matters less what words we use than that they be genuine and sincere. If said in a mechanical "shrinky" way, comments like "I can tell you're unhappy" or "I hear your feelings" are likely to set them off. In dealing with Sheri, Rachel, for example, might have said in heartfelt tones, "This is really hard because you never know how those pictures are going to turn out no matter what you wear." Or, "I'd love nothing more than to come up with a brilliant solution for you, honey, but I don't seem to be able to find one."

Our adolescents look to us as mirrors of reassurance that say, "You're competent. I think you can handle it." When that mirror reflects our anxiety and frustration, it confirms our children's fears that perhaps they aren't competent, perhaps they can't solve their problem, perhaps their despair is appropriate. When the mirror is red with anger, it tells them we don't appreciate their feelings. If we muscle in assistance but have a resentful attitude, we're nonetheless closing them off, even as we try to help them.

Some assertive expressions that would have let Sheri know she's capable of solving her problem would be: "Look, I know you want me to fix this, and you think driving to Allison's is the only solution, but I'm spent in the driving department, and I guess I'll have to let you just be mad at me. In the meantime, I really do trust that you can come up with an alternative." Rachel might have reminded Sheri, "You've asked for my help. I've given it to you. I know I'm not doing what you want and that you're upset. I'm sorry you feel so frustrated about your dilemma."

If the argument is clearly out of control, we need to call it to a halt by saying something like, "This is not working for either of us. We need to stop now. Let's take a break, and we'll get back together with our wits about us in a few minutes." As the parent, we should take *equal* responsibility for the conflict, even though we may feel our child is more at fault for having pulled us into the argument.

We can, of course, offer problem-solving suggestions, but we shouldn't be offended if they don't work. In fact, given how frustrated the adolescent is likely to be with herself, the situation, and us (as a displaced focus), she will most likely enjoy rejecting every good idea we pose. This way, the teenager successfully forces us into "co-misery." An adolescent psychology tip here is helpful: be co-miserable; be empathetic. This will help diffuse the hysteria.

When one person sees another becoming hysterical, the temptation is to help. Unfortunately, the help usually amounts to minimizing the problem, offering solutions, or reminding the person to calm down and keep the issue in perspective. Intense feelings are often overlooked.

Freud posed the famous question, "By God, what do women want?" We might imagine Sheri's father coming into the room, scratching his head, wondering what in the world is happening between his wife and daughter. He'd say, "What do they want? How can I help?" He might be under the illusion that he could help with a solution such as, "Why doesn't she just wear something different?" Needless to say, this isn't likely to work. What women want is sincere validation: "Don't fix me, but be with me." When troubled, men usually want this too, but their quest for validation might be expressed differently — through a nonverbalized need for space, tolerance, or comfort.

How can we "be with" our adolescents, yet simultaneously give them room to breathe? It's tricky. When I talk to parents about this, I use the phrase "I'll go make some tea for us," which is a metaphor for any nurturing statement that communicates we aren't leaving them high and dry. We want to find a comment that "breaks set" but still keeps us connected in some way. While we don't want to follow them around when they may need a moment of private reflection, it often helps to check in with a brief, nonengaging, supportive comment that lets them know we care, such as "I appreciate that you're in a real jam" or "Hope you're doing O.K. with this" or "Let's talk again in an hour and see where we are."

A consult would be advised if tirades begin to dominate your communication and your adolescent's unhappiness is persistent. It's possible that emotional storming is not just a developmental phenomenon but a depression or an anxiety disorder, and only a professional evaluation will determine this.

Bear in mind that using some blend of the guidelines is not likely to leave any twosome completely happy: resentfulness and frustration are likely to linger. What we're trying to do is *minimize* damage to the relationship. We want to support the adolescent who is in a blitz and address the main issue (blue sweater) as deftly as possible. Because of the multitudinous feelings that can be packed into any situation, sometimes the best we can hope for is to avoid the two- or three-hour screaming battles that I so often hear about in my practice. When a row winds down to mere mutual disappointment between mother and child, this is often a major achievement.

Tornadoes as Centrifuges

Sometimes, valuable information separates out as a result of the whirling that occurs in an emotional mother and daughter interchange. While we're rarely aware of it at the time, a little nugget might drop to the center, which can be there for us to examine when the spinning stops. If a mother has a good relationship with her daughter, she might be able to revisit the episode, saying, "I'm sorry about my part in the argument. What do you think was happening there?" The mom might discover something important was behind the hysteria.

Imagine, for example, that Rachel and Sheri were folding laundry together the next day, and Rachel alluded to their argument. Sheri might tell her mother that she was upset about the blue sweater because she felt like her mother was controlling her decisions. If only her mother hadn't come on so strong about the sweater, she might have worn it. Perhaps Rachel would then replay a picture of herself marching efficiently into her daughter's room, holding forth the dry-cleaned blue sweater as a fait accompli. Perhaps Sheri had needed more time to mull over this big decision. Through deft handling of the argument's residue, Rachel could gain insights into her parenting. Sheri might disclose that something entirely unrelated had been upsetting her: perhaps she had been spurned by a friend or embarrassed in class by a teacher.

Between some mothers and daughters, there can be a tacit understanding about a need to dispute; many mothers will stay engaged and do their part of the dance, when most fathers will more easily separate. The more feeling-oriented and close to his daughter the father, the more threatened and affected he is by the conflict. Because they care so much, fathers often feel compelled to enter in, but the feelings are usually too confusing and intense. Not knowing where to begin, they bungle or opt out altogether. To some dads, the tirades can seem like pure misbehavior. Tomorrow's pictures and blue sweaters just don't pull them in; it takes more compelling subjects like sex, drugs, and bad boyfriends.

Studying mother-daughter conflicts, Terry Apter believes that daughters often keep after their mothers because they want to gain recognition and validation.[5] They fight for confirmation in an effort to be seen as a competent, unique person who is not simply an extension of their mother.

There is a critical distinction to be made between a mother's role in a situation when a daughter is in a preexisting emotional state, looking to be rescued (as with Rachel and Sheri), compared to a situation in which, for example, a daughter challenges her mother with an outrageous outfit or proposal. In these situations, daughters may need to do a little verbal sparring with their moms as they seek to hear their mothers voice respect for their independent choices. Unfortunately, the opposite can ensue, and the mother criticizes the outfit or the plan. Even if they feel they must veto the idea at hand, mothers need to validate their daughters' competence and right to autonomy. Fathers and daughters, mothers and sons, and fathers and sons may experience transactions similar to Rachel's and Sheri's, but mothers and daughters seem to be the combination most at risk for highly emotional, extended arguments. When individuals are of the same gender the intensity can be greater, as our children attempt to establish their unique selves.

Attention Deficit Disorder, Stepparenting, and a Deviant Peer Group: Ricky, Bev, Charlie, and Kent

"All this violence on the news every night. We're worried sick about Ricky," said Bev, a sprightly brunette, whose concerns spilled forth like water gushing from an open spigot. "You know, I told you on the phone he's been on Ritalin since he was seven. Sometimes I'm up practically all night worrying. Our divorce was tough on him, but Ricky's dad and I get along fine, so that part's O.K. But, Ricky's hanging out with deadbeats. I know he's smoking cigarettes 'cause I smell it on his breath. He lies through his teeth and says he isn't. Well, I guess I did too at thirteen. But, you know, he just hangs out every day after school with these guys. I'll bet they're drinking too. I don't think they're a gang or anything, but they're scum of the earth, that's for sure. They're stealing cigarettes from the Stop & Shop. Ricky got caught for that, and then he has the nerve to tell me he's not smoking."

Bev, who worked as an office manager for a fishing export company, and her reserved ex-husband Kent, an insurance salesman, had made an appointment to see me because they were worried that their thirteen-year-old son, Ricky, in cahoots with a wild peer group, was on a path to delinquency. I saw it as a positive sign that Ricky's biological parents had wanted to come in together, as it often takes some engineering on my part to pull a divorced couple together for a parent consultation. At a later session we would also add Charlie, whom Bev had married two years ago, three years after her divorce from Kent, who remained single. As will become apparent, Ricky's three parents had some significant issues to deal with, but the families were functioning well because they rose to the occasion of every problem presented to them.

In addition to my work with his parents, Ricky periodically checked in with his pediatrician, who had prescribed Ritalin after diagnosing him at age seven with Attention deficit and hyperactivity disorder (ADHD), known generally as ADD, which can occur with or without hyperactivity. Because there are no laboratory tests to diagnose ADD, it can be difficult to judge exactly where high-energy, rowdy, inattentive behavior leaves off and ADD takes over. High distractibility, impulsivity, and often hyperactivity are the hallmarks of ADD, which is three to four times more prevalent in boys than girls. If we stir together the biology of ADD, the more aggressive male physiology, the sociocultural influences of strong, dominating, stoic male role models, and demographic, environmental, and family stressors, we have a potentially dangerous concoction.

Bev was savvy about the risks for her son, even as she sympathized with his ADD. "I sure can relate to it," she said. "I've always been a little hyper, and it got me into plenty of trouble in school, just like Ricky." Now in her late thirties, Bev had found a way to harness her high energy and use it to her advantage in her work. Though she thought of herself as disorganized because she was always on the go, switching from dock surveillance to warehouse checks to bookkeeping to order processing, her liveliness became a strength. That Kent could never keep up with her had been an issue in their divorce. Bev's "hair-trigger temper" and volubility had also taken a toll on her first marriage, just as they now resulted in fireworks between her and a similarly brash and brazen Ricky.

The crisis that brought Bev and Kent into my office began when Bev threatened to separate Ricky from his wild peer group by pulling him out of public school and placing him in a nearby parochial school. Though they could scarcely afford the tuition, the parents saw it as a way to "get Ricky away from his lowlife friends." Ricky was "a follower," explained Bev. "This pack of hell-raisers is in the gutter and juvie is around the corner." Ricky strongly resisted the idea of changing schools. After a fierce argument with Bev, he ran away to a friend's house for two nights.

Bev and Kent had other concerns about Ricky, related in part to the developmental havoc of his being thirteen: Should he be allowed to take buses all over town? What about the loitering downtown? What about his problem with homework, which he completed erratically? Ricky often failed to turn in assignments he had, indeed, finished. As an active grade schooler, Ricky had tested his parents' and teachers' patience (rock throwing, malicious teasing); he clearly was what we call a hard-to-parent child, and with the onset of adolescence, his mischief making was becoming more threatening.

In a consultation session, as people tell me their history and describe their current dilemma, I keep a mental checklist of protective variables versus risk factors. In my mind I tick off plusses and minuses — strength, strength, risk, risk. Afterward I have a list that circumscribes the problem, tells me what we need to work on, and also pinpoints strengths that I can enhance.

What I've discovered is that people are often more painfully aware of their risks than of their strengths that can help compensate for vulnerabilities. While the stresses of divorce were necessarily a tick on the negative side, Bev and Kent had separated in as amicable and reasonable a way as possible, which alleviated some of the danger. Under a joint custody arrangement, Ricky spent a week on and a week off with each of his two caring, involved parents. Bev and Kent agreed to live in the same neighborhood so that school and shuttling would be manageable. However, they did have to deal with Ricky's inevitable stress due to his weekly transitions.

Likewise, Ricky's ADD could be chalked up as a risk factor, but because his parents had taken steps to deal with it at a young age, it remained a small rather than a large problem. Early identification of this kind of problem helps parents plan ahead, engage the child's energy and strengths, adjust to what life with an ADD kid holds, and stay on top of schoolwork like a bee on honey. A huge strength in this case was that Ricky was still in school and was pulling mostly C's. While this may not seem like an applaudable achievement, for a boy with ADD, this is a definite plus. Like so many kids with this disorder, Ricky was quite smart (cumulative IQ of 120), but traditional classroom education, geared for kids without ADD, had tapped into all of Ricky's weaknesses. He had trouble sitting still and listening for long periods, and he was unable to structure his time for task completion. Consequently, because his school situation had highlighted his deficits, Ricky's self-esteem suffered miserably in his important social role of student. Another tick to the risk side.

Kent, Ricky's biological dad, was a definite plus. An involved, invested dad, he frequently ran interference with Ricky's ongoing school problems. Kent had an extended family who appreciated Ricky's enthusiasm in helping out Grandma and babysitting for cousins. There was, however, a little hitch with Kent. While married to Bev, Kent had reacted strongly to her negative forecasting about Ricky's future. Identifying with Ricky's vulnerability, Bev was constantly on him, after him, and around him. Consequently, what developed between Kent and Ricky was a type of parent-child coalition that can occur between two unlike family members. Trying to smooth matters out, Kent had become Ricky's advocate, in a way that was not entirely helpful. As he endeavored to counter Bev's "bull dogging" of Ricky, Kent had earned a reputation for passivity, and for minimizing Ricky's problems, writing them off as "Bev's obsession." Kent insisted he did not take the diagnosis of ADD lightly, but he did feel protective of his son, constantly exposed to his mother's fire. In earlier years, Kent has resisted therapy for Ricky, but recent concerns about his peer group had airlifted him into consultation.

Another strength in this family was Charlie, Ricky's stepfather. A couple of years younger than Bev, Charlie was a low-key man with native smarts, who worked as a carpenter. *Only too easily and often does a stepfather come into a home and see a lippy, forgetful, disruptive child and feel he has to clean it up. Lacking an attachment and a history with the child, stepparents can overcontrol in their efforts to set matters straight.* Because the child remains loyal to his biological parents, negative energy and criticism can easily be displaced to the stepparent, who becomes the bad guy.

Charlie, on the other hand, had an easygoing temperament and the good judgment not to try to control the situation. From the outset, Charlie had remained on good terms with both Kent and Ricky, making it clear, "Ricky's already got a father." Though Charlie hadn't read any of the excellent advice books on stepparenting, he seemed to have an intuitive grasp of what did and didn't work. "I don't go out of my way to take Ricky on," said Charlie, "but if he takes me on, I let him know I'm not going to stand for it." Charlie let Ricky know what his limits of tolerance were with direct statements like "Cut it out" or "I don't like that." He expressed himself in clear, clean assertions instead of threats, and thus avoided a power struggle, which would have created a new risk in this family's situation.

Charlie was highly supportive of Bev's parenting efforts and authority. He let her vent without criticizing her for using her sharp tongue, which was exacerbating the situation. He had the excellent instincts to let Bev handle her own battles with Ricky, without triangulating by defending her. Many stepfathers fall into a triangulation trap, particularly when mothers haven't been sufficiently authoritative. It virtually always fails because mothers need their own power, credibility, and working relationships with their children instead of relying on the precarious support prop of a stepfather.

Bev and Charlie had been wondering whether Charlie should structure his workday as a carpenter so that he could be home during the after-school period. Upon entering junior high, Ricky had become a latchkey kid, and he hadn't handled the freedom and responsibility well. Wouldn't it be a good idea for Charlie to come home at 4:00 in order to supervise Ricky more closely? My advice was definitely not. We needed to preserve what was working, that is, the strengths of which the family might not be aware. To put a stepfather in charge of a vulnerable child can be disastrous; the biological parents need to remain on the frontline.

Ricky's Peer Pressure

When parents come into my office bashing their child's friends, the fixation on peers often turns out to be a red herring. Typically, there is a deeply embedded family problem to root out, which has contributed to the choice of a deviant peer group. Acting out socially is symptomatic of other issues therapy can bring to the fore. For "peer problem" cases, part of what I do is track the "strength and risk" checklist to determine the overall scope of the problem. Another important step is to assess whether "those friends" truly are a destructive influence or whether they simply don't happen to be the friends the parents would choose for their child. After all, a boy like Ricky does not have easy access to the high-achiever group and is likely to remain on the fringe.

In Ricky's case, however, his deviant friends were a central problem rather than a red herring. While the family portrait had smudges — divorce, ADD, Bev's "mouthiness," and Kent's protectiveness (played out as passivity) — there were plenty of bright spots too. After talking with Ricky, it became clear he was in a precarious place with his peer choices and was moving toward a rough group of delinquents who were pulling him into illegal activities. His friends were not of the ilk who look seedy but remain essentially harmless. Ricky had chosen a truly at-risk bunch, and his parents needed to take steps to extricate him from this group. Because of this family's many strengths, the situation with Ricky's peers was more an obstacle to surmount than a problem systemic to the family.

Researchers studying children at risk for negative peer influence have identified these central factors: low peer status; poor school performance; closer to friends than to parents; low self-esteem; family in strife.[6] Bev had described Ricky as "a follower" in his group, and his academic problems rendered him at risk for identifying with peers on the fringe. Furthermore, Ricky was spending too large a percentage of his time with this peer group, in hopes of belonging and gaining status via this association. On the plus side, Ricky was without one of the most destructive of risk factors: alienation from family. Although he had run away from home, this move was more a response to Bev's threat to change his school than a symptom of estrangement.

To turn the situation around, Ricky's parents negotiated a plan with him. They postponed making a decision about changing his school, but they also revamped his after-school time. I advised Ricky's parents not to hit the peer issue head-on.

Close friends are sacred turf: to tread on them is to tread on your child. Parents should control what is within their means to control. Since friendship choices are not up to parents, they would need to instead direct their efforts to how Ricky spent his time in general. Ricky's parents needed to get him busy with more prosocial pursuits so he would be less available to hang around downtown. ("Prosocial" refers to interactions that enhance social skills, caring, cooperation, responsibility, and collaboration.) Every afternoon after school, Ricky was signed up to attend a program at a neighborhood Boy's and Girl's Club. Not only would this program help keep him off the streets, it would provide the structure he needed to follow through with his homework. Ricky loved sports, but he would not be allowed to participate in these activities until his homework was completed. Fortunately, Bev could manage the logistics of the after-school program. Who can say how much of today's delinquency might be prevented if all parents of at-risk kids would work together with community services to establish a network of prosocial activities?

Instead of attacking Ricky's friends, Bev and Kent made an effort to encourage other friendships. My suggestion was not to pretend that they liked his deviant friends, for Ricky would see through it. An honest statement would be, "Yes, I prefer your company when you're around [someone else]." If they went camping for the weekend, Ricky could take a friend — but not one of the wild ones. Bev asked, "What should we do when one of Ricky's zero buddies is at our house doing something we don't like?" I advised her to act directly toward the friend the way that she felt. Bev should uphold the household rules, and if she has an issue with one of the friends, she should simply let him know that the behavior is not acceptable in their home.

Nevertheless, I cautioned her against becoming the household warden. Bev had totally written off Ricky's friends as a bad lot. I advised her to evaluate them individually. Bev viewed Ricky as a vulnerable kid, and her Mama Bear tendencies led her to overreact. If Ricky were left suddenly without any friends, he would feel isolated, angry, depressed. Bev and Kent should forbid contact with the friends with whom he had shoplifted, but they should try to build some rapport with the more acceptable of his friends. They might even make efforts to get to know these friends' parents and join forces with them to promote safe pursuits.

Bev, Charlie, and Kent should continue setting things up for low-key, fun times with Ricky. Charlie and Ricky shared an interest in baseball, so they might, for example, go to a batting cage together. *When parents put more energy into positive parenting, especially during rocky times, adolescents usually feel more secure about their home life and thereby are often less inclined to choose deviant peers.* All three parents in this vignette realized that an increase in appreciative statements and a decrease in nagging and criticism would improve Ricky's morale. Bev had to work the hardest on her parenting style. Ricky was a difficult kid, and if Bev attended to each and every one of his mistakes — "You left your homework on your desk." "You forgot your lunch." "You lost your new jacket." — she would be negative with him most of the time. All parents of ADD kids can identify with the dilemma of the ongoing negative. In order to keep a minimally acceptable ratio of, say, three positives for every one negative, Bev would have to ignore more of his minor mess-ups.

Little by little, Ricky's parents edged him out of his deviant group, sometimes reacting/restricting, sometimes letting go/guiding. At the same time that his parents were forbidding some of Ricky's peer activities, they emphasized the advantage of not changing schools; in other words, this was a give-and-take solution. The transition out of his wild group slowly occurred, and Ricky was in no man's land without his close friends for some time, which was hard on everyone. What allowed this family to stay the course was a combination of qualities. Importantly, the strong parent-child attachments were there. The family represented a definite resource; the parents had the competencies and potential to all work together for change, instead of splitting and polarizing. The peer issue had galvanized them into cohesive action, which held Ricky together during the phase when his peers were no longer a key source of support.

Family systems theorist Salvador Minuchin made the point that what distinguishes normal families from pathological families is not the absence or presence of problems per se, since families of all types will encounter difficulties. Of critical importance is what the family does with their problems.

How a family functions as a whole — the family system — determines whether they can adapt, problem-solve, and seek help when needed: Does the family have the ability to respond and restructure flexibly? Do members have appropriate boundaries? Are they mostly warm and positive as they interact with one another? Some of the challenges that Ricky and his family faced could easily have shaken another family apart, but they possessed many family system strengths and exemplified Minuchin's theory in action. What they were able to do with their problems was impressive indeed. Following up on counseling recommendations, Ricky's parents became very clear about what they would or wouldn't allow Ricky to do, and thus they — rather than the friends — remained the central force and authority in Ricky's life. By taking a stand, they steered their son off his socially deviant track and out of harm's way.

Bulimia: Mary's Double Life. The Fehr Family

The perfect body, the perfect face, the perfect clothes, the perfect personality, the perfect family: none of these conditions exists, of course, but to some they remain sought-after ideals. When an adolescent pursues the socially promoted stereotype of the perfect girl to an extreme — thin, nice, always good and never angry — instead of achieving this flawless state, she risks developing an eating disorder. Anorexia nervosa is a psychosomatic illness (an illness stemming from an interaction of body and mind) in which one starves to emaciation. Those who suffer from this disorder become severely malnourished. In extreme cases, anorexia can lead to mortality.

At least five times more common than anorexia is bulimia nervosa, likewise psychosomatic in its origin and potentially life threatening, though it usually occurs among normal-weight women. Bulimia involves bingeing and purging, usually by self-induced vomiting. What these disorders also have in common is an obsession with weight, shape, and body image as a measure of self-esteem.

Anorexia and bulimia represent problems of identity. Their significant increase in incidence in the last twenty-five years in western society requires that we acknowledge the influential role of sociocultural context. Since the late 1960s and early '70s, abnormally slender body weights and shapes have been idealized, worshipped, longed for, and suffered for by females in our culture. Although boys, too, can fall victim to eating disorders, the statistics are drastically lower for boys, just as the sociocultural pressure on boys to be slim is less. At what point, women must ask themselves, does idealization of the slender female body become exploitation?

Sixteen-year-old Mary and her parents, Vanessa and Michael Fehr, came to the Adolescent Clinic at the University of Washington for an evaluation and treatment of Mary's eating disorder. Because her dieting, bingeing, and vomiting had been an ongoing pattern for longer than six months, her condition was easily diagnosed as bulimia nervosa. A year before, Mary had begun dieting, hoping to slim down before starting high school. In six weeks, she took ten pounds off a frame she viewed as "pudgy," but decided to lose at least another five "just to be safe." Everyone in the family supported and approved of Mary's dieting until Mary experienced a fairly predictable backfire effect common to those who diet severely: dieting stimulates strong food cravings, which is the body's natural response to nutritional deprivation. Then the dangerous cycle begins: dieting to lose weight, bingeing as a reaction to fasting, and vomiting to purge calories and avoid possible weight gain.

Tearfully, Mary explained, "At least half of my energy every day goes into trying to keep on my diet, and then I hate myself while I find a secret place to eat and then get rid of it. I swear to myself I'll never do it again, that I'll try to be good and get back to my diet, but I always end up gorging and throwing it up." Mary went on to describe how she lived a "double life." On the outside, she made it look like she "had it all together." She got good grades, had a cute figure, and put on a smiley face, but inside she was tortured by her efforts to keep her social facade in place.

Mary showed other characteristics typical of both bulimia and anorexia.

- She possessed a distorted body image. Though her thighs were slight, she referred to them as "bulky," and though her stomach was flat, she called herself "fat."
- She maintained perfectionistic ideals for herself. Even after receiving high marks on tests, she was depressed because she felt pressure to maintain that level of achievement.
- She had low self-esteem. Despite glowing accolades from teachers and other adults in her life and an impressive list of accomplishments, she never felt "good enough."
- She tended to repress, minimize, or deny negative feelings. Since feeling angry automatically made her feel guilty, she thought she should try instead to just be nice.
- She had obsessive thoughts and rituals related to food.
- She was exceedingly sensitive and anxious about interpersonal conflict. She avoided "sticking up" for her views or herself, even when she felt she was right, because she feared losing friends, feeling guilty, or other outcomes.
- She lacked a unique identity. Not having reflected much on life, she was unable to express opinions about religion, politics, or sexual mores; likewise she couldn't articulate distinctive preferences or desires or visions for her future. Regarding the "Who am I?" question,

she was in a fog. Questions about what distinguished her uniquely as a person (aside from her activities) made her extremely anxious, but she settled on "being a nice person."

Family Matters

In addition to this painful individual snapshot of Mary, there was the family picture to consider. As a whole, the Fehr family typified those with an adolescent with an eating disorder. Vanessa and Michael were pleasant, friendly, and unerringly polite. They upheld values of kindness, social conformity, and family closeness. *The type of closeness they described moved beyond a realistic desire for harmony between family members and into a pattern of enmeshment, a hallmark of families with eating disorders. Enmeshment signifies a condition of blurred boundaries.* Family members with distinct boundaries understand it is acceptable to be different from one another, to have conflicts and ambivalent feelings about one another, and internal lives not totally known to others. In contrast, families with blurred boundaries often feel anxious and sometimes extremely distressed by normal differences and privacy.

During the Fehr family interview, individuals spoke up for one another, censored their own responses to avoid hurting or offending another family member, and displayed extreme sensitivity to each other's feelings and ideas. "Mom knows me better than I know myself," commented Mary, with a hint of resignation. "She says things I'm thinking before I say them. She literally reads my mind. It's kinda scary."

Vanessa and Michael were physically and emotionally overprotective, to the point that Mary had very little sense of autonomy and competence. Her parents worried intensely about her sleep, her friendships, her appearance, her school performance, and her safety in ways that made Mary angry and uneasy, but she was averse to showing it. It was not until later in treatment that Mary was able to voice these negative feelings directly.

Unwritten rules prevailed in their rigid family milieu. Everyone knew the importance of tidiness, acting nice, and not showing anger. Nonetheless, contradictions existed. Mary pointed out that her nine-year-old brother "could sass Mom, wear what he wanted, and have some privacy." Despite her obvious frustration with being treated differently than her brother, she said she put up with it because family reaction would be intense if she were to pursue an independent direction. "I don't speak up about what I want to wear because it's not worth it. It upsets Mom, and then I feel guilty." Although the family valued its code of "glossing over" problems — as Mary was later to call it — they lived in a chronic state of unresolved conflicts and unhealed resentments. To keep their differences under wraps, they avoided arguments and instead triangulated, capitulated, or internalized their conflict.

So protective of one another, so frightened of old hurts, and so upset by ambivalent feelings are families like the Fehrs that present and past difficulties do not readily emerge in therapy. Sometimes it takes six to twelve months before family problems relating to the eating disorder become unveiled and well understood. One year into therapy, we unearthed significant unresolved resentments in Vanessa and Michael's marriage. Vanessa derived little emotional satisfaction from her relationships with her husband and with her son, and out of this disappointment she had developed an inordinate focus on Mary as the center of her life. Separated from her extended family, she had "given up" her East Coast ties to move to the West with her husband; moreover, she continued to harbor an uneasiness about converting from Judaism to Lutheranism, Michael's faith. According to Michael, "nothing was ever enough," despite the fact that he had provided his family with a comfortable lifestyle and involved himself in family activities far more than any of his business partners. While he admired Vanessa's devotion to her children, he longed for her to feel more satisfaction with her life, with him, and with his contribution to their well-being. As it turned out, each of the family members felt they could "never do enough" to please others; a cycle of starving for approval, bingeing through episodic explosions of anger, and purging in an effort to deny problems became a family-wide theme, as did each individual's lack of internal self-acceptance.

Just as many young people with eating disorders have a double life, so too do their families. In their social world, they often come across as happy and content — a perfect family. Unspoken resentments and deep disappointments are often covert. Left unacknowledged, these hurts can only fester and isolate family members. Recovery for adolescents with eating disorders can take two to three years of therapy, although individuals with extreme cases, personality disorders, or abuse histories often require lengthier treatments.

Seeing Mary and her family at the adolescent clinic had the advantage of providing the multidisciplinary treatment eating-disordered teenagers need. Because Mary was vomiting three to four times a day, she needed a physician to monitor her electrolytes (specifically her potassium level). Her distorted ideas about nutrition and almost phobic attitudes toward anything but salads required intervention from a skilled nutritionist. Mary also saw a psychology intern for individual therapy and the intern and me in family therapy.

What a huge undertaking it is to establish a new self based not on ideas of perfection generated by society at large but on a true, authentic self. Some of the issues I worked on with Mary and her family included learning how to identify, accept, and express negative feelings; how to tolerate, manage, and negotiate conflict with others; and how to tend to one's own feelings, while appreciating those of others (that is, establish relationship boundaries) — all within a family that had little sense of how to negotiate these delicate interpersonal maneuvers. Also of critical importance, the relationship between Mary and her mother needed repair. Mothers are often "blamed" for enmeshment problems, so treatment sometimes overemphasizes individuation issues and the daughter's need to express her anger.[7] A mother-daughter relationship can often be rejuvenated more effectively by exploring some of the social pressures on mothers instead of blaming them. As Mary and her family addressed their issues, they worked to match up the "selves" they presented to one another and to the outer world with what they really felt and thought. Thus, the schism of their double lives changed from good and happy on the outside — while bad and sad on the inside — to a greater integration of a myriad of emotions and thoughts, which were more or less consistent internally and externally.

Dieting and Its Dangers

The pressure to be thin in our culture is enormous. Hardly a girl escapes the feeling that some part of her body should be thinner or smaller. Social comparisons intensify during adolescence, and the desire to "measure up" along the lines of appearance can take precedence over other areas of self-concept.

While only around 5 percent of adolescents will fall prey to a full-blown, diagnosable case of bulimia or anorexia, a much larger percentage of adolescent girls (50 percent or more) diet restrictively. In one college study, researchers found that 61 percent of women surveyed exhibited some form of an eating disorder such as chronic dieting (with or without pills or laxatives), binge eating, or deliberate purging, but these behaviors did not occur frequently enough to be diagnosed as bulimia.[8] Dieting will not necessarily lead to the formation of an eating disorder, but the physiological urge to binge after fasting and the terror of regaining weight puts girls at risk. True, research has documented the harms of obesity, but most girls with eating disorders were not medically overweight when they first started dieting.

What variables determine which girls are likely to progress from dieting to an eating disorder? Although this phenomenon is not completely understood, it is thought to be based on some combination of biological, psychological, and family characteristics, loosely analogous to those in the Fehr family. Given the increased frequency with which teenage girls have dieted in the last two decades, specialists are analyzing sociocultural forces and the need for social change — for greater acceptance of a realistic range of body shapes for women in our weight-conscious society.

Health concerns about the harms of excess weight must be balanced with our growing knowledge of the harms of dieting, especially for young women. Even if couched in comments about health, most dieting in girls is about appearance. Parents usually have the best of intentions when they encourage their child to diet, for parents, too, belong to the culture that values thinness. Moms, in particular, can fall into the trap of complaining about their own bodies, of not eating with the family because they're dieting, and of expressing concerns about their daughter's weight.

A former patient of mine, now in her late twenties and recovered from an eating disorder, describes below what it was like to be a girl who felt compelled to fashion herself into a person she could never be. In our life achievements, as in our body types, perfectionism rarely serves people well in a search for health and well-being. Each of us is a profile of strengths and weaknesses, and it out of this mix that we experience the richness of human relationships.

This former patient tells of the painful discontinuity between her confused inner feelings and the outward image she put forward, as she fervidly pursued her goal to be the "perfect girl." Although her story is about recovery from an eating disorder, it is also about an adolescent figuring herself out in her social world. After years of hard work, she eventually not only made peace with the imperfect mix of who she is, but also came to "enjoy" her life. Her story follows:

It was part of being perfect — slim hips, no fat, able to make my body do anything. A part of me I could control absolutely. I was the one who controlled what I ate. I was the one who trained beyond the team schedule. I became a perfect shell, hiding every ounce of my confusion and self-disgust. The only view I felt even vaguely comfortable with was the view from the outside.

It all worked for a while. When I was in college and on a lightweight crew team, I had the perfect body for it. The closer I got to fat-free invincibility, the more praise I garnered. And then there was the perfect body, so highly sought in the region where I was raised — also fat-free, but waify, feminine. It wasn't maliciousness on my family's part; it was just that things on the outside, measurable successes, are more comfortable for them. When I went home from college for Christmas my mother wanted to know how I had become so slim, for advice on her diet. My great-aunt, always concerned about whether or not I had a boyfriend, followed me around at the annual Christmas party, commenting on how "darling" and "thin" I was. I would often feel confused, thinking that there must be more than one perfect, that my body had to be two things at once. Every compliment I received in those years had the echo of a nail in an empty metal pail. None of them filled me up; in fact, they made me more anxious, but I still needed them.

Then, while still in college, I began to realize that no matter what my weight or my level of fitness was, I would never be happy with it. Every day was a struggle to keep to the narrow path of perfection. But perfect was always somewhere else, outside myself. I began seeing a therapist, which helped me start to feel safe just sitting still and feeling. And, I also saw other women and friends dealing with similar things. All around me were strikingly strong, vibrant women starving themselves too. By my senior year, I got past despising the sloth in others, and became angry at the fashion magazines, the televisions shows, the movies, the families, and everything else that told them — or rather us — that we had to be something we weren't. I think that getting angry was the first step. I still ran miles, I still obsessed about food, but I knew it wasn't what I wanted.

If there were one story of how I brought myself out of this and got to where I am now, I would tell it. But there isn't, just as there isn't one reason I was anorexic in the first place. I began picking out feelings from inside me, learning about myself — how I reacted to things — and then I started trusting those feelings. Doubt about my body image became a clue to the fact that there was something I couldn't handle, and that I had better figure it out. I still work at soothing myself when I am uncomfortable with emotions, but now from the inside. When my mother asks me about my accomplishments rather than my desires, I stop and feel that she is different from me, separate, and that I am what I want. I am not perfect about taking care of my feelings, in fact, I am not perfect about anything, but I enjoy my life.

6

The Slippery Slopes of Sexuality

Goal: Accept your adolescent's sexual awakening. Help your child appreciate sexuality as part of a healthy human identity, and assist him or her in becoming sexually well adjusted and responsible.

WITH some degree of exaggeration and some degree of seriousness, health care professionals claim the need for sex education from birth to age one hundred. Though an overstatement, what we're trying to get at with this recommendation is an acceptance of sexuality as a healthy, ongoing part of life. Educating children about sexuality begins early in their lives, as parents use anatomically correct names for body parts, show physical affection for a spouse, and respond clearly to children's questions at a developmentally appropriate level. During puberty we gear up to address physical and emotional issues related to sexuality more directly.

Let's assume most parents know they *should* talk with their child about sexuality, just as we know we should make that appointment with the dentist or doctor. But with sex, it's awkward. We feel shy, they feel shy, so we leave too much to osmosis, when we should be doing everything we can to interpret sensationalized messages in the media, provide straight facts and information, and help them understand sexuality. Imagine, for example, what adolescents might conclude solely from the contradictory pro-sex and anti-sex messages both overt and subliminal in American culture: "Just Do It"/"Just Say No." We don't expect our children to get behind the wheel of a car and know how to drive; we give them lessons. We don't expect them to be able to pick up a violin and know how to play, and we don't expect them to plunge into the water and know how to swim. But, too often, we cross our fingers and hope our children will emerge at some point in their twenties with a healthy sexuality that is equivalent to perfect driving skills, the facility to play Bach sonatas, and a strong butterfly stroke.

What keeps us from carrying out "should" can be highly complex; the slopes of discussing sexuality with adolescents are slippery indeed. Finding a foothold can be tough. Sexuality is a broad topic encompassing more than the act of intercourse, and it is best handled as a series of informal exchanges instead of the single "sex talk," when we sit them down and bring out the educational pamphlets. There is a profusion of issues to cover, and there are many ways to talk about them, which need not relate to the parent's or the adolescent's sexuality directly. *Most of the comments we make to our adolescents about sex should be within the context of discussions about relationships and/or about sexual phenomena in the world, not about their or our experiences specifically.*

Lectures, interrogation, or personal references from parents can make teenagers groan with disgust and dread; they want to protect their privacy, as do we. Though most teenagers lack a place to find clear information about sexuality, most would rather skip it than endure awkward, invasive talks. Relatively few of the conversations we have with our children should impinge directly on their sexuality, but that small percentage of the time when we speak forthrightly is sometimes a far better experience than we might have imagined. Parents should, however, prepare for some back-sliding, since most adolescents will register resistance to our efforts.

Sexuality is a wonderful part of life, potentially a source of great pleasure, but we need to create an awareness in our kids of possible hazards along the way: unwanted pregnancy, sexually transmitted diseases, abuse, harassment. We fear our child might become the victim of a sexual hazard, and we also want to guard against our child becoming the perpetrator of abuse or harassment. Keeping our children safe in these regards can be likened to developing their immune system response: they need to receive some kind of deliberate, healthy exposure that enables them to develop self-protection. In the same way that we take our children to a health care provider to be inoculated, parents are likewise responsible for their children's "psychological immunization" against dangers related to sexuality. As young people become more knowledgeable about the complex array of sexual issues potentially affecting them, they tend to become better prepared to handle and fend off the perils of sexuality.

Our job as parents is to help our adolescents understand their sexual feelings, impulses, and reactions, be in control of their sexual choices, and understand the range of complicated sexual phenomena in the world today. We want them to develop the capacity to participate in sexual relationships in conscious, caring, and consensual ways that do not harm themselves or others. Without immunization, our children are at risk, but with healthy, guided exposure, they can make safer decisions for themselves and others. And, once immunized, our children's good health will allow them to experience the joys and fulfillment of a life open to exploring, learning, and evolving. Teens do not become sexually well adjusted either by being shut off or protected from sexual experience or by being so free to explore that they are overwhelmed with more than they can integrate into positive learning experiences.

Coming of Age: Puberty Dawns

A hundred and fifty years ago, menarche, psychological maturity, marriage, and childbearing all occurred within a period of a couple of years, typically from ages sixteen to eighteen, if not younger. A century ago, it might have been possible for parents to give their child "the talk" at puberty, in anticipation of marriage, and allow sexuality to unfold from fragments of information. We might also argue, however, that our ancestors were not always initiated into sexuality and human physiology in entirely healthy and clear ways, for mistakes and misunderstanding have been part of sexuality's legacy.

No longer do we have a brief span between the onset of puberty and childbearing, yet in many ways we continue to operate according to the old biological and sociocultural expectations. Today, it is not unusual for girls to start menstruating at age ten, which means that hormonal changes bringing about menstruation can begin as early as age eight. Psychological maturity happens in the late teens, and some young people now postpone marriage for another ten years, until their late twenties, when they are more economically independent. Many adolescents have at least fifteen years from the time their hormones begin moving them to have sexual interests and desires until the time they can actually fulfill those yearnings in a marital situation. Abstaining from sex until marriage becomes an unrealistic expectation for some, given this chronology.

Bodily changes during adolescence are rapid and confounding to an adolescent. Our job is to make sure they have lots of information about what's happening with their bodies, whether it be menstruation, breast development, genital growth, or nocturnal emissions. Girls should be taught what happens to boys and vice versa. With the exception of infancy, this is our most accelerated period of physical growth; no wonder teenagers spend so much time before the mirror — they're changing right before their own eyes! To the point of frenzy, pubescent teenagers analyze themselves: "Am I normal?" "How do I compare?" "What do I look like?" "What do I feel like?" Because emoting is more socially acceptable for girls, we're often privy to the exasperated outbursts and sighs of woe from our daughters, but our sons are also experiencing their share of angst as they too ponder their imperfect reflections. Parents frequently complain that their teenagers don't share the bathroom fairly. This is true; they don't. The mitigating factor is that their obsessive mirror gazing is more about vulnerability than vanity.

Only too easily can parents slip into jovial teasing about an adolescent's new physique, making wisecracks about bra sizes, voice cracking, or jock straps. It could be that such meager attempts to be funny rise out of our personal discomfort with their new bodies, for their transformation signals the beginning of the end of our child-rearing years. Keeping conversations light and using self-directed humor to defuse tension can be effective, but our crass jokes are insulting. All teasing about their bodies and sexuality is off-limits.

We can be ready to reassure our kids and empathize with them when they send us cues that they want to talk, but we also want to appreciate that sexual awakening involves many private experiences, which may include wet dreams, sexual fantasies, secret crushes, and masturbation. Whenever possible, we should help them maintain privacy in acutely sensitive matters.

Another point of consideration about puberty is the disproportionate growth rate of girls versus boys during the early teen years. In general, there's a two-year difference between girls, whose periods begin at an average age of 12.6, and boys, who mature at the average age of fourteen. Any sixth-grade class contains a motley mix of tuned-in girls with finely etched features and bodies growing shapely, towering over scrawny or pudgy boys happily wearing the T-shirts their mothers bought for them. If interest in boys is strong, some early developing junior high girls will bypass boys in their class and seek out high school boys. To discourage these relationships, parents can encourage lots of friendships and a variety of nonromantic social experiences for their young teenagers and try to delay the onset of serious dating in general.

The Dating Dance

Puberty ushers in some pairing off into couples, which generally starts around age fourteen. Teenagers today are less likely to "date," but they do "go out." Though early adolescent one-to-one experiences are highly anticipated, the awkwardness of being with someone of the opposite sex makes the actual experience something of a letdown. The draw is to be known as someone who is sought after, but once alone together, young adolescents become tongue-tied; it's too intimate. Talking on the phone is much easier; you can play a CD for the person, put her on hold, or talk to a friend who's in the room when the conversation lulls. Any parent observing their thirteen- or fourteen-year-old son or daughter in a couples situation is likely to notice how much fun they *aren't* having together. Parents probably have more cause for wariness when young teenagers showing up at the door are smooth, poised, and articulate instead of bumbling, blushing, and gaze-averting.

It could be the awkwardness of it all that has brought about the group dating trend. Instead of going out as twosomes, teenagers often travel in larger (psychologically safer) packs. They mingle in a group and check each other out, free of commitment to a specific person. They dance alone or line dance (a metaphor for group inclusion), eliminating the need for pairing up. Typically, a second stage of dating occurs when some kids within the group pair off. Usually it is only older teens who become a couple independent of the group. (Today, a couple isn't said to be "going together," but "seeing each other.")

A type of pairing that's more prevalent these days is the "good friend" duo. Though they go out together, these friends of the opposite sex purport to have no romantic interest in each other; a teenage girl's best friend might take in a movie with the best friend's boyfriend, for example.

Nonetheless, a lot of flirting can go on in these relationships. In their pure form, these platonic relationships become opportunities to learn about the opposite gender's culture in a situation semi-free of sexual static.

Looking Sexy

One of our more difficult parenting experiences occurs when we wake up to the realization that our child looks, acts, and feels "sexual" and intends to go out in the world that way. How we wince when we notice, for example, a daughter showing off her budding breasts by wearing a little T-shirt and no bra or a son grooving pleasurably to highly sexualized music. We worry we've lost our ideological hold on them.

From the dawn of time, those who are younger have been borrowing attributes of adulthood in an effort to appear more sophisticated than they truly are. It is not only the children of the present who sometimes slather on too much makeup, squeeze into tight clothes, or carry themselves with adult affectation. What parents sometimes forget to take into account is how uneasy teenagers can be with their borrowings; they put on the thick eyeliner for a dance but upon arriving, might head directly to the bathroom to wipe it off.

Understandably, parents can get riled when their child wears something that suggests "sexual availability." *Discussions about clothing choices are usually most effective when they occur in a general context; it's far easier for an adolescent to make objective judgments and decipher an outfit's erotic message when it's on the back of a model or an actress instead of her own.* But, what do we do when the risqué piece of clothing is, indeed, on our child? While it is the parent's responsibility to share opinions and preferences, harsh judgments can ignite bad feelings.

In a classic scenario — let's say your daughter is wearing a low-cut blouse — parents have basically three options: disallow the revealing blouse; tactfully offer your perspective but let the adolescent choose what to do; or say nothing. Values, hot buttons, and specific family context will dictate which of the calls we're likely to make. What we especially want to avoid are blurry expressions of outrage that fall into none of the above categories, like, "I can't believe you think you're going out the door like that!"

What about the first option? Before deploying one of our parental "no" bombs, we want to keep in mind that we have only so many nonnegotiables; each time we render a solid, "I'm-not-budging" decision, we lose a little rapport from having usurped control in an area where they may need and benefit from practice. No matter how kindly we deliver our nonnegotiable, we need to be prepared to suffer the consequences of its not going well (that is, potential anger, backfire leading to behavioral acting out, "ruined" day, refusal to go out). If, however we feel strongly that the piece of clothing is truly offensive, the decision to exercise parental authority respectfully is available.

While the second possibility is dicey and often fails, I include it among parenting choices because it can work in some families. We might offer a comment aimed at increasing our child's reflectiveness and convey our honest impression: "I've got to admit, I'm uncomfortable with your wearing that blouse," or "I'm concerned about the impression your blouse will make." Some kids may pick up such a dropped hint and, in their own time, head back into their rooms to change, not so much out of compliance, but because they, too, have been conflicted over whether their choice was "too much." Defensive and hostile on the outside, some kids may be secretly relieved when their parents call them on their over-stretch. On the other hand, a lot of kids will feel chastised by this kind of parental observation. Sensitive and self-conscious, adolescents put a lot of thinking and effort into what they're wearing. Any remark (even a compliment!) might be interpreted as critical; the conversation goes haywire, and we don't get the desired end. Once we've let our adolescent know what we think, we need to trust that she is competent to make her decision about what to wear, one way or another.

The third response — to bite one's tongue — is worth considering because, in reality, in these types of situations there isn't much that's likely to work. Why say anything? Confronted by our editorializing, teenagers sometimes wear what they have on out of pride. Remember, clothing is prime territory for identity exploration; what she puts on today may not be predictive of tomorrow. Moreover, why not let the peers do some of the socializing for us? If a teenager wears something that truly pushes the limit of acceptability, according to their standards of what's too sexualized, other kids will almost always let her know. Peer teasing will put a teenager back in a baggy T-shirt quicker than any parent comment.

Whether they be clothing issues, rules and restrictions, or permissions and approvals, parents sometimes "choke" with decisions relating to their child's sexuality and let things go by that in retrospect appear to have been ill considered. Perhaps, for example, you've slipped up and let them go to the house of a friend of the opposite sex without parents at home, and realize you need to reverse that permission. Perhaps you let them watch an R-rated movie but now have second thoughts. While consistency is always preferable, it's never too late to admit, "The decision to allow you to do X was a mistake on my part. I now realize it would be better if Y." Or if it applies, you might let them know you're adjusting to changed circumstances.

We should always avoid subjecting our children to our arbitrary whims, but there is no reason for us to feel we have to live with a bad decision. Kids may rail and say, "But you let me wear a halter top to school before!" A response can be, "Yes, I did, and I'm sorry to be doing an about-face with this. I've thought this through more fully and I now see that I shouldn't have, so you will have to make do with this new rule."

The Pleasures and Perils of Pornography: Charlotte, Randy, and Tad

Recently, while I was facilitating a workshop on adolescent sexuality, a tall, bright-eyed woman with a strong southern accent waved her hand from the front of the audience and asked, "Well, I know men like looking at sexy pictures, but I was beside myself when I found porn magazines in my fifteen-year-old son's dresser drawer. What should a parent do in such a situation?"

I asked the woman, whose name was Charlotte, if she would be willing to share more of her story with the group; I've found that people's specific dilemmas can be a better springboard for discussion than generalizations about sexuality. Charlotte explained that after a quick look at her son's magazines, she slammed them shut and impulsively stuffed them in a garbage bag. Not a word did she say to her son, for she knew he would figure out what happened. Besides, tossing the pornography enabled her to remove the material she found truly objectionable from her son's line of vision, while avoiding the awkwardness of a confrontation.

When her husband, Randy, took out the trash that evening, he was puzzled to see the magazines. To Charlotte's explanation, he had reacted with dismay. "Getting aroused by this kind of material is what healthy, red-blooded, American boys do," Randy had claimed. He proceeded to normalize the phenomenon of pornography, whether it be magazines, movies, or the porno channel on cable TV, and they were currently at an impasse about Tad's access to this kind of material.

As one might imagine, the ensuing discussion in the workshop split down the chromosome line, with most men expressing more liberal views about pornography and most women raising reservations. Shrugging his shoulders, one brave spokesman for the freethinkers posited the view that pornography evoked pleasurable fantasies that could lead to better sex and that, on the whole, it was relatively benign "as long as it wasn't the kinky — you know — perverted stuff." A woman countered that we were not talking about adults but adolescents, who might not have the maturity to censor the "sick stuff" from the acceptable material.

She noted the difficulty in drawing the line between soft and hard porn. Although sex with animals was clearly depraved, what about images of a man with multiple partners, a woman masturbating in a public place, or children in sexual poses? One person expressed the view that pornography sometimes became repetitious and boring; another commented that while pictures in some of the better-known magazines were usually "pretty good," the stories, articles, letters, and ads were definitely outside the sexual mainstream. As the debate heated up, a man burst out, "Hey, what about the First Amendment?"

I thought to myself, "Hey, what about educating our kids about some of the issues and controversy involved in pornography?" The discussion reflected the variety of opinions, values, and emotions that come to the fore as a diverse group of people debate the complexities of human sexuality. Because attitudes about sexuality reflect one's identity, upbringing, and life experiences, people have distinct ideas and biases to air. Because sex, and more specifically pornography, is at once a moral and highly emotional issue, a discussion can become as incendiary as any I know.

I stressed that we should be aware of the values our adolescents might absorb from this exposure to sexuality. We should take it upon ourselves to discuss these values with them if we discover they are seeking out pornography. A parallel situation occurs when our kids watch violent films or view ads suggesting good times will be had from drinking, smoking, or showing off with sex-typed behaviors. We want them to be capable of decoding all types of media, including pornography. The difference between objectionable films and ads versus pornography is that open critique of media distortions is more plentiful, while a solid analysis of the messages pornography sends is rarely available to adolescents. Tempting though it may be to minimize something relatively small like a couple of *Playboys* under the dresser or a visit to an erotic Web site, we want to keep in mind that our kids are impressionable and their ideas about sexuality are formed cumulatively.

Some of the angles to consider are that pornography rarely represents intercourse in the context of loving relationships, which is the way we would like our children to know, experience, and prefer sex. Moreover, it depicts sexual attraction based primarily on unlikely physical attributes, eliminating notions of desire based on interpersonal qualities. Since real-life women and men rarely look like those portrayed (in the absence of implants, dieting, or cosmetic surgery of various kinds), pornography creates false expectations. Sex in pornography frequently presents men dominating subordinate women, who may even show pleasure from explicit victimization. Sadomasochism is plentiful. Although pornography has not been proven to play a causal role in sexual offenses, some researchers argue that it is part of a general socialization that promotes sexual aggression against women, if only by the attitudes it influences.[1] While many adults claim, "I can handle this stuff, even though I'm not into it," this statement begs the question of whether our sons and daughters can. Given some of the sexual preferences depicted in pornography, we need to let our adolescents know that pornography distorts, exaggerates, and misrepresents most people's sex lives.

We might also clue our children in to who the women are who dance in topless bars, pose for pictures in hard-porn magazines, or earn a living by participating in sex flicks. Often, they have been victims of incest or sexual abuse. Rarely is the decision to market their bodies a chosen affirmation of their sexual nature. Most of them simply "ended up" here, and the road that took them to this end is frequently a sad tale.

Because adolescents are curious about sex, we might consider supplying or having around some books or publications that present more realistic versions of sexuality, such as *The New Joy of Sex*. These books are plenty sexy and will teach them about lovemaking in explicit detail but don't have the problems associated with pornography. We might argue that it is often because of the unavailability of more legitimate publications that adolescents resort to sneaking a peek at more disturbing material.

The pros and cons of pornography, as debated among members of the workshop, echoed the opposing points of view of Charlotte and her husband, Randy. Ideally, both Charlotte and Randy should listen to each other's ideas and feelings about Tad's access to pornography, try to respect each other's differences, and focus on negotiating a policy with their son with which they both can live. *Parenting often involves moving off a position one would be more comfortable keeping, and when we do compromise, a more balanced parenting philosophy can emerge.*

If her husband were to persist in his pro-pornography stance, Charlotte might offer her son some material she felt was more representative of her views of sexuality, saying, "Dad and I have some differences about this, and here is my perspective for you to consider."

Mothers and fathers are both responsible for providing their child with information about sexuality. Out of their own discomfort, parents often pass the buck on sex ed to the parent of the same gender. There is no reason to believe that sons should receive information about sex exclusively from their fathers and daughters from their mothers. Because boundaries between opposite sex parents and an adolescent will necessarily be different from those between parents and children of the same sex, what's appropriate will vary. Nevertheless, an ongoing dialogue with both biological parents about sexuality has the distinct advantage of offering two points of view, which are bound to be somewhat unique because they represent male and female perspectives.

Myths and Excuses: Why We Don't Talk About Sexuality

Since most parents know they *should* discuss sexuality with their adolescent, it can be helpful to mull over some of the obstacles that keep us at base camp, contemplating our assault of this formidable topic. First and foremost, many parents feel ill equipped for the journey, held back by an intergenerational legacy of silence. Parents of today's teens may have come of age during and after the sexual revolution of the '60s, but we were brought up by parents of the '30s and '40s, and our heritage is one of discomfort, confusion, and insecurity when talking about sexuality. We lack role models, and attitudes change slowly, especially on matters fraught with taboos and riddled with cultural contradiction.

Another stumbling stone from generations past is the fear that if we provide information about sexuality and contraception, we may encourage sexual activity. Though research has refuted this notion, this objection continues to be raised. *Adolescent girls whose parents have communicated with them about sexuality have not been found to be more likely to be sexually active than those deprived of such parent communication.* (I would bet it's the same for boys, but research is scant on boys' sexuality, since we have a bias toward worrying mostly about girls.) According to some studies, the degree to which adolescents receive sex education was actually shown to relate to a lower incidence of girls' sexual activity. And, importantly, of the sexually active adolescents, those who had more sex education were more likely to use contraception regularly.[2]

Some parents worry about getting tripped up by their child's questions about their own sexual experiences, which they would prefer not to answer. If family secrets are disturbing the parents, creating "hot buttons," parents might consider clearing up the mystery — but only if it appears to be affecting their child rearing and the child is mature enough to absorb its impact. Parents can draw the line with private details such as when they first had sex. Only a small percentage of adolescents will be assertive enough to gun for specifics, but if they do, a clear option is available. Parents can respond in respectful though in no uncertain terms that they believe disclosure of personal matters would serve no helpful purpose and, in fact, could be very distracting and burdensome to the adolescent's own decision-making process. To defuse the topic, parents can calmly respond, "To my mind, knowing what I did would be neither helpful nor germane." While I have heard of special circumstances where revealing intimacies worked, for the most part this is a boundary parents can keep without apology because what we did — virginal until marriage or sex at age fifteen — is likely to be irrelevant.

Another barrier blocking parent-child discussions about sex is the assumption our kids have learned everything they need to know from a sex ed course taken through school or a community resource. Most adolescents would beg to differ; so would many experts in the fields who have noted the inadequacy of school sex education programs on grave problems such as adolescent pregnancy, sexually transmitted diseases, and AIDS. Unfortunately, even when parents do talk with their kids about sex, it is likely to be the so-called "birds and bees" or "facts of life" discussion, which usually is redundant with course material.

Parents have the unique opportunity to individualize discussions about sexuality and relationships and to intersect with their adolescent at critical moments, when an adolescent most needs and wants information. A sex ed course has the standard limitation of being necessarily gauged for a *group.* It is likely to tell some adolescents more than they want or need to hear at the time and to tell others far too little, depending on what is going on in an individual adolescent's life. In therapy situations with adolescents, I've found that a sex topic that brought on boredom, rolling eyes, and disinterest one week might become of urgent importance weeks later, all because of changed circumstances. Maybe a friend just had an abortion; maybe they just started to masturbate; maybe a romantic relationship has blossomed and they're flooded with sexual feelings. Since we can't always predict when a sexual issue might be salient to them or when they might be ready for a new level of analysis of an old precept, we want to hone our active listening skills and be ready to talk at a moment's notice.

Time and again I hear four loosely related statements from parents explaining why they don't communicate openly with their teens about sex. The often-repeated lines are: "We've had the talk, and I told her to come to me if she has any more questions"; "Every time I try to bring it up, she shuts me off"; "I know I should, but I don't know how to approach the topic"; and "I want to talk about it, but haven't found the right opportunity." Each of these statements represents parents slipping their way down the slopes.

First of all, parents might have noticed what research corroborates: Sol Gordon, a major figure in the field of sex education, has found that kids stop asking questions actively after about age eight. Parents may say to their adolescent, "Do you have any questions about sex?" Chances are the teenager will respond, "No," so the parent adds, "Well, if you do, let me know." Now all the pressure to initiate a talk is on the teenager. *If we expect our kids to come to us with their confounding concerns about one of life's greatest mysteries, we're kidding ourselves. In most cases, we need to go to them.* We need to prove we're comfortable with these discussions and that we can be trusted. Otherwise, they're not likely to believe it's safe to bring up a highly charged or taboo sexual issue, even if they are in great emotional distress.

If kids are uncooperative or even downright rude when parents try to discuss sex with them, we should ask ourselves what might have triggered the resistance. On the one hand, adolescent discomfort with our efforts to talk about sex is completely normal; expect some rolling of eyeballs. Teenagers want to seem cool and informed; "I know all that stuff," they might say. On the other hand, if our teenager's reaction is intense, we should consider revamping the approach. Most teenagers will be repulsed by discussions with parents that are intrusive, patronizing, judgmental, anxiety provoking, full of scare tactics, or manipulative. Some entrées are better than others.

Some Tips for Carrying Out Conversations About Sexuality

Parents who lack confidence or feel uninformed may need to do a little groundwork before engaging in a conversation about sexuality. Reading some books, attending a workshop, talking with friends may help. If certain anatomical words stick in your throat as you say them, practice glitch-free pronunciation. Consider seeking out a group of like-minded parents (particularly those with older teenagers who have traveled this tricky terrain) who can function as a sounding board as you rehearse your thoughts and ideas. Because this book focuses on relationships, the parenting process, and how information can be conveyed, parents may want to refer to books listed in the reference section at the end of this book for background on topics like human physiology, puberty, contraceptive methods, abortion, sexual violence, sexually transmitted diseases, and pregnancy.

Below are several ways to broach sex topics. Whatever the approach, tone and attitude are critical. Although there will be times when we have to be direct (perhaps we find a condom under their bed, or an open letter on the dining room table referring to intercourse), most conversations should be eased into in low gear rather than kick started. Remember, however, even the deftest of maneuvers can fail miserably. A disheartened mother told me about her efforts to use an anecdote to raise her daughter's awareness. The mom related a story about her friend who worked at Planned Parenthood, describing how this friend counseled a young girl who couldn't believe she'd become pregnant because she'd only had intercourse one time. The daughter responded brusquely, "What's the little lesson in that story, Mother?" Sometimes we're so big in their lives and our "lessons" are so transparent that we'll lose ground in our efforts.

What is optimal is not one big talk but many low-key talks over a period of time. Issues should be raised in a matter-of-fact-way with some casual indifference about whether it will "take." Be assured that something will filter in, and if we reach a conversational impasse, we should drop it because, ideally, we're having these conversations in advance of a crisis, when we have some leeway and there's nothing pressing. Most of our conversations about sex should be agenda-free. If we have a passionate objective, our child, who knows us like the back of his hand, is likely to stonewall. We want to acknowledge the pinnacles and pitfalls in a healthy, nonintrusive way. These exchanges might take place in a car, while folding laundry, gardening, or hanging out together in the kitchen, as if sexuality is an element of the air we breathe.

Following are seven techniques that may be successful:

1) *Seize natural opportunities as a springboard for global questions or generalized musing.* News stories and ads provide daily opportunities to communicate with children and adolescents about sexuality, which is the ideal way to conduct sex education. We might hear a broadcast about domestic abuse, and — without moralizing or grandstanding — comment on the dynamics of dominant/submissive romantic involvements; we might refer to an ad and talk about media exploitation of sex. Or, we might use a newspaper piece on rape on college campus to talk about sexual violence. With any questions we ask, we want to convey honest interest in their opinions; we're not trying to hammer in a point, even though we might like to!

2) *Use the Socratic method: ask questions to provoke independent inquiry.* This approach can be particularly effective in reviewing movies. Rent a video that has a sexual theme (is there one that doesn't?). Choose one that might inspire a *thoughtful* exchange of ideas. TV shows, including soaps, which are replete with melodramatic and manipulative romances and gender stereotypes, can work too. Again, we don't want to bash or moralize as we assess the movie, but we do want to pose some questions that require judgment and evaluation rather than correct or incorrect responses. We might use a phrase like, "It really disturbed me when [something] . . . what did you think?"

3) *Introduce a hypothetical situation with someone else as the subject.* As with all these approaches, we need to pick our time, make sure everyone is loose enough to exchange opinions, and try to link our hypothetical query to a natural opportunity so we're not springing an idea on them. Let's say, the topic is contraception. A conversation with a son might go something like this: "What would you do if a friend told you he was having unprotected intercourse with a girl he didn't really know very

well? Would you feel comfortable talking to him about the risk of her getting pregnant or about his risk of getting a sexually transmitted disease?"

In all likelihood, the son would respond, "I dunno. It depends."

A possible rejoinder would be, "Yeah, I probably wouldn't have the nerve to confront a friend unless he was a close one." As with all these techniques, we want to stay one step removed and keep the intensity down, as we talk about someone else. The dialogue then might travel to questions like, "How far would you go to try to keep this friend out of trouble?" "Would you actually get him condoms?"

4) *Practice the please-inform-me approach.* Here, we want to be a little humble, realize we're from another generation, and relate to them in a way that stimulates chatting, without teaching per se. We want to stay open-minded, keep it light, and be ready to be enlightened. Most teenagers have thought a lot about sex, and whenever we're able to acknowledge their good ideas, we should seize the opportunity. To introduce a topic — safe sex, for example — we test the waters. A possible opening question with a daughter might be, "You've had that class on sex. Do kids make jokes about the curriculum? I know we sure did." Based on the daughter's response, parents might consider telling a funny story about sex ed. In this way, the parent and the adolescent join together to share a mutual perspective on an experience. (Too often, the dynamic is parent point of view versus that of the adolescent.) If all is going well, the parent could reflect, "It's incredible what stands between life and death. You know, just a little piece of rubber. There's so much to know about safe sex, like the technical stuff that has to go on, you know, the engineering of how the guy gets a condom on in the midst of passion. Do you think kids today are more willing to discuss some of the nitty-gritty of safe sex because of AIDS?" Another possible query might be: "Speaking of safe sex, did they cover homosexuality and bisexuality? They sure didn't in my sex ed class."

Typically, a teenager might question the parents, "Why are you so curious about sex all of the sudden?" The answer is, because it's *important.* Times have changed: the issues are different, more complex, and more dangerous. There needs to be no apology for trying to get your kids to think about these matters.

5) *Let your child overhear a discussion you have with a spouse or a friend.* Much information can find its way to a young person through their eavesdropping. Simply let them be around while we're having a heartfelt

conversation about an area of concern to us. The topic can be anything —
sexual molestation, AIDS, sexual harassment in the workplace, or any
aspect of a love relationship (theoretical, not gossip). Adolescents who
overhear adults deliberating over any complicated issue usually receive a
lot of food for thought.

6) *Respond directly to their cues.* Sometimes, in the most subtle of ways,
our adolescents will let us know they're looking for information about
sexuality. Since we want them to open up, we should take care not to
dominate or judge, especially if they seem tentative. This might happen,
for example, when an adolescent is questioning his own sexuality. A family
might have a high school son who begins asking questions about gay
culture and bisexuality in a nervous or anxious way. It would be appropriate for parents to provide their son a conversational opening by asking
him whether he has any personal concerns or wants to talk to a counselor.
Even if he doesn't want to pursue the question of his own sexual identity,
the parents could reassure him that it's not unusual for young people to
have bisexual or homosexual feelings, but that the whole process of figuring out a sexual identity requires time, meaningful exploration, and support from others.

7) *Be a Role Model.* Although this approach is nonverbal, it may be one
of our most powerful ways of exposing our children to the wonders of
human loving. Parents who are able to model healthy sexuality, who enjoy
each other, and who show affection (in a nonexhibitionistic way) for each
other are teaching their child about the value of sexuality within a relationship. In this way, the adolescent learns of the wonderful reciprocality
between a love relationship and good sex, which can deepen and enhance
the relationship itself.

When a Teenage Relationship Is Headed Toward Sex: Ellen and Rivka Kellerman

"It's not like I'm in the dark ages. I know that the majority of teenagers
have sex by the time they finish high school. It's just that I really don't
think Rivka is ready or that she knows what she'd be getting into if she
were to have sex with her boyfriend." Though Ellen Kellerman was an
articulate, well-educated woman with a genial sense of humor, she struggled to find words for what I've come to see as archetypal parental anguish
over their child's initiation into sexual intercourse.

People come to therapy for various reasons, some with overwhelming problems that will take years to resolve, and others, for a circumscribed one- or two-time consultation over a specific issue. What I've learned through these consultations is that healthy families, like the Kellermans, can hit a bump, seek out information, put it to use, then proceed on a smoother course. Ellen's daughter, Rivka, age sixteen, had been seeing Jared exclusively for two and a half years, and their relationship showed signs of increasing intimacy. Because conversations between mother and daughter about sex had been going very badly, Ellen sought my guidance.

"What are your concerns about Rivka starting to have sex with her boyfriend?" I asked. I could anticipate some of her answers, but I wanted Ellen to verbalize her thoughts, which would help me gauge whether Ellen was expressing her thoughts in a respectful "hearable" way that would further dialogue between mother and daughter or in a way that would close down conversation.

Taking a big breath, Ellen presented her case. "Well, I've thought about this a lot, as you might imagine. It would be naive for me to think that Rivka is not seriously contemplating having sex with Jared. They're very close, and I notice how Rivka lights up when Jared puts his arm around her. At sixteen, she's mature in many ways. But I solemnly believe that no teenager should have intercourse. I think it creates an emotional vulnerability that no teenager can ever foresee before actually having sex, so how can they truly make an informed choice about whether they are ready?"

I was impressed with Ellen's thoughtful statement. Perhaps all Ellen needed from me was explicit permission and encouragement to speak her mind and share her ideas with her daughter. But, when I said as much to her, she became distinctly uncomfortable.

"Well, you see, I have told Rivka this, but she becomes furious. She tells me it's her decision, which I guess it is. She seems to interpret anything I say as one more effort to pull her away from Jared."

I took a gamble, "Is it?"

"No," she retorted flatly. "Jared is a very nice boy. Even though he is not who I would ideally pick for Rivka, I've come to appreciate him as a person and to see how they meet each other's needs." Ellen explained that her daughter tended to be "uptight, perfectionistic, and emotional," while Jared was more laid-back and accepting. Easily ruffled by a tough home-work assignment, a grade, or a verbal jab from a peer, Rivka relied on

Jared's easygoing temperament as a soothing balm. Implicit in Ellen's description of Jared, however, was a cavil that he was neither very academic nor very ambitious. Anyone with Ellen's piercing intellect would judge this as a fault.

"I admit, I didn't have a lot of good things to say about Jared in the beginning, but I've made a real effort to be more accepting of him." Perceptively, Ellen went on to mention the "Romeo and Juliet" effect, describing how criticism of Jared could cause her daughter to "run to him."

"The truth is," she continued, "Jared is very good for Rivka, and vice versa. But, she has me pigeon-holed where I was two years ago, so when I try to talk to her about my feelings about sex and my views about waiting, she writes me off as trying to sabotage her relationship with Jared *again*."

Ellen and Rivka have cinched up over the issue of whether Ellen approves of Jared or not, unable to move to another level of discussion. *When a person possesses a rigid (sometimes defensive) perception about an attitude or position we hold, and we genuinely believe ourselves to have a different stance, our only recourse is to state our position firmly and confidently then prove it through our actions.* As I listened to Ellen, I wondered whether Rivka was truly failing to see her mother's sincere acceptance of Jared or whether Ellen was still unintentionally conveying rejecting messages about Jared or about sexuality. Was there a discrepancy between what Ellen overtly said and what her "unconscious parent" was communicating to Rivka? Perhaps Rivka, like many adolescents, had stopped talking to her mom, having concluded, "She would never understand what I'm going through. Virginity is all she cares about. My parents want to control me. They wish I was eight years old again so they wouldn't have to deal with this."

Hoping to fill out the picture a little more, I asked Ellen, "What does Mr. Kellerman think about the possibility of Rivka having sex with Jared?"

"David? Oh, he's old guard. This subject is for mothers and daughters. Actually, to give him credit, he has participated in discussions about sex with Rivka, more than most fathers. But he's a lot more conservative than I am. I almost want to keep him out of it because I'm afraid he'll come on so harshly that Rivka will run right to Jared." I took note of the fact that Ellen had twice expressed a concern that Rivka might "run to" Jared.

"Tell me more about the conversations you've had with Rivka about sexual intercourse."

"Conversations? Battles, you mean," said Ellen, rolling her eyes. "She basically tells me it's none of my business. She says that when she's ready, she's ready and that it's her life."

"Can Rivka define what 'ready' is?" I asked Ellen.

"No. She just says that she knows she loves him. But I don't believe teenagers are capable of loving each other in an enduring way that can hold up to the responsibilities and pressures of a sexual relationship. I guess I believe there has to be something more than romantic love, but I have trouble describing what that 'something' is. I become tongue-tied, so Rivka wins the debate before I really get started. I feel like I'm failing Rivka and myself. I need to try harder because Rivka dismisses me as neurotic and out of touch."

As described by her mother, Rivka sounded feisty. Had Ellen been more intrusive and controlling with her daughter than she appeared to be in this session? What had triggered Rivka's irascibility? Ellen was very attached to the notion that sex is off-limits for teenagers. *Although most of us would share Ellen's preference, when a parent is intense and adamant about virginity, it can thwart conversation that might truly help a teenager with a decision.* A family session would help me assess if it was just Rivka's nature to be headstrong and private or if something was exacerbating the parent-daughter dynamic. Ellen, however, had set certain parameters around this consultation; Rivka would never come in, and her husband believed she had blown matters out of proportion.

I reiterated to Ellen that she was off to a solid start by talking with Rivka about the emotional vulnerability that happens in sexual relationships and the unanticipated complexities that sexual relationships bring. The beauty of this tack is that it avoids the moralism ("Nice girls don't") that can be so guilt-inducing and unproductive. Parents can try to help their child visualize what it would mean to cross over into a state of sexual activity. We can explain that most people find sex to be very powerful. After we've had intercourse with a person, not only are we likely to feel more tied to and possibly dependent on them, but from that time forward we must deal with an expectation that sex will continue. Once initiated, it's tough to return to abstinence, and it can be excruciating when the relationship ends. Since one day's sense of love, trust, and readiness for sex with a person can so easily be followed by another day's sense of loss, betrayal, and regret, any of us had best ponder this decision with humility. Knowing all this, parents desperately want to save their children from the potential wounds of premature sexuality. Sometimes, however, adolescents can't hear our sound message because it becomes lost in what appears to them to be an anti-sex judgment.

We're treading on thin ice when we use age as the sole criteria for not having sex. Teenagers, especially sixteen-year-olds, are not likely to be convinced they're "too young," given the prevalence of sex among adolescents. Approximately 50 percent of today's youth aged fifteen to nineteen are sexually active (more of them boys than girls), with increasing prevalence as they age. Because so many adolescents have sexual intercourse by their junior and senior year, age is a meaningless measure of readiness for them. Age is, however, relevant for many health care educators, who caution against early sex. When thinking is less mature and egocentrism inhibits the capacity for mutuality in a relationship, the social and emotional costs of a sexual relationship are greater.

Sexual Decision Making: Guiding Teenagers in Evaluating Their Readiness

Sexual decision making refers to a whole range of decisions adolescents necessarily make as their bodies and minds mature. It pertains to sexual attitudes, values, and behaviors: What kind of person am I sexually attracted to? How far do I go with a boy/girl? Am I secure in saying no and slowing things down, or do I worry too much about losing him/her? What do I think about having sex? What kind of commitment should I have from my partner? What do I do about contraception? Am I scared about feelings of attraction to people of my gender? Although teenagers usually deliberate privately — and we want to respect their right to do so — parents can have talks with their children to aid their decision-making process.

Like Ellen Kellerman, many parents search for convincing reasons why teenagers should postpone having sexual intercourse. A good approach, which I reviewed with Ellen, is to focus on the type of relationship most compatible with sexual involvement. *Because most of our children will decide whether or not to have sex within the context of a relationship, we want to highlight the relationship as the main topic and sex as a subtopic.* Parents can become mired in the "not-ever" mode, spinning their wheels about abstinence, wishing they never had to acknowledge their child's sexuality, so it may not occur to us to sharpen everyone's thinking about *when* an adolescent might be ready. The dialogue between parent and adolescent is more likely to remain open if we drop abstinence as our sole agenda and move to a "*When* you have sex, you ideally also want . . ." I have found that most adolescents become so anxious about the shortcomings of their current relationship that it swerves them over to where they need to be: defining the kind of relationship they want to be in before they embark on the complex and intimate journey of sexual activity.

When talking to an adolescent about the kind of partnership wherein sex works best, we want to emphasize that no one should engage in sex to try to create a relationship that isn't already there. Over the long run, mixing sex into an already clouded relationship serves only to complicate matters. Though this vignette pertains to a daughter, our sons desperately need to deliberate over their decision to become sexually active and to be supported for choosing not to have sex. Given current gender expectations, it can be tough for boys when they're in love and not pushing the sexual envelope. The following points apply to boys and girls alike. A person is usually most comfortable having sex when:

- She respects her partner and the way he conducts his life in general. After the more transient romantic whirlwind subsides, she likes the overall picture of who he is as a person, which includes how he treats friends, family, other adults, and children, how he functions in school, what his future plans are, as well as basic character traits.

- She feels respected and cared for by him and knows that her feelings are considered important to him. There is a mutuality in the relationship, meaning that both partners have their needs met in a balanced way and that opposing needs/wants can be negotiated successfully. Both people feel a comfortable balance between their desire for closeness and togetherness and their desire for autonomy (apartness) and independence from one another. Neither person feels pushed, coerced, or exploited by the other. Each feels safe to say "no" to the other, without a risk of reprisal (that is, the loss of the relationship or other negative consequences).

- She views the relationship as stable and secure. In other words, she has known her partner well, over a period of time, and has experienced the relationship as relatively gratifying, without significant ongoing turmoil or crisis. She trusts the relationship not just because of a "feeling" or words and promises but because actions have given her good cause for trust.

- She communicates effectively with her partner. She feels listened to and able to articulate her feelings and preferences, as is he. Conflicts are generally resolved in a satisfying way. Discussions have included contraception, pregnancy, sexually transmitted diseases, and AIDS. She knows in the abstract that the relationship could end in the future and has accepted the emotional risks that are likely to accompany that loss. She realizes that sexual intimacy would intensify the loss.

Ellen Kellerman's Quandary

"If that's the kind of relationship one needs before having sex," said Ellen Kellerman, responding to the above description, "I'm not sure I should be having sex with my husband."

We laughed, and I admitted, "It's had that effect on others." *When we say, "Teenagers are too young to handle all the emotional and physical complexities that accompany a sexual relationship," we're talking about the presence of criteria like respect, trust, stability, and communication in their relationship.* In actuality, teenagers usually don't have the optimal conditions for adding sexual intimacy to their relationship. Although it's another question altogether whether adults do, they usually have more resources and maturity to draw on. When I talk to teenagers about the concept of relationship-based sex, some become crestfallen or teary-eyed, as if yearning for a bond they wish existed. Others react cynically, claiming that this kind of relationship is a fiction. Whatever the case, relationships like this are rare among adolescents. This is why many teenagers who become sexually active do feel vulnerable, hurt, and confused once a sexually intimate relationship ends.

But what about Rivka? I asked Ellen how she thought Rivka might evaluate her bond with Jared. Somberly, she responded, "The irony is, she and Jared might actually have a relationship pretty close to the one you just characterized. Now I'm really confused."

I'm impressed with this family. Not only might sixteen-year-old Rivka have a mature love relationship, she also has a mother who is willing to recognize and admit it, though doing so undermines her personal goal of persuading Rivka to postpone sex. I then said to Ellen, "You know, you can acknowledge that Rivka will make her own decision to have sex, one that may or may not work out for her, without your having to be absolutely comfortable with her decision and without your having to surrender your preference."

I wanted Ellen to understand a notion related to parent-adolescent boundaries: *as our children move toward late adolescence, not only will they disagree with us on important matters, they will increasingly be in the position to act on their own. Parents and children need to be able to accept and tolerate one another's differences without harming their relationship.* Letting that idea float in Ellen's mind, I returned to a hunch I had earlier in the session with Ellen. Was something driving Ellen's intensity? Why was she so concerned about Rivka's "running to" Jared? I asked, "If it seems to you that Rivka's relationship with Jared is solid, could we explore a little more why you feel so disturbed about your daughter having sex during adolescence? Is there anything in your or your extended family's sexual history that makes this a particularly loaded question — more loaded, that is, than it would be for other parents?"

Ellen became pensive. "Nothing between my husband and me, but, now that you mention it, my mother did have to get married because she was pregnant. Is that what you mean?"

"You tell me. Was it a problem? Is the issue of your mother's pregnancy important to you?"

Ellen rested her head against the back of the chair and shut her eyes. "I had no intention of getting into this, but I can see your point. Actually, it was a big issue." As if letting the skeleton out of the closet, Ellen described the sadness of her parents' marriage. Better educated and from a wealthier, more socially prestigious family, Ellen's mother had come to view her father as a huge disappointment and her own life possibilities as dramatically curtailed because of her marriage. "I detested how critical she was of him, but I also felt sorry for her because she felt like her life was wasted. Maybe Rivka has picked up on my fear that she will get into a similar situation and end up having to get married like my mother."

"If Rivka were to sense that source of anxiety, what do you think she might be feeling?"

"Resentment! Unfairness! Like she wants to get away."

What had started as a relatively straightforward consultation on teenage sex had become an eye-opening session for Ellen. She pondered whether her ferocity about abstinence might actually be driving her daughter away. Before our session, this bright, responsible, dedicated mom had been truly unconscious of how her own mother's secret had impacted her agenda for her daughter. In a therapy session, these types of break-throughs typically happen when people are deep into their stories, often very near the end of the hour. While most parents are uneasy about their adolescent becoming sexually active, Ellen, burdened by her background, was riddled with anxiety. I suggested that she share the source of her anxiety with Rivka. From what Ellen had told me about her daughter, it seemed as if Rivka would be capable of appreciating why Ellen was par-ticularly sensitive about adolescents and sex.

"What are the risks of sharing your mother's background with Rivka at this point?" I asked Ellen.

"Probably none," she responded, realizing that she owed her daughter an explanation. "Rivka is old enough to be discreet, and it would probably account for some of her grandmother's nastiness and my 'neuroticism.'"

After a pause, Ellen added, "You know, Jared is not Jewish, and that really is another sore point. I've tried to shield Rivka from this, but David is very unhappy about it. That's what I meant by his 'conservative values.' I actually think Jared's not being Jewish rankles him more than the sex."

I told Ellen it was quite valid for her and her husband to have reservations about Jared's religion. In truth, we're likely to have many sound reasons why our child's partner is lacking; it's as natural for parents (like David) to object to those shortcomings as it is for us to object to their having sex. Knowing us well, our children respond to our telegraphing negativity, often without understanding its source.

Rivka was being distanced by family-of-origin secrets and by her father's qualms about Jared's Protestantism. Leaving parental concerns unspoken had created misunderstanding: Rivka judged her parents as rigid, controlling, and unappreciative of Jared, just as it had robbed her parents of the opportunity to express and own their religious values and historic sensitivities, while also respecting Rivka's burgeoning values.

Ellen and I spent the remaining minutes of the consultation discuss-ing the many compelling reasons why her daughter was not like her mother. Given Rivka's youth and the years of college and life experiences yet to come, the chances of her marrying Jared were probably small. Moreover, should Rivka decide to have sex with him, she could use contraception. Though Ellen preferred abstinence for her daughter, Rivka could remain a well-adjusted adolescent from a healthy family and also be having intercourse with her boyfriend.

Shaken by her revelations, Ellen scheduled a follow-up consultation. When I again saw Ellen, to her knowledge, Rivka remained in a holding pattern with Jared. Mother and daughter had been talking more; it still wasn't easy, but no longer were they deadlocked. As I had recommended, conversations remained indirect, with a strong emphasis on appreciating what Rivka was going through, but without invasive prying into the when, where, and why of what was happening between her and Jared. Once Ellen had given her daughter the gift of revealing the family secret, they seemed better able to discuss Rivka's affection for Jared. Ellen was coming to grips with the inevitability of her daughter's advancing sexual involvement with Jared over their two-year relationship. Recognizing Rivka's clarity of thought and mature functioning in most areas of her life, Ellen realized she needed to trust her daughter's judgment, separate her own anxiety from Rivka's situation, and accept that Rivka will have preferences and experiences different from her own.

Every parent deals with their adolescent's sexual decision making within a unique family context, made up of factors such as the parent's own sexuality, the adolescent's current relationship, biases developed over the years, and family-of-origin issues, all of which color the picture of how we think, assess, and talk about our child's sexuality. Sometimes, we hide behind a statement like, "I don't believe teenagers should have sex." Since we don't usually explore our sexual backgrounds, since teenage sex is accompanied by numerous risks, and since most of our friends would agree with this statement, we rest on this assumption, until an adolescent tests us on it, and we have to push for deeper analysis. Most adolescents are unlikely to either accept or see the inherent wisdom of this curt thumbs-down statement, and it falls dramatically short of giving them a means to assess their readiness and of providing them with the information they need to keep themselves psychologically and physically safe.

Contraception and Safe Sex

Understandably, many parents freeze up at the thought of their teenager having intercourse, but they nonetheless want to make sure their kids are knowledgeable about preventing pregnancy and sexually transmitted diseases. They ask me, "How can I talk about contraception and safe sex when I don't believe my adolescent should be having sex in the first place?" Hoping to forestall their child's sexual debut, many parents let their discomfort block discussions about safe sex.

How can we handle this dilemma? First, as parents, we can maintain our preference that they hold off on having sex. That said, we then engage in what some people see as doublespeak — we inform them straight out that we believe they should not have sex as teens, but if they do, they should be smart about it. Parents are repeatedly in the position of advising, explaining, teaching, and warning against undesirable or risky behaviors. Nonetheless, we know — and our adolescents certainly know — that they will make up their own minds. Should they decide to partake of an activity of which we'd disapprove, we want to urge them to do whatever it takes to prevent injury or negative consequences. *Our job is to share our preferences, our knowledge, and our values. We should encourage our adolescents to take precautions, for no study has found that encouraging precautions increases the incidence of the undesirable or risky behavior.*

Sol Gordon, who has written widely on sex education and teenagers, calls these parental urgings No, Buts. While it's not ever really necessary for us to approve of certain kinds of teenage behavior, we do need to get used to appending qualifications to our restrictions. A No, But statement dealing with sex might be: "I expect you to wait until you're [whatever level of maturity or circumstances applies to your values] and have formed a mature relationship with your partner before you have sexual inter-course, but if you decide otherwise, I want to make sure you're committed to using a condom." This type of warning does not condone sex because the parent's position is very clear.

We might also make an analogy between these statements and the idea of an insurance policy. We don't plan on our homes bursting into flames, but we carry fire insurance in case it does; we don't count on having medical catastrophes or car accidents, but we try to have backup. In our efforts to guide our adolescents, we may not expect them to have sex at an early age, but we've instituted a type of safe-sex insurance policy: a plan for how to proceed if it happens. Only if they violate the original clause will they need to put the plan into practice.

Some parents ask "If 50 percent of teenagers are having sex, what's the profile of adolescents who become sexually active versus those who don't?" Some — like Rivka, should she pursue sex with Jared — make a relatively responsible decision to have sex because they're in a committed relationship. In contrast, most of the young (under age fifteen) teens who are having sex are doing so without a stable, mature relationship and without much weighing of the pros and cons. Most of the very young sexually active adolescents have other significant problems, such as neglect or abuse in their families. They seek or push for sex to get the love they lack at home. Studies have shown that risk for early sexual activity is associated with poverty; a large single-parent family; a prior teen pregnancy in the family; low academic motivation and achievement; low self-esteem; family conflict; problem behaviors such as drug use and delinquency; and more socially permissive standards in their homes.[3] In socially permissive families, parents are unaware of their children's whereabouts and activities, don't maintain standards of discipline, neglect to create rules for dos and don'ts of dating, and basically give the teenager too much freedom. Social permissiveness also correlates positively with risk-taking behaviors, like drug and alcohol use.

Among samplings of teens who are sexually active, there are always one-quarter to one-third of them who are not practicing birth control, despite their wish not to become pregnant. Why not? Many adolescents who are having intercourse (and many adults) are confused and ambivalent about their sexual involvement, which results in inconsistent contraceptive use. They have misinformation about the reliability of the rhythm and withdrawal methods. They worry about the pill and its possible side effects, about the awkwardness of managing condoms, and about their partner's attitudes and expectations. Shame and denial are prevalent.

"Well," some people are inclined to respond, "if teenagers feel bad about having sex, why don't they just not do it?" With a complex behavior like sex, saying no isn't that simple. *Our societal taboos and adolescents' negative feelings about being sexually active don't appear to act as a fail-safe deterrent to teenage sex, though they may succeed in preventing the use of contraception.* As the data on teens who become sexually active reveals, some teens are propelled into early sex for reasons related to early emotional deprivation or family problems. A mere campaign about saying no cannot undo the power of the social variables placing these kids at risk for early sexual activity. Moreover, when feelings such as guilt and shame prevail, teenagers often remain "psychological virgins," in denial about the reality of their sexual behavior. If teenagers spend their psychic energy repressing the reality of what they're doing because they believe it's bad or wrong, their energy will not go toward rational, responsible decision making.

Another process that can thwart contraceptive use has been called by David Elkind "the personal fable" or the "myth of immunity." This myth, which likewise operates with a lot of risk-taking behaviors, prompts adolescents to think, "Those statistics don't refer to me. It won't happen to me. I'm special."

If teenagers are wafting in a period of guilt, ambivalence, and denial about their sexual activity, their unprotected intercourse can place them at risk for contracting sexually transmitted diseases, most lethally, AIDS. One would hope that the increased incidence of AIDS among teenagers and predictions about its further increase in the next ten to twenty years would motivate parents to encourage safe sex through condom use, instead of reinforcing denial through guilt, shame, and moralism.

At the very least, most parents will want their kids to refrain from having sex until their psychological maturity matches their biological maturity. *A goal consistent with contemporary realities is that when young people decide to have sex, it should happen with high consciousness instead of denial, in an intimate, mature relationship with another person, and with enough awareness of what they're doing that they will practice safe sex. High consciousness and competent decision making are our ultimate goals because this is the best means of ensuring their safety.* Achieving this end takes talking, thinking, assessing, and a certain amount of parental soul-searching. It takes educating our children about the complex concept of what it means to be a sexual being and a morally "good" person at the same time, which can enable them to proceed with their eyes open and act responsibly in their sexual decision making.

Gender Judgments

I was heading out of my office at the Adolescent Clinic at the University of Washington when a medical colleague flagged me down in the corridor. "You'll never guess what happened!" she began. The day before, she'd arrived home unexpectedly early to find her eighteen-year-old son having sex with his sixteen-year-old girlfriend in his bedroom. She handled the situation like a pro, but, in the retelling, her tone conveyed a certain satisfaction that her son — a "late bloomer" — was sexually active. "Well, at least he was using a condom!" she added breezily.

Among the several issues raised by this mom's discovery are three: How do we weigh a teenager's right to privacy with our obligation to inform the teenager's parents about behaviors of which the parents may be unaware? (In other words, should this mom share what she knows with the girl's parents?) Do we feel differently about our adolescent sons having sex than we do our daughters? What about household rules around our kids' sexuality?

Whether it be sexual behavior, risk-taking adventures, or other problems, telling other parents about unique information we're privy to is always a difficult judgment call with several issues to evaluate. Certainly, when the teen's behavior or action is destructive or life-threatening (for example, drug use or attempted suicide), their right to privacy is superseded by our moral imperative to try to help them. Therefore, we have to inform others. This generalization aside, we must look not only to the specific behavior or action and its circumstances, but also to the specific teenager and the family — its dynamics and its values. Much depends on how well we know the other parents; teenagers are sometimes capable of appreciating when our loyalties, allegiances, and friendships necessitate disclosure.

My colleague's situation was complicated by the fact that she knew the girlfriend's parents only as distant acquaintances, couldn't predict how they would react, and therefore felt reluctant about telling them. In my experience at the adolescent clinic, I've found that most kids will initially resist including their parents in private matters; usually, the adolescents who eventually relent are those whose family context can be trusted to absorb their news. When teens plead wrenchingly and urgently that their parents will react violently, they're usually right. We want to have empathy in the abstract for the other parent as we mentally wear their shoes, but, unfortunately, sometimes informing other parents about their child's sexuality endangers the teenager.

In the aftermath of her discovery, my colleague talked with her son about what it means to become sexually active and about birth-control and safe-sex obligations. But, at the time we spoke, she hadn't made any decision about conferring with the girlfriend's parents. A possible solution respecting both the girl's right to privacy and the colleague's obligations as a responsible adult would be for the colleague to have a one-on-one with the girlfriend herself. She might say something like, "It's your decision to engage in sex, and since I've become aware of this, it becomes my responsibility to make sure you've thought this through and that you're having sex with conscious intent and with proper precautions." She could talk to her about birth control and safe sex and suggest *strongly* — if not urge — that she consider being open with her parents about her sexual activity.

The second issue raised by the mother's discovery: most parents do experience a higher heart rate when their daughters (as opposed to their sons) become sexually active. Some parents are apologetic about their double standards, but others are unapologetic, as they articulate the greater risks and responsibilities for girls — namely pregnancy or the potential trauma of abortion and the age-old cultural biases that hold girls to stricter sexual standards.

Overcoming quick judgments is challenging, since they're often ingrained. Nonetheless, in forming judgments about a teenager's sexual involvement, we want to look at the full range of issues for each teenager, regardless of gender. We can avoid gender-biased assessments by evaluating a particular teenager's level of maturity, personal sense of responsibility, relationship situation, and current family life.

One reason parents expend more nervous energy over their daughters' sexuality has to do with perceived motives for sex. Teenage girls are more likely to be sexually active as an expression of "love" and "relationship," whereas boys' intent can sometimes be suspect, given the levels of testosterone coursing through their veins and the goading they receive from peers. Some parents are understandably wary, should their daughters be devastated by a boy's possibly more casual, less committed approach to sex. Again, analyzing specific situations is always preferable to slipping into generalities about girls versus boys.

Another increasingly obsolete gender bias concerns responsibility for birth control. Traditionally, this burden has fallen more upon girls than boys, but ironically, since adolescent girls can feel more guilty about having sex than boys, boys are sometimes able to think more rationally about the potential dangers of unprotected sex. We miss a vital opportunity if we counsel our daughters about birth control but neglect our sons. Often the male partner plays a critical role in insisting upon protection, which challenges the stereotype of boys being "out for sex" without having much of a sense of responsibility. My colleague was rightfully pleased about her son's wearing a condom, and he probably played an important role in that decision.

To be sure, some boys like the thrill of sex without contraception because they believe they'll experience greater pleasure without condoms, or perhaps they want to impregnate a girl. Some boys don't want to deal with the responsibility of taking precautions, buying condoms, and learning how to use them. They deny the risks of unprotected intercourse or don't care because they believe birth control is the girl's job. However, AIDS is calling us all to attention and modifying our thinking, just as it is spurring parents to educate their sons as well as their daughters about safe sex.

The third issue: Was it exceptional for my colleague's son and his girlfriend to be having intercourse within the comfort of his own bedroom? While plenty of teenage sex still takes place in cars and bushes, teenage sex frequently occurs in the family's own home. One can surmise that this phenomenon correlates with more working-parent families, which can lead to less supervision of teenagers and greater access to an empty home.

Household rules are each parent's call to make. Guidelines depend upon criteria reiterated throughout this book — where the teen is developmentally, past experiences, family values, and family-of-origin issues. At a minimum, families can insist on an open-door policy when teenagers of different sexes are together in a room. Teenagers will accuse their parents of being "obsessed with sex"; they'll express disgust at what we presume they're doing; they'll be outraged at our "suspicious minds" — all effective means of wearing parents down. Most parents won't want to make it any easier for their teenagers to engage in intercourse than it already is, and logistical deterrents (having sex on top of twigs and tree roots is less enticing than a double-spring mattress, for example) can be a way to slow down advancing sexuality.

A Sexual Trauma: Joseph, Roberta, Rose, and Luke Green

Talking with me in my office were a dad, distracted and depressed; a mom, careworn, strung-out, and angry; and a fifteen-year-old daughter — a six-month survivor of a violent rape, who sat listless and silent. Tears pouring out as profusely as her complaints, Roberta (the mom) felt that her family had been "ripped apart" since the rape. Their situation had gone from bad to worse, the family "collapsing completely," to use her words. "I can't handle it one more day. I'm ready to burst," she sobbed. Subdued and enervated, Joseph Green was a counterpoint to his wife. He felt like a "shadow" or a "damper" had descended on the family. If

Roberta expressed herself in catastrophic language, Joseph's was gray, icy blue, and lifeless.

Later, I learned what was behind this initial devastating family portrait. Even before the rape, the family had been in a state of disrepair and dysfunction. After the rape, they progressed from shell shock to family breakdown. The challenge that lay before them was to rebuild the family with a foundation and structure that would support healthy development for all its members.

In recording some family history, I learned that prior to the rape Roberta and Joseph had considered Rose "lost" to them. Resisting and disobeying her parents, she had felt "out of reach" since the age of thirteen. Dealing with Rose had absorbed much of their energy, which they resented because it took them away from their three other younger children.

Aside from their children and their jobs, much of their lives had revolved around their church. Rose, however, had balked at church attendance and had rejected the youth group. She had also been caught sneaking out at night, had come home drunk on numerous occasions, and had associated with tough boyfriends.

Though both parents believed in strong discipline, Roberta, who worked as a bank teller, carried most of it out, having a stronger, more vocal personality. She had by default assumed the role of "bad cop." A forklift operator, Joseph had been pressured by his operations plant manager into working double shifts, and for the last couple of years he had been exhausted by the overtime he'd felt compelled to put in just to keep his job. The family felt they needed the money from Joseph's extra shifts, but his schedule left Roberta "holding the bag" — a sore spot in their marriage.

I asked Rose to tell me about the rape because I needed to assess where she was in the recovery process. Outside a hamburger stand, Rose had been given a flyer with a map to a keg party to be held that evening in an isolated field several miles from town. Rose told her parents she was spending the night with a friend, but then went with a group of girls to a party where alcohol flowed freely and some kids headed to the fringes of the pasture to have sex. Feeling woozy from the alcohol and needing to relieve herself, Rose wandered off from the center of the party. In a far corner of the field, she was attacked and raped by an older guy whom she recognized. Though no one had heard Rose's screams, her friends, anxious about her absence, had gone in search of her, and upon finding her, had taken her to an emergency room.

In our worst nightmares we see our daughters being attacked in a dark alley. In actuality, only about 20 percent of rapes are committed by a stranger. The vast majority of rapes are perpetrated by a male the female has known, which means it is likely a woman will walk of free accord into the very situation that puts her at risk.

The type of party Rose attended was problematic at her rape trial, because she chose to be present at a place where alcohol was served and sex was happening. Rose's credibility was shattered by the defense attorney, who exploited her history of sexual relationships. In the end, however, the nineteen-year-old rapist, who had a long record of previous charges, was found guilty and sent to prison.

A rape indictment can make a huge difference to the victim and the family. For a short time, the conviction bolstered everyone. Rose went through therapy at a sexual assault center and seemed to be emotionally stable. However, the family tilted out of balance, as Rose's attendance in therapy dwindled, Joseph withdrew more into himself, and Roberta wailed at those around her in her quest for healing.

Six months after the rape, a depressed Rose, suffering from rape flashbacks, spent most of her day curled up in a blanket on the couch staring at the TV, resisting going to therapy or school. Joseph began working more hours than ever, while Roberta found herself again abandoned and burdened, needing to take a leave of absence from her job to enhance the home life of her other children and be with her depressed daughter.

Blaming the Victim

Rose and her parents were plagued by many plaintive "if only's." There is no underestimating the guilt and self-blame a rape victim can feel, even if attacked under circumstances completely beyond the victim's control, like a break-in to an apartment out of the blue. Expectedly, Rose continued to dwell on what she might have done differently: "If only I hadn't gone to that party." "If only I hadn't been drunk." "If only I'd stayed with my friends at the party." And, a notion that haunts most who have been raped, "If only I'd fought back harder." Likewise, Rose's parents speculated, "If only we'd been tougher on her." "If only she'd stayed more involved with the church like her brothers and sisters." "If only we'd been able to get through to her before she got raped."

Sometimes when kids end up in real trouble after a pattern of red flags, parents will "if only" themselves to a destructive degree, wishing they could turn back the clock and heed the signs. Rose's parents were searching for a reason for the rape, and thus they mistakenly linked her "disobedient" behavior and their parenting directly to the rape. Though a girl who is taking risks like Rose is possibly more susceptible to rape at a party like the one she attended, even a teenage girl without Rose's red flags could be the victim of the same scenario. "Good" girls go to keggers, experiment with alcohol, and need to find a private bush too. We need to watch out for "blaming the victim" (and her family) in our quest to understand and explain a traumatic story. Sometimes blame happens inadvertently, out of a self-protective mechanism, as we try to piece together reasons why the circumstances don't apply to our family or our children. Rose's case was a mixed picture because she certainly was engaged in problematic risk taking, yet this disaster at this party could have happened to almost anyone.

That the crime against Rose was sexual in nature added to everyone's sense of guilt, for Rose's sexuality was a preexisting family issue. Rose's burgeoning sexuality had distressed her parents, and they believed they could best deal with it through increased threats, admonitions, and church attendance. Open discussions about sexuality, talks about risks of sexual violence at unsupervised parties, and decision making on matters related to sex were unheard of in this family; chastity was the only acceptable option.

Research has emphasized the importance of rape information to dispel myths, alert girls to risks, and diminish victim blame.[4] Boys and girls alike need to be educated about rape; in one key study, out of 432 adolescents surveyed, only 21 percent of them believed it was unacceptable for a "guy to hold a girl down and force her to have intercourse" across all situations described.[5]

Rose represents a young person who has experienced the worst of both worlds: she was taking behavioral risks through her drinking and her abandoning of the conventional track socially and academically; moreover, her lack of self-esteem, black sheep role in the family, and void of understanding about sexuality rendered her psychologically naive. Parental efforts to scare Rose away from sex had been heard by her as condemning judgments branding her a loser and a bad girl. Rose had no opportunity to understand what had fueled her reckless lifestyle (issues to be covered shortly), nor did she comprehend its risks. Clearly, no one should pass judgment on the Greens for the maelstrom tugging Rose its way, for they, too, were naive, troubled, and unable to deal effectively with Rose's behavior.

The Greens' family patterns had neither worked for them in the past, nor were they serving them well in the present. As disciplinarians, these parents functioned in a way characteristic of many families who constantly battle with their children. Of the authoritarian school, they came down on undesirable actions with harsh punishments, believing this to be the only way to control behavior. Rose stonewalled their attempts to communicate with her. Prior to her rape, reprimands had been leveled at her for curfew violations, phone calls that went on too long, homework, attitude, peer choices, and appearance. At present, Rose was still on the couch and needed no discipline, but the young children in the family were acting up more than ever. The Greens described their current home scene as either depressing, because of Rose's and Joseph's posttraumatic blues, or high-stress, because of Roberta's irate reactions to sibling fights, chores left undone, or the general chaos.

To a large extent, the Greens' ineffective discipline methods were tied in to parental exhaustion. For all of his goodness, piety, and family conservatism developed from his evangelical leanings, Joseph had defaulted on his parenting responsibilities. His daughter's trauma had taxed his ability to cope. Family wounds and massive guilt prevented this family from resolving their trauma.

Who Sustains a Crisis and Who Doesn't: A Family's Coping Responses

After several sessions with the Greens, it was apparent they had come to me not only with the trauma of rape but with a problematic family background that included deep parental conflict over family roles and Joseph's work schedule; a mishandling of sexuality; and a pattern of overpunishing, rarely praising, and rarely communicating in warm, open, and effective ways.

Those who study how families cope with trauma emphasize that stress and upheaval are not absolute and contained in a crisis itself; some families grow stronger in the process of adjustment while others disintegrate. As families search for their bearings, trying to recover from a crisis such as a rape, preexisting family strains and hardships impact the recovery process, making it difficult for them to find their way.

What families like the Greens must cope with is the crisis plus the aftermath of the crisis, often referred to as the pileup.[6] This situation can be likened to a car crash followed by a multicar pileup, which can be more damaging than the initial wreck. Preexisting family strengths such as good communication skills, open-minded perspectives, high tolerance for other family members, role flexibility, and lack of substance abuse enable families to reorganize and rise to the challenges ahead and minimize pileup. Family vulnerabilities — fragile emotional states, interpersonal and intrapersonal conflicts, skewed perceptions of the meaning of the crisis, unresolved family-of-origin issues, inflexibility — mingle with circumstances to induce greater stress. The Greens were vulnerable, without a buffer of family strengths to help them weather their trauma, and the result was a family system breakdown.

Research indicates that families cope more successfully with crisis when connected to a supportive community. The Greens' primary support system was in their church, but after the rape, this base began to wobble. Attending church as a family, they endured sneers and stares that made them feel like "lepers," to use Roberta's expression. Previously viewed as pillars of the church, the Greens learned that several member of the congregation, clinging to tenets of "decency," wrote ungenerous letters about Rose to the church board during the trial. Though the pastor tried to shield the Greens from these rumblings, sentiments swirled around the family: "She was asking for it," "She should have known better," "What kind of girl did they bring up?" Ultimately, the Greens separated from their church. Perhaps Joseph's words best expressed the poignancy of this loss: "I feel as if the ground has slipped away from underneath me."

Joseph had been more intensely connected to their church than Roberta, for his father was a minister within this particular denomination. Indeed, another preexisting rub in the family had been Joseph's family-of-origin issue with his domineering father, who exacted strict obeisance to the literal word of God. Throughout their marriage, Roberta had been somewhat put off by the vehemence of her father-in-law's religion, and had been trying to persuade her husband to switch churches. Following the rape, Joseph suffered from an overwhelming crisis of faith. He was angry at God for letting this happen to his daughter; he felt turned upon by the church he had devoted himself to; and he had to cope with his father's judgment and disappointment when he left the church. During the trial, Joseph had focused all his wrath on the rapist and all his energy into a conviction. Down the line, he was drained and deeply disturbed by his loss of faith in God.

The Greens' postcrisis pileup included their loss of support resources, their long-fermenting family problems, and their maladaptive coping responses. Instead of bonding as a family, they became isolated from one another. The more Joseph withdrew and internalized his problems, the more Roberta emoted. "She keeps dwelling on it," said a deeply suffering Joseph, who couldn't tolerate his wife's need "to carry on so."

The Greens' therapy was multifaceted. Certainly, Rose had additional work to do to recover from her rape. She began studying martial arts, and with this group she chose to reenact her rape. This had an enormous impact on her because she was able to fight off her assaulter, which symbolized her new life as an empowered person who could protect herself. Her parents attended a "graduation ceremony," and they also reported feeling healed at a deeper level following the ceremony.

A child's recovery from a sexual crisis is inextricably linked to parental support. To be capable of providing support, parents, too, must mend. Thus, therapy addressed the pre- and postrape conflicts in Roberta's and Joseph's marriage, as well as the various injurious patterns and dynamics in the family at large. I urged the Greens to research different churches, and during the time we worked together, they found a generous church community. Joseph's new pastor helped him accept a new idea of God as a supportive force and presence in his life, as opposed to a God who dictated his will. Once Joseph's spiritual crisis had been alleviated and he united with Roberta in efforts to rebuild family ties, they likewise revamped their approach to discipline. The younger children "settled down to a dull roar," explained Roberta, and there seemed to be more warmth, patience, and flexibility all around. In a situation like this, it's hard to pinpoint exactly why everyone started to flourish. With as many positive changes happening as there were, I often see it as pure synergy.

If we were to plot the curve of the Green family's relative health, we'd see that prior to the rape, the family was limping along, functioning poorly. The crisis was such a strong blow that it held them together during the rape trial. Following the trial, the family plummeted into a state of almost total dysfunction. Family members were living with enormous shame, and they had no means of letting go of their pain. Indeed, they were considerably worse off during the six-month period after the trial than they had been during their initial nightmare. The irony is that the tragedy, which forced the Greens to deal with previously ignored problems, provided the impetus for the family to become healthier than they had ever been. Through therapy, Roberta and Joseph brought their problems to light and found a new understanding of themselves and each other. And it was the healing within the family that enabled Rose to shake herself free of her destructive behavior and become closer to her family.

Few parents can claim they are actively addressing all of their existing family problems, just as few can credit themselves with having thoroughly educated their child about sexuality. In our hearts, we know it is best to embrace both jobs. Even if we somewhat neglect them, things often turn out all right because there are adequate resources and family strengths to carry the child through adolescence safely. Nonetheless, every story about a sexual and/or family tragedy alerts us to the fact that we cannot count on good fortune and simply adequate family health. By educating our adolescents about sexuality and bolstering family functioning, we can create a buffer should we encounter a crisis.

The sexual world seems more complex than ever and the traditional directive — "just don't until you're married" — is inadequate guidance for adolescents who need to prepare themselves to be competent in today's world. When discussions about sexuality include not only cautions about sexual risks but thoughts about love, loss, family life, interpersonal dilemmas, and strategies for decision making, we're preparing our children for sexuality within the context of healthy and loving relationships. This should be our goal. Difficult though it may be to find momentum while ascending toward this goal, reaching it is possible. And if we miss a step, mistake our reach, or momentarily lose direction, it's the taking of the journey to enable our children to be sexually healthy that can make a difference.

7

The Wide-Open Range of Risk Taking

*Goal: Distinguish between normal and problem risk
taking; enhance your adolescent's awareness of
unhealthy risk; stimulate a spirit of responsibility;
and, as appropriate, restrict and minimize
risk-taking behaviors.*

WHEN taking risks, we move out of
neutral territory and into areas where personal judgment and "should I or
shouldn't I?" decisions arise. By turns frightening, stimulating, dangerous,
and rewarding, risk taking involves thrill seeking, arousal, being special,
being on the edge, stretching, and feeling stronger. Through risk taking
we grow intellectually, emotionally, and physically, but we also get in over
our heads.

Because the tasks of adolescence include experimenting with identity,
pushing for independence, and searching for personal values, adolescence
itself is a condition of risk taking. What, after all, can they safely do with
their youthful zest? Though motivation for pushing limits varies from
adolescent to adolescent, risk taking ranges from relatively safe testing, like
Chris's sneaking out to a concert in Chapter 1; to minor crises, like Terry's
and Sam's vandalism in Chapter 5; to concerning patterns, like Ricky's
choice of a deviant peer group in Chapter 5; to significant pathologies,
like Fiona's conduct disorder and suicidal behavior in Chapter 1. Many
behaviors that eventually become problematic may start out as relatively
innocuous risk taking, then cross a line to become more dangerous.

Risk taking is a double-edged phenomenon: if we want our children to grow up as unique individuals aware of their own limits, they need a certain amount of freedom to explore in order to gain competence and personal insight. On the other hand, parents need to protect their children from harm. Sometimes these two inclinations — to permit freedom and to safeguard — leave us waffling.

Let's say that a family has an adolescent son who impulsively accepts a ride from a teenage driver who careens down narrow streets at top speed, barely escaping an accident. The son is quite shaken. Any sane parent would have wanted to restrict their child from setting foot into the car in the first place, thereby avoiding any possibility of danger.

The boy has had a harrowing experience, and he decides that next time instead of blithely hopping into someone's car, he's going to make sure he knows the driver better. What a valuable lesson this adolescent has learned, but it took a mistake, and a risk, to learn this lesson. And then again, this story might have had a less fortuitous ending.

One way to envision our child-rearing task is as a journey. We're trying to get our children from point A to point B. As with any trip, we constantly reorganize, adjust to change and to hazards along the way, and make decisions about when to push forward and when to hang back. The ultimate question — will my child make the trip unscathed? — is never certain. This uncertainty, this ambiguity, lies at the heart of being the parent of an adolescent.

How, then, can parents enable the safest possible trip through the teenage years, given our children's need for independence, exploration and risk taking, and also for protection? This question poses profound dilemmas. In our efforts to both let go and watch over, there are several working strategies to juggle. *If there is any one thing we can do to insulate our children from truly problematic risk taking it is this: our best protection comes from being the strongest, highest functioning family possible.*

When we're functioning in the ways the optimal families in this book illustrate, when we're open, flexible, and accepting of who our children are, yet clear in our boundaries and in our expression of limits and authority, we're setting the stage for our children to act in their own best interests. Parents who problem-solve with their children and work with them to stimulate awareness, responsibility, and healthy habits are, de facto, making their child's journey through adolescence safer. We can supervise our kids, know where they are, and adjust the reins of freedom and control accordingly.

A healthy family is a powerful force in keeping harmful risk taking at bay because healthy ways of operating are internalized by our children and guide their judgments. Diana Baumrind and her colleagues followed families over a twenty-year period and found that the distinguishing characteristic among children who had a low incidence of problematic risk taking was that they had parents who were both *authoritative* and *responsive* to their children's needs.[1] This parenting style was consistently associated with adolescent competence and deterrence of harmful risk taking.

Parents can also minimize deleterious risk taking by attending to adolescent milestones, and by not giving too much freedom too early. In one sense, there are developmental milestones parents are aware of — the first date, the first bus ride with friends, the first rock concert. While most parents will want to set their own standards, there's a case to be made for being somewhat in sync with other parents whose judgment we respect, for if we hold our child back unreasonably, we may lose their trust and damage the relationship. After all, it is their developmental *need* to stretch. That said, we nonetheless want to measure each of these first steps carefully to make sure our child isn't pushing ahead too quickly. By exposing our children little by little to life's new adventures, we improve the odds of their developing the skills to handle them.

Many years lie between the onset of puberty and a child's leaving home, and, ideally, we want each of those years to have markers signifying new permissions granted and new competencies gained. Freedoms that are appropriate for seventeen-year-olds are usually wildly inappropriate for thirteen-year-olds because young teenagers have not yet gained the competencies required to travel the larger territory safely.

What about risk-taking milestones most parents dread — the first puff of a cigarette, the first act of outright defiance, the first flirtation with law breaking? While there's no timetable indicating that a certain risk-taking behavior is normal for one age group but not for another, there are some patterns: middle schoolers are notorious for sneaking out, for example, and high schoolers are given to stealing Stop signs and driving fast. *A general rule is that the earlier certain risk-taking behaviors emerge, the more of a problem they represent and the more activated the parent must be in efforts to slow risk taking down.*

Some young adolescents assume a convincing posture of ersatz independence: "No sweat; I can handle it. Back off; I know what I'm doing." If your child's competence is an issue, keep a relatively firm grip through limit-setting, supervising, and following up on details in nonoppressive ways that still allow for growth to take place.

On the other hand, some adolescents are overwhelmed by the pressures they face. It is, for example, within the realm of possibility that a middle schooler who feels pressure from his peers to sneak out of the house at night might actually come to you and earnestly ask for help with ways to save face. In this situation, you can help empower your child by practicing refusal skills: "I've got a game tomorrow and if I'm out at night it'll mess me up." Or, "My parents would find out for sure and ground me forever. I'm not willing to take any chances." Or, "I'm not into it. You're my friend and I expect you to support me in my decision," Or, plain and simple, "No thanks. No way." Some kids may want and need to practice this kind of dialogue with parents.

An excellent means of protecting a child is to create an ongoing dialogue about risk-taking issues. To do so, we need to be savvy about our techniques. Parents should not necessarily conclude something is wrong if their adolescent gives them the cold shoulder, should they try to sit down to discuss risk taking, especially in high school. In fact, you're in the huge majority if your adolescent throws you overboard in this situation. By high school, most kids have had their fill of safety lectures and have developed a certain integrity about their own abilities. Our continued instruction implies their lacking — an unwelcome message to most mid- and late adolescents.

Another technique for minimizing risk taking is to make sure your adolescent is involved in healthy extracurricular activities. It can be difficult to strike the balance between over- and underscheduling — too much hurrying versus too much drifting. Adolescents need unstructured time, but for some kids, unsupervised time translates into increased opportunities for risk-taking behaviors. An advantage of structured activities is that they provide adolescents with skills or talents that boost their sense of identity. Adolescents with strong identities tend to be less likely to push into dangerous areas to discover who they are.

A great challenge for parents is to distinguish between developmentally normal risk taking and problematic risk taking, which can keep us from either overreacting or underreacting as we attend to our adolescent's missteps. Risk taking exists on a continuum, ranging from behaviors that are generally considered positive (running for class office, competing in sports, standing up for one's principles), to those that cause moderate concern (very isolated incidents of pranks, truancy, vandalism, small experimentation with alcohol or marijuana), to those that are considered health-compromising and pathological (patterns of destructive and/or deviant behavior). How do we know whether a behavior like cutting classes or making prank phone calls represents something of a lark, rooted in the adolescent's exploration of a new identity and new autonomy, or is a deeper issue that may require clinical intervention? *Although there are no hard and fast measures to go by, important criteria are the frequency and intensity of the risk behavior as well as the adolescent's age and overall life adjustment.* When a teenager is regularly taking risks — drinking, acting out, breaking rules, becoming alienated from conventional standards of behavior — and parents' efforts to reduce the problem are not succeeding, a psychological referral is recommended. Even if your adolescent is only in the beginning stages of experimentation, you have legitimate grounds for further clinical evaluation, especially if you are questioning your parenting skills. In these situations, parents can seek out a clinician specializing in adolescent health who will help determine the required level of intervention.

When Risk-Taking Opportunities Are on the Rise

By high school, many of the risk-taking behaviors that parents most fear become more logistically possible or simply more probable. In addition to sexual activity, three areas of concern are dangerous driving, cigarette smoking, and alcohol and drug use.

The possibilities for risk-taking behaviors increase when teenagers get their driver's licenses. Most adolescents relish their new identity of "driver" and the freedom it entails. Parents, however, are usually aware that automobile fatalities are the leading cause of death among teenagers; indeed, driving is the most legal and most lethal mix of adolescent risk-taking activities. Nevertheless, compared to other areas of risk taking (drinking, smoking, taking drugs, sneaking out, lying, and pranking), parents have unique leverage because driving involves a distinct privilege: it's a behavior that requires explicit permission from parents.

Because we have the keys and they want them, we are in the position to use the various guidelines for minimizing risk taking to full effect. We can use our parental authority to not allow too much freedom too soon. We can devise rules about when, where, how far, and with whom they can drive. (How many teenagers can be in the car at one time? When can they drive and have music playing? When they can drive on the freeway?) We can dole out the privilege of car use contingent upon responsible behavior and rescind this privilege when they take undue risks. Whereas conversations with a sixteen-year-old regarding illicit activities are usually difficult to pursue, conversations about driving practices are legitimate territory because they must earn our seal of approval.

Importantly, we can set up problem-solving situations with our young drivers: "How would you handle it if a friend in the car insisted you drive faster so he wouldn't be late for his curfew and get grounded?" "What would be a good way of convincing a friend who has been drinking not to drive?" "How would you defuse a situation where a friend wanted to race cars?" "What are some things you could do to reduce distraction while driving, since this is a major cause of accidents?" "How conscious or aware do you think you'd be of becoming groggy behind the wheel? What are some measures you could take to keep from getting drowsy?"

Though parents can use their clout to discuss rules about driving, it is trickier to discuss cigarette smoking. What's the best way to nip this dangerous habit in the bud? Interestingly, research has found that efforts to deter teenagers from smoking by linking the habit to cancer have been only marginally effective. Only when the antismoking campaign was directed to things that mattered to teenagers in the present did the message begin to have an impact. Instead of presenting cancer statistics, real though they are, we stand a better chance of getting through to our kids if we talk about how unattractive smoking is or how it makes clothes and breath smell bad. We can talk about how it affects athletic performance, how it controls you instead of you controlling it, and how images in the media and advertising manipulate people into thinking smoking is glamorous or cool. As is also the case in discussing alcohol and marijuana use, that cigarette smoking is illegal for young people and possibly addictive is not a highly compelling argument to teenagers. If we focus on observations that are relevant to our kids' perceptions, we stand a better chance of jarring them into awareness.

According to a prominent survey of drug-use trends among American youth, 87 percent of adolescents by their senior year reported having experimented with alcohol at some point in their lifetime and 51 percent reported having consumed it within the prior month.[2] *As much as we want our teenagers to abstain from drinking entirely, if nearly 90 percent of them have by their senior year experimented with alcohol, a realistic strategy is to do whatever we can to postpone the age at which it begins, minimize use and risk, and promote healthy decision making.*

Two parental responses to the prevalence of alcohol in youth culture are the hard-line "don't you dare" forbidding response and the overaccommodating "I might as well let them drink at home to keep them safe" enabling response. Each of these reactions can be problematic, particularly for high schoolers. Parents will want to be direct, unambivalent, and absolute in their policies on drug and alcohol use with their middle schoolers. Because experimentation among high schoolers is so prevalent and often beyond our control, we want to shift our emphasis to their competent decision making instead of relying on the power of our negative sanction. It's crucial to keep our kids talking to us. Reiterate the message, "Be smart. Use your good sense. I know teenagers drink, but it's *risky* and involves serious dangers."

Whatever the risk-taking behavior, whenever mistakes are made — theirs or ours — we can try to make them "usable" mistakes. Each problem well handled offers the potential to develop greater competency.

In the Scheme of Things: Meg, Peter, and Sasha Hathaway

Although Meg Hathaway is a good friend of mine, she didn't tell me about her daughter's drinking incident until about a week after it occurred. "I'm glad you didn't tell me what was going on," I leveled with her, "because you and Peter figured this situation out beautifully by yourselves and my advice might have interfered with your instincts." When confronted with a problem like the one Meg describes below, the best step might be to make some phone calls and gather ideas, if not from a psychologist, perhaps from other parents. The Hathaways used their own resources to devise a solution they believed was right for them. Below is Meg's tale of what happened at fifteen-year-old Sasha's first Tolo, a high school dance to which girls invite boys.

I don't know how I could have been naive enough to be hoodwinked by a group of ninth graders. Maybe I was distracted, caught up in the evening, thinking about the fun things like who my daughter's date would be for her first formal high school dance, what she would wear, how she'd do her hair, or the practical things like transportation. Even though Peter, my husband, had to catch a plane early the next morning, I wanted the kids to have a safe place to go after the dance, so I was more than happy to have a small postdance party — seven couples including Sasha and her date Duncan — at our house, and to be the parent who would stay up and supervise so Peter could go to sleep. The girls would sleep over here, and then I would take the boys to Duncan's house, where they would spend the night, in time for their 2:00 A.M. curfew.

Was the wool ever pulled over my eyes! Perhaps all the plans whirling in my mind kept me from catching on, but I guess I also have to admit that I thought alcohol was a distant threat. I wasn't ready for these kids to be determined to drink and to be so calculating and devious about it. I now know that they had the whole thing planned! They had the beer, some of it stashed in bushes on the beach to drink before the dance and some of it stashed in Sasha's room for the party at our house. Renting the limo made it possible to have the driver drop them off at the beach to drink and then pick them up again, no questions asked. I had objected to the limo because it seemed a bit much, but little did I know the limo was as much about drinking as it was about making Tolo special.

I imagine a scene at the drugstore where my daughter deliberately buys Tic-Tacs and a small bottle of mouthwash to fit in the purse she borrowed from me! I have a hard time believing this level of scheming was possible of her.

I also keep playing back how aglow the girls were when they left in the limo to pick up their dates. I was enthralled by the excitement, but all the while the deception was brewing. When the kids arrived back at our house after the dance around midnight, there was no figuring out the kids had been drinking. Apparently, they had a "parent script" all worked out! They'd determined beforehand they would talk to me for only a few minutes so I wouldn't have time to get suspicious, then complain about their high heels, which would give them an excuse to hurry up the stairs. It worked like a charm. They put their sweats on and smuggled more beer from Sasha's room into the basement playroom for the party.

I watched TV to stay awake, all the while keeping my ears open, figuring that as long as there was some kind of noise below the kids were neither having a wild ruckus nor pairing off quietly for sexual enterprises. I called downstairs to see if they needed anything, and at one point, I dropped in to replenish the snacks. Everything seemed fine. As 2:00 approached, I gathered the boys into my car to take them to Duncan's. Then things began to unravel.

I still can't believe I didn't catch on. Greg, one of the boys, vomited in my car, and I said, "Oh, dear, are you all right? It must have been those greasy chips." I swerved to the curbside, where Greg hopped out of the car and again threw up. I felt sorry for him, thinking how embarrassed he must be, so I commiserated with him. The boys in the car joined in and cleverly covered for Greg, explaining to me that he hadn't felt well at the dance. I dropped the boys off, returned home, and bid the girls goodnight.

Then the phone rang — Duncan's mother — and I felt like a complete idiot. Greg had become violently ill at Duncan's house, rolling on the bathroom floor. Alarmed, Duncan's parents began asking questions and quickly discovered the "flu bug" Greg told them he'd caught was alcohol-based. When I learned the kids had been drinking I woke Peter up, and we set the wheels in motion to transform the evening into an experience the kids would not soon forget. Feeling duped, I was determined to no longer be so gullible. Peter and I first confronted Sasha alone and then the girls as a group. A couple of them became teary-eyed, but most were still as stones. Peter stayed at home with our younger children, and I, with Sasha beside me in the passenger seat, drove each girl home, waiting in front of each of their houses as they told their parents what they'd done.

I wrote a letter to all the parents (girls and boys), which I've included below, and later Peter and I held a series of meetings. My letter explains the issues I raised with the girls during the car ride to their homes.

Dear Tolo Dance Parents,

Peter and I would like to share our reflections and some further information about what happened Saturday night. After a call from Jackie Hunt, Duncan's mom, regarding Greg's "illness," we called Sasha upstairs, and she admitted there had been drinking on the beach and, we're sorry to say, at our house while we were upstairs.

Initially, when Peter and I spoke with the girls, they were unwilling to talk, but during the long carpool to everyone's houses, they began opening up. I realized it would be unfair to ask the girls to tell on each other, so I asked each of them to be responsible for making her own statement. It was a quiet drive until I made it clear that unless someone spoke up, I would drive slower and slower, and we would be in the car together for hours.

Sasha broke the ice, and eventually each girl took a turn. The girls expressed feelings of shame over letting all the parents down and their failure to be responsible. They said that they had been "punished enough" by the way they felt at 4:00 A.M. and by the thought of confronting parents at that hour. They felt that all we needed to discuss was "what the parents would do as punishment," since the details of what, why, and how were already water under the bridge.

The girls asked me whether I was really surprised and disappointed or whether this was "sort of expected." I said that this was somewhat irrelevant. The illegal nature of their activities, the trust they had lost, and the health concerns of binge drinking were the issues we needed to address.

Interestingly, there seemed to be no awareness of the meaning of personal liability — that is, my liability as the responsible parent hosting the party. Some did not understand the phrase guilt by association, so I underscored that they were all guilty, even if they personally hadn't gotten drunk.

I asked the girls to predict what they thought would happen in their houses after this type of behavior. To my dismay, one of the girls quipped, "So what are my parents going to do — take away my phone?" I realized that Peter and I have never had any serious discussions with Sasha about drinking and its consequences; this episode reminded me of our need to make clear statements about expectations and consequences.

Our family has crossed a new threshold. Peter and I want to apologize to all of you for what happened under our supervision.

Sincerely,
Meg Hathaway

The parent meetings were valuable for me because I learned about the different parent attitudes. We don't necessarily share all of the same values, but I was heartened to discover that most parents were similarly shocked by what had happened. Because of this incident, in certain situations my radar will be up, and I'll seek more information in the future. I feel comfortable enough with these parents that we plan to get together on other issues. I have my own ideas; I'm not looking to them to set standards for my family, but I like to bounce ideas off other parents. I now know who I can call and say, "Am I the only mom in the world who won't let her daughter . . . ?" This working relationship with the parents of Sasha's friends will be worth its weight in gold.

Since the teenagers drank under their watch, the Hathaways suffered personal embarrassment, but they did not glaze over their own culpability. In fact, they took a true risk by opening up the situation as they did. *A well-handled alcohol crisis can, paradoxically, be a wonderful bad thing for a family because it forces parents to come to grips with the issue of teenage drug/alcohol use, which many health care professionals consider a major task of raising an adolescent in today's society.* The Hathaways faced their parental responsibility without denial, minimization, or preoccupation with what others would think of them. They devised an effective solution, doing all they could to turn the situation into a reasonable crisis that would teach the teenagers a lesson. Their strategy was to make the teenage drinking episode something of an ordeal for parents and teenagers alike.

A brilliant tactic on Meg's part was to slow the car down whenever the girls were not forthcoming, dragging out the trip all the longer. Although she pointed out to them that what they had done was illegal, she didn't waste all her fire on this point. More effective was her flipping of the equation on the girls: you put me in a bad position; I was liable. Meg and Peter established a relationship with the other parents, creating a network for the future. Rightly so, the Hathaways were frustrated by the fact that the teenagers had not been apprised of parental expectations regarding drinking until after the deed was done. Nevertheless, they made the most of this opportunity to deliver a clear, authoritative message on adolescent substance use. There is no assurance that these kids won't drink again, some maybe all too soon, but they will do so with more awareness of their personal responsibility and the Hathaways' negative sanctioning.

Drugs and Alcohol: When? Where? What? How Much?

Studies have shown that many healthy, normal high school juniors and seniors drink occasionally on weekends and still manage to stay on top of their grades and athletic activities. Though a parent's job is to impede use, at some level, with an adolescent who is on track, there is no single right way to inhibit substance intake.

Many different approaches will get us to the same desirable long-term outcome: a well-adjusted adult who, at most, uses alcohol conservatively and primarily in social situations. In particular situations, with particular factors at play, parental responses to substance use vary depending on the type of drug and circumstances of use, the teenager's age, temperament, overall well-being, history of previous substance use, and reflectiveness when confronted by the use.

The Just Say No anti-drug campaign is a solid tool for grade-school children (ages six to eleven) who need to hear a clear negative directive on substance use. An unqualified message appeals to their black-and-white, concrete thinking. During middle school, many adolescents feel some pressure to take risks — smoke cigarettes, shoplift, experiment with alcohol and marijuana. Helping middle schoolers with ways to say no continues to be an appropriate tack.

For high schoolers, the problem with relying completely on the Just Say No approach is that it offers only one strategy — total abstinence — which is about a 10 percent possibility for today's high school seniors. With alcohol all around them, they hear our prohibition once; they hear it twice; and then they don't hear it at all. If there is a single area where a lot of "good" teenagers lie to their parents, it's with alcohol and drug experimentation. The price parents can pay for a controlling "don't even think about it" or an outraged "if I ever hear about your drinking . . ." is a closing down of discussion, which robs us of a chance to enhance our children's thinking, especially *when* alcohol use occurs. Indeed, we may need to reserve our sternest no's for drinking and driving or harder drugs such as crank and crack. Parents *can* influence their adolescent's use of alcohol, but it takes flexibility, openness, warmth, and well-honed listening skills to keep the dialogue open.

Predicaments illustrating the inadequacy of abstinence as the only subject on the table occur regularly in families with high schoolers. A classic scenario involves a teen confiding in his parents about intentions to attend a party where alcohol will be served. We can feel like we're in a real bind when our child's honesty — a virtue we want to reinforce in every way possible — brings about consequences our child will see as negative.

Even if we have every intention of forbidding him to go to the party, we'll need to resist an automatic no and *communicate* in nuance as we deliberate with him. Independent of a decision about the party, we can express our heartfelt appreciation for the honesty. A possible response would be, "It took a lot of courage for you to be straightforward with me about this. I want you to know how much I value and admire your honesty. I am really sorry that I can't let you go to the party."

Many parents want some signs to help them discriminate between different types of alcohol use, which require different parental responses. Although evaluators rely on different classification systems to assess levels of use and chemical dependency, what they all have in common is the concept of a drug-use continuum, ranging from abstinence to addiction.

The drug-use continuum is not about condoning or enabling. Parents can and should be unequivocal with their message: "Drugs and alcohol are dangerous for teenagers. I expect you to neither drink nor use drugs." Then, as recommended in the previous chapter on sexuality, we become comfortable with the ambiguity of "No buts": for example, "I am asking you explicitly not to drink, but if you do, make sure you call me for a ride if you need one."

Instead of zeroing in on one yes or no question — Is my child drinking or using drugs? — we should reserve our most intense scrutiny for tracking when, where, what, and how much substance taking is taking place, making sure our child stays on the safer end of the continuum. To assess where an adolescent is on the continuum, evaluators ask questions like the following, which parents can likewise consider:

- What substance might he or she be using? How dangerous is it? What is its potency and potential for addiction or lethality?
- How frequently is he or she using it and over what duration of time? Is he or she trying to achieve an occasional mood change or attempting to alter reality in a significant, ongoing way? Can we identify a pattern?
- In what types of situations is he or she using the substance? Is it primarily social or recreational? Does he or she seek it independent of a social context?
- Is he or she compelled to seek the substance despite negative consequences (such as impairment of daily functioning, loss of friends, problems at school or with family relationships)?

The drug-use continuum runs from stage zero to stage five. Though individuals can remain at a stage without advancing any further, progression is always possible. The description below of these stages is limited to adolescents, though it's clear to see how behaviors along the continuum apply to adults. An adolescent is at stage zero only if he is a total abstainer. This is parental nirvana.

Stage one users are generally defined as experimenters. These are the investigative teenagers behind the garage, curious about the effects of alcohol. Any substance use in a middle schooler, even experimentation, should be considered a serious problem and dealt with strictly. If a high schooler is experimenting, we want to have a talk to let him know we take this matter seriously and perhaps enact some consequences, but we don't want to overreact, especially if the teenager is sick, embarrassed, and humiliated. Most parents would hope their adolescents progress no further than this point along the continuum.

At stage two are recreational users. In this category we place teenagers who drink or smoke marijuana while socializing with their friends. They neither use drugs on every social occasion nor do they go out of their way to make sure it's on hand for a good time. In these situations parents should establish a policy of ongoing monitoring and determine what consequences to impose when their child is found to be using. *Parents can and should be authoritative in making judgment calls about their adolescent's use and in imposing consequences based on this call.* Parents need not prove beyond a reasonable doubt that their teenagers have been using; rather it is incumbent upon the teen to present a clear, unambiguous picture of sobriety. An effective way of monitoring use is to establish a check-in policy at the teen's curfew.

If there is a history of alcoholism in the family, discuss this with your teenagers and *warn* them. Because the chances of progression are much higher for teens with alcoholism in their family backgrounds, even recreational use is risky for them.

Stage three users are generally defined as regular users. Substance-seeking behaviors set in. Partying with alcohol and/or marijuana is routine, and experimenting with other harder substances (cocaine, psychedelics, and so on) is common. Teenagers in this category use mainly on weekends, and they are beginning to experience negative impacts on their school, extracurricular, and family lives. Regular use in any teenager should raise a red flag. This is the point at which parents are well advised to seek consultation and consider a formal drug/alcohol evaluation.

Drug abusers, at stage four, are compelled to use substances on a daily (or almost daily) basis in order to have any sense of well-being. They seek a drug-induced state (drunk, stoned, high) and will lie, steal, and violate other codes of conduct in order to procure and use drugs. Indiscriminate in their choices, they mix drugs freely. They almost always have significant problems in their school, family, and social lives. Despite disruptions, such abusers typically deny they have a problem, claiming they could stop if they wanted.

Those at stage five — alcoholics/addicts — are both physiologically and psychologically addicted. Teenagers at stages four and five are desperate to use substances and require significant intervention for recovery.

Though only a fraction of adolescents who try a substance experimentally or recreationally develop drug-dependence problems, parental watchfulness is required all through the adolescent years. Since our goal is to keep our kids from advancing along the continuum, the further an adolescent travels along it — using drugs more frequently, experiencing more adverse effects, seeking substances in more pressing ways — the louder our alarm bells should ring.

To be sure, we never want to minimize the seriousness of alcohol and drug use by adolescents. Nonetheless, an important longitudinal study has pointed out the extent to which adolescent drug experimentation occurs in a healthy family environment. This study followed more than one hundred children and their parents from the age of three to the age of eighteen in an effort to investigate the relationship between psychological health and drug use.[3] When the children reached eighteen, the researchers classified them into three groups based on their use of marijuana: abstainers, experimenters, and frequent users.

The results of the study strongly suggest that the experimenters are psychologically healthier than either of the other two groups. Compared to the experimenters, the abstainers were observed to be "anxious, emotionally constricted, and lacking in social skills." Frequent users, compared to the experimenters, were "alienated, deficient in impulse control, and manifestly distressed." The mothers of both the abstainers and frequent users were perceived to be "cold, critical, pressuring, and unresponsive to their children's needs." Although findings about the fathers of frequent users were inconclusive, the fathers of abstainers, relative to fathers of experimenters, were "unresponsive to their children's needs, authoritarian, autocratic, and domineering."

Mild experimentation with drugs seems to be the byproduct of a family environment wherein some risk taking will naturally occur — but not too much. Children raised in an environment of trust, openness, flexibility, and authority are likely to experience a range of choices that is closed to children in rigid, authoritarian families. Likewise, children in permissive families are likely to explore too great a range. Ideally, we want *excess* risk to be inherently undesirable to our children as they stretch and grow stronger, while not putting themselves in jeopardy.

Halting the March Along the Risk-Taking Continuum: Juan/John on the Brink

When I work with families, the more deeply entrenched the problems, the more in need is the family of a comprehensive systemic change to build its strengths. If I'm counseling an adolescent whose risk-taking behavior has become truly problematic — that is, endangering to himself and others — merely educating him and his family about the dangers of his behaviors is like putting a Band-Aid on a gaping wound. In telling the story of Juan/John, I hope to illustrate the kinds of system changes that need to happen when a family's problems have accumulated and an adolescent's risk-taking behavior has become a clear and present danger.

If there ever were a dedicated, overworked, often exhausted group of employees, counselors in today's public schools are they. I received a phone call from a counselor responsible for no less than 250 students, urging me to take on at the University of Washington Adolescent Clinic the case of a particular boy. Fifteen-year-old John, also referred to as Juan, was on the verge of flunking almost everything, was suspected of drug and alcohol use, and was becoming increasingly defiant with his teachers. This young man lived with his divorced mother and his grandfather, both of whom had emigrated from Cuba in the early 1960s. His Caucasian father was out of the picture.

The clinic was swamped with referrals at the time, but the counselor's plea made it difficult to pass on the case. "John is a kid that could go either way. He has so much potential that it would be a shame to have him slip into the abyss of the flunkie–druggie criminal subculture." The counselor went on to explain that she had about fifty more cases she'd like to refer, if only the parents would follow through. She believed that John's mother, Mrs. Haines, would follow through because she'd detected an intense investment on Mrs. Haines's part the last time she'd come in for a parent conference. When Mrs. Haines learned that the clinic determined charges on a sliding fee and costs to her would be minimal, she agreed to try a consultation.

I call John/Juan "J." because his name was a question. His grandfather insisted on referring to him as Juan, while his mother was adamant that he be called John. When I first met J., I immediately knew why he had inspired a rescue attempt by the counselor. J. had an inviting grin, large dark eyes, and expressive brows. His manner emanated warmth, good nature, and responsiveness. He expressed himself in honest, uncomplicated language. When asked what he did after school he replied, "I like playing basketball," with a simple shrug of his shoulders, a smile, and direct eye contact, which is unusual for a child with significant behavioral and conduct problems.

Even though we request the presence of all family members living at home to attend the initial interview, Mr. Jimenez, J.'s grandfather, failed to show up. Mrs. Haines was disheveled and looked defeated. She described how J., as an underage driver, had wrecked her car, broken curfew continuously, talked back to her, and made "bad" friends.

Her own hardships were considerable: she was a single parent; she held a sewing job at a sporting goods factory despite threats of layoffs; she suffered chronic back pain and financial strains; and she'd missed child support payments from her ex-husband, who had abandoned them to start a new family when J. was four years old. As Mrs. Haines began to tell her story, with a trace of a Spanish accent, J. peppered it with his own perspectives and often humorous clarifications. Even when J. gave his mother a hard time, it appeared to be playful teasing. When kids interrupt with aggression, hostility, and defiance, it can signal significant family distress and relationship difficulties. But when interjections are made with warmth, humor, and mutual regard, I am inclined to see the interchange as potentially reflective of spontaneity, trust, and flexibility — family strengths to be sure. Nevertheless, the lack of a parent-child boundary between Mrs. Haines and J. was evident from the start. The bantering style of their disagreements and tangential presentation of problems made them appear on equal footing. On the other hand, their affection for each other was also evident.

Most of Mrs. Haines's and J.'s conversation consisted of haggling over who caused the other the most grief. J.'s main complaint was that his mother nagged him, treated him like a delinquent, and constantly raised the issue of J.'s possibly being a gang member, which J. resented.

"You don't know who I am if you think I'm into a gang. That isn't me," he protested. He felt his mother should appreciate that he always got home safely, albeit late, that he hadn't been arrested, and that he was still attending school (usually). Ignoring her son's reassurances, Mrs. Haines fretted that J. had lost all respect for her authority, could flunk out of school at any time, could fall prey to pressure to join a gang, and could end up in jail or dead on the streets. I felt that both J. and his mother were each a little right and each a little wrong. In actuality, J. exhibited a great deal of common sense as he defended himself, and he did not seem to be drawn toward gang affiliation at this time. Anxious, exhausted, and culturally dislocated, Mrs. Haines had overreacted in depicting her son as something of a delinquent. But she did have legitimate cause for concern. Statistically, under 10 percent of today's kids become seriously involved in drugs and delinquency, but in high-risk, high-crime neighborhoods like the one in which J. lived, the percentage leaps above the national average.[4] That J. had not yet had a run-in with the police was a fortunate circumstance; his late-night partying and underage drinking had certainly exposed him to that possibility. His neighborhood was teeming with negative role models and opportunities to act aggressively and break the law. Whenever we have a riled-up, risk-taking kid, without firm family grounding, living in a problematic neighborhood, it's entirely feasible he could over time pro-ceed to a dangerous dead end, which was exactly what we wanted to prevent with J.

As the initial interview proceeded, several family strengths emerged. J. voiced great concern over his mother's health, and it was clear that Mrs. Haines admired J.'s intelligence and wit. If they avoided sensitive topics, they truly seemed to enjoy each other's company. Whenever I complete a first interview and realize I've laughed a lot with a family, I feel optimistic that humor and good feelings will supply some of the flexibility needed to help them tackle their problems.

My objectives for the second session were to assess the degree to which J.'s drinking was problematic and to get a sense of how vulnerable he was. He told me he enjoyed drinking on weekends, rarely drank during the week, had been drunk fewer than five times, and had never ingested alcohol when by himself. He acknowledged that he helped procure beer for him and his friends. Although he preferred beer, he smoked marijuana on rare occasions. One time he had taken hallucinogenic mushrooms, but because they had upset his stomach, he had no intention of trying them again. On the drug-use continuum, I classified J. as a regular user. Substance use was interfering with his life responsibilities: he argued with his mother continuously about his weekend activities, broke curfew, and showed signs of moving away from conventional standards for adolescent behavior. He was flunking out of school and becoming alienated from sources of positive influence — adults and peers alike.

Like most adolescents, J. rejected the possibility that drinking could ever become a problem or preoccupation for him; playing basketball meant far too much to him to "screw up" his body with drugs. Convincing though he was, J.'s assurances held little sway with me. Most adolescents with risks for progression into drug dependency will protest similarly.

To evaluate J. further, I drew upon another diagnostic model. In the 1960s and early 1970s, researchers studied problems such as adolescent pregnancy, drug abuse, and delinquency as separate from one another. Interestingly enough, the various predictive models for these behaviors began to resemble one another. In other words, the factors that lined up to predict teen pregnancy were similar to the ones that were associated with drug abuse. One comprehensive model was developed by Richard Jessor, whose research identified variables linked to a host of risk-taking behavior in adolescents — cigarette smoking, delinquency, early sexual activity, and alcohol and drug use. His model also identifies factors that served to protect adolescents from those outcomes.[5] Using this model helps me to establish broad family-wide treatment goals. Parents, too, can refer to this model when they have questions about the level of risk of any teenager.

Here I apply an adapted version of Jessor's model to J. Next to the various factors, I write "yes" for present, "no" for absent, and "some" for somewhat present.

Domain	Risk factors	Protective factors
Biology/Genetics	Family history of alcoholism: NO	High intelligence: YES
Social Environment	Poverty: YES	Quality school: SOME
	Role models for deviance: YES	Cohesive family: SOME
	Conflicting values between peer group and parents: YES	Neighborhood resources: SOME
	Opportunity for illegitimate activity: YES	Interested adults: YES
		Models for conventional behavior: SOME
		High controls against deviant behavior: SOME
Personality	Low perceived life chances: SOME	Value on achievement: NO
	Low self-esteem: SOME	Value on health: YES
	Risk-taking propensity: SOME	Intolerance of deviance: SOME
Behavior	Problem drinking: YES	Church attendance: NO
	Poor schoolwork: YES	Involvement in school or clubs: NO

This assessment of J. revealed his mixed profile and clarified the need to arrest his progression along the continuum. What could propel him along the continuum were several critical risk factors such as poverty, deviant role models, problem drinking, and poor school performance. The protective factors that could keep him from negative progression included high intelligence, interested adults, and value on health. If we could strengthen the "somewhat" protective factors and transform each into a "yes," we would bolster J.'s chances.

Reframing Mrs. Haines's Outlook

My initial treatment goal was to increase family cohesiveness — a critical protective factor. Mrs. Haines's authority needed to be enhanced; conflicts needed to be reduced; and boundaries needed to be firmed up. I would then be able to move on to other issues: reducing J.'s contact with deviant peers, insisting that he participate in prosocial and school activities, and structuring his time to focus on homework completion and school achievement. I also hoped to work with available resources in the school and Latino community to build his sense of identity and help J. invest in future goal-planning.

Unfortunately, there was a snag in my initial goal of family cohesiveness. J. had enormous control in doing whatever pleased him. His mother was so overwhelmed by her physical, emotional, and financial stresses, and her despair was so pervasive, that she was unable to mobilize herself to help him. Mrs. Haines not only had significant back pain, but her depressive symptoms included frequent weeping, sleeping and eating problems, extreme fatigue, and low energy. Although J.'s risk-taking behavior was of great concern, it would have been naive for counseling to focus first on, say, his problem drinking because J. had no intention of following an abstinence policy. Furthermore, Mrs. Haines had no ability to enforce one. Because we had a systems problem, we had to back up and put energy into the system in a stepwise fashion. To have any chance at curbing J.'s risk taking, I would first need to tackle Mrs. Haines's undiagnosed depression, for her bleak and hopeless outlook could block other efforts.

Parents who are pessimistic, exhausted, depressed, powerless, or hopeless will not be able to make it to base one in trying to help their child with problematic risk taking. Therapy, first of all, had to tackle Mrs. Haines's feelings of despair and adjust her self-defeating perspective. She also needed support in her parenting role. In adjusting Mrs. Haines's perspective, I used a classic tool in any therapist's toolbox, called reframing. During her first individual appointment, Mrs. Haines said, "I have no power over my son. I can't control him." I reframed her crippling outlook by responding with a more uplifting but equally valid point of view: "What you're doing isn't working, but that's why you've made the effort to come here. You need help. It's too hard to try to do everything that is needed by yourself." If Mrs. Haines truly believes she has neither power nor control, then the window of possibility for helping her son is shut tight. With reframes we take a little lever and pry open the window, offering some hope for what can be done. Mrs. Haines can have an impact. She cares deeply and should be applauded for not having given up on J. Other examples of reframing follow.

Mrs. Haines's statements:	My reframes:
"J. is totally out of control."	"As you've said, J. needs your greater authority."
"J. has become a kid I don't even know anymore."	"Your power struggles leave you unable to enjoy the best parts of your relationship together."
"We have a broken-down family."	"You have a crisis situation. It's a good time to rebuild the family in a way that works better."
"I have no one to help. First my husband leaves me and now my son will probably leave. It's hopeless."	"We need to build your hope by building your strength."

At the end of our session, I set forth three goals for her, none of which pertained directly to J. Since she had so little power over J., I didn't want to set her up for failure, and it was critical to keep her in therapy. I asked her to talk to a doctor about an antidepressant medication, which might alleviate her back pain as well as her depression, to attend her church activities, which she valued but had curtailed because of her anguish over J., and to bring her father to the next session. Inevitably, Mrs. Haines asked, "What about John?" I told her that I agreed with her about the seriousness of J.'s problems, but that until she had more strength and support, she would not be able to work on goals with her son. I hinted that I had plans in store for overhauling J.'s situation, but first we needed a "treatment team," which meant bringing another adult on board for daily help since therapy was only once a week. As things stood, J. was perfectly indifferent to his own drug, alcohol, and school problems. I needed to strengthen Mrs. Haines's base so that eventually her force would effectively mobilize his.

Bringing in Grandfather and Burying the Hatchet

Research on adolescent substance abusers has documented the difficulties of treating adolescents from single-parent (mainly single-mother) families. Impoverished young males growing up in dangerous neighborhoods and lacking positive male models and/or fathers have much working against them in their challenge to reach adulthood safely and successfully. Although on the drug continuum J. was a regular user and not an abuser, many circumstances within his family were consistent with those of drug-dependent teens. It is nearly impossible for single moms like Mrs. Haines to turn a drug-use situation around by themselves.

Why? we might ask. In some cases, social variables such as time away from home at work, a dangerous environment, and poverty overwhelm parental efforts to control adolescent risk-taking behavior. Some solo moms do not have it within their emotional means to maintain parental hierarchy and authority. Fearing the child's anger, rejection, or power, these mothers have a difficult time maintaining a clear parent-child boundary and thus become permissive. Up against the abundant risk-taking opportunities available to teens today, many single parents give in to their despair, believing themselves powerless. Social isolation, poverty, psychosocial stressors, neighborhood violence, lack of community resources, and alienation from family supports combine to create the conditions that breed drug problems among teens today. To treat a drug-abusing teen from a single-parent family, research has found that the prognosis is greatly enhanced if other adults or family members are brought in to provide additional support.[6]

If feasible, I make strenuous efforts to engage an absentee, biological father and put him in a coparenting role. In reality, it's not doable with every dad. While I did put Mrs. Haines in touch with legal-aid counsel who would help her collect on her child-care payments, I had strong evidence that J.'s biological father had moved on to his next family, wiped his slate clean, and would never look back. Although we tend to associate deadbeat dads with poverty, men on every rung of the socioeconomic ladder heal the pain of marital failure by creating new lives for themselves and discarding the old.

That left only Mr. Jimenez, J.'s grandfather. Another reason to include Mr. Jimenez had to do with the value Hispanic/Latino cultures place on family, patriarchy, and hierarchy.[7] Although it was important to empower Mrs. Haines so she could realize her own full parenting potential, J. needed a male role model as much as Mrs. Haines needed parenting support. In Hispanic/Latino cultures, machismo refers to a type of maleness that impresses or influences others. J.'s alliance with his risk-taking friends was putting him at risk: he needed to learn how to garner respect through means other than alcohol use, defiance, and illegal activities.

Only with the greatest of reluctance did Mrs. Haines agree to bring her father to the next session. I saw a former fiery self emerge as she described how the house belonged to her from the divorce agreement, but out of financial convenience, she and her father lived together. She alluded to their many conflicts, ranging from her resentfulness about leaving Cuba at age four (I later discovered she inherited many of her ill feelings from her now-deceased mother), to his disdain for her love of a "worthless gringo," which had made it necessary for her to elope against his objections, to his I-told-you-so attitude when the marriage failed. J. laughed at the suggestion that we include his grandfather in the sessions, saying "It sure would be weird," but he seemed surprisingly willing if not enthusiastic about the idea. He let on that he liked his grandfather, but they kept their distance, primarily because of the feuding between his grandfather and his mother.

What immediately caught my attention about Mr. Jimenez in the first all-family session was his dignified bearing and formal presence. He wore a suit, held his head high, and stood as erect as a hemlock seeking light in a dense forest. He had fled Cuba when Castro came into power and the island aristocracy emigrated to Florida. Before addressing J.'s issues, we spent some time talking about his transition and adjustment to American life, his failed business in Miami, and his move from Florida to Seattle after his wife's death.

LK: Mr. Jimenez, what do you think should be done about J.'s behavior — his drinking and staying out past curfew, his school performance, and so forth?

Grandfather: His mother has no control. Juan does whatever he wants. His mother lets him walk all over her. Juan is headed for trouble.

(I noticed that Mr. Jimenez showed his concerns about family problems in exactly the same way Mrs. Haines had expressed her fears for her son — criticism. A lot of what seemed severe in tone, however, was a cultural tradition of patriarchal authority. J. listened respectfully and did not interrupt to defend himself as he had with his mother.)

LK: Yes, you're right about that. That's why we are here. What do you think should be done?

Grandfather, shaking his head with a mixture of disgust and exasperation: Juan shows no respect. It's a big problem here in America. I see it everywhere — how the children treat the people in the street, how they act toward their parents — and everywhere the drugs and the guns.

(Twice, I've heard that Mr. Jimenez doesn't know what to do about his grandson either. In fact, I hear the same globalized despair I heard from his daughter — another similarity between these two who supposedly have very few connections.)

LK: You said that Juan walks all over his mother. Does he walk all over you too?

(This question was a gamble because I was mining for strengths and didn't want to give Mr. Jimenez an opportunity for continued criticism. But, having observed the rapport between grandfather and grandson, I felt it was a safe bet.)

Grandfather: No, Juan is respectful toward me. Juan is a good boy, but he is following the American way of being a teenager, being wild and doing as he pleases.

(Juan sinks low in his seat, but maintains his pleasant smile as he watches the interchange between his grandfather and me. Mrs. Haines looks fearful of where this conversation might be going. She seems angry and resentful of her father's disparaging comments about her parenting. I'm trying to steer clear of his fault-finding at this time.)

LK: Mr. Jimenez. I notice that you call your grandson Juan and his mother calls him John. What do you make of this difference?

Grandfather: I am telling you that my grandson knows nothing of his Cuban side. He understands me at home where I speak only Spanish, but he refuses to address me in Spanish. He chooses friends who are black, and most of them don't even know where he gets his dark color because his last name is Haines, and he doesn't tell them of his heritage. His mother does nothing to help because she chooses the American ways too.

Mrs. Haines [*unable to contain herself*]: Papa, you brought me here when I was four. You decided our family should come to America. I didn't choose it. I am just living the life you chose, but you keep blaming me for it.

Grandfather: I didn't choose that good-for-nothing husband of yours. You had lots of Cuban boys to pick from in Miami.

(Quickly we had arrived at the heart of the conflict between Mrs. Haines and her father. Unburied hatchets have a way of being flung around in therapy sessions, which invites a therapist to get on with the necessary resolving, healing, and burying. But first the flinging had to stop.)

LK: But that marriage brought you your grandson.

Grandfather: That is true. That is true. He is the only good thing left in my life. But I do not even see him much because this is how things are with my daughter. I stay in my basement apartment and try to avoid trouble. But I worry about what is going to happen to him if he leaves school and joins a gang and does the drugs.

(At this point, each member of the family looks to be choking back tears. I, too, am affected by this strong man's expression of painful isolation, his anguish over his family, and his feelings of ineffectuality.)

LK: This is exactly why we needed you here too. We want your help. [I turn to Mrs. Haines.] Mrs. Haines, would you accept your father's help if he offered help that you were comfortable with?

Mrs. Haines [in a hushed, nearly inaudible voice]: Si.

As much as she knew she needed her father's help, it was a dark thing for Mrs. Haines to open up this relationship, so frightened was she of inviting this judgmental patriarch into her life. She saw him as negative, overbearing, and superior, and as party to her own life failure. Her grudge was strong. But, therapy would include helping Mrs. Haines to assert herself and ask for the kind of support she needed with J. I would work with her on her feedback to her father.

The parallels between these two parent-child relationships (J. and Mrs. Haines, Mrs. Haines and her father) were striking. In each case, there was ongoing criticism and complaint by the parent, resistance and defiance in the child, and escalation of anger and threats in the parent. These factors intensified the power struggle and ultimately created distance between the parent and child. More than likely, this pattern had been behind Mrs. Haines's elopement and was recycling itself through the next generation, predisposing J. to distance himself from his mother. In the same way that I would be helping Mrs. Haines express her needs and perceptions to her father, I would be interceding between J. and his mother. He, too, needed to make her understand how counterproductive her constant criticism and griping were; but he also needed to increase his tolerance level for his mother's ways.

Juan's Resiliency

Once Mr. Jimenez joined us, our sessions were infused with a whole new energy. As Mrs. Haines worked on being heard by her father, she gained a new appreciation for J.'s need for respect from her. She began to see how her "pelting" of complaints was keeping her son from obliging; as J. put it, "Why would I want to come home if this is what I get?" Medication helped Mrs. Haines's depression, level of pain, reactivity, and irritability. On a behavioral level, we assigned Mr. Jimenez the important role of monitoring J.'s homework and after-school time and of helping to get J. signed up for some prosocial activities. Mr. Jimenez kept in contact with J.'s counselor at school, and together they bird-dogged his progress to help him improve his grades. A few times a week Mr. Jimenez would take J. with him to the library, where he went daily to read international newspapers. Their relationship blossomed.

Mrs. Haines attended church more regularly, and she became involved with a Latino mothers group. The three generations in this family represented different speeds of cultural transition, with Mr. Jimenez keeping to the "old" ways, Mrs. Haines resisting these traditions, maintaining little of her heritage, and J. remaining clueless about his ethnic roots. As J. developed a deeper relationship with his grandfather, he could reclaim his Cuban identity. But this road had its bumps. At one point, we had to deal with Mr. Jimenez's racism, for he was highly disapproving of J.'s African American friends. In his wonderful, straightforward way, J. explained to his grandfather, "These guys are great basketball players. That's why I hang out with them. You're reading too much into this." When Mr. Jimenez visited J.'s school, he was struck by the number of kids who, like J., were of unidentifiable ethnicity, and thus he began to view his grandson's mixed racial identity as part of a larger phenomenon.

As our sessions continued, I became more and more confident that J., who had been on the brink, was unlikely to progress into problematic substance abuse, delinquency, or school failure. The family appeared to be growing closer across the three generations. Boundaries between J. and his mother grew more firm. Mrs. Haines let slide some of J.'s lippy taunts, while J. did the same with his mother's fretting. Between Mrs. Haines and

Mr. Jimenez there seemed to be less defensiveness, less hostility, greater tolerance, and a greater willingness to resolve conflicts.

Of the fifty or so family cases the high school counselor (in the beginning of this vignette) had hoped to refer to the adolescent clinic, one has to ask, "Why did J. rise to the top of the list? What gave him the edge over all those other kids living in dangerous environments?" Who are the kids who make it against the odds? Various researchers have identified a constellation of personal, family, and environmental characteristics that correlate with resilience. Resilient adolescents tend to have a group of some of the following characteristics in common:[8]

- Good care/safe environment
- A strong relationship with a caring adult
- Appealingness/social skills
- Good intellectual skills
- Talents valued by self or society
- Positive self-regard
- Religious faith or affiliations
- Socioeconomic advantages
- Good schools and other community assets
- Good fortune

A critical resiliency factor in J.'s case was the positive attachment figures in his life: his mother, who (chronic pain and depression notwith-standing) did not give up on him and followed through on counseling appointments and recommendations, and his grandfather, who supplied additional parental support, served as a positive male model, and worked to resolve the family feud that pervaded the household. J.'s intellectual skills, which enabled him to benefit from his grandfather's and the school counselor's monitoring, were another important variable.

In contrast to J., an adolescent who, for instance, has a learning disability, is from a thoroughly disadvantaged environment, and has not a soul on earth as an advocate has three big strikes against him. Also significant, J. had a friendly disposition and an appealing demeanor. Kids like J., who had won everyone's heart, can be a magnet for available resources. Even in an environment of limited resources, a child with a likable personality and an easygoing temperament will pull more out of that environment. Indeed, it can be difficult to make the extra phone calls and the special plea for a kid who comes across as contemptuous, mean-spirited, and rejecting of help.

Without his family's intervention, J. might have reached the troubled state the high school counselor described as "the flunkie-druggie-criminal subculture" of today's youth. Indeed, J. was on the brink. But in many ways he did not fit the classic profile of a child headed for conduct problems. Conduct disorder (the preferred term for delinquency) is a persistent pattern of norm or rule violation, characterized by aggressiveness, destructiveness, deceitfulness, and/or law breaking. Children at risk for this disorder can be identified as early as four to eight years of age. They tend to be angry, aggressive, have poor social skills, and little ability to control their emotions. They usually have significant difficulties with school and at home in early childhood. To this constellation of features add poverty, severe parental neglect or abuse, and a crime-torn neighborhood, and we have a picture of the risks that lead to adolescent drug abuse and conduct disorder because of the way these problems, if left unaddressed, snowball to create increasing failure in all areas of life. As problematic as J.'s situation was, it was moderated by strengths like his temperament, social skills, family support, intelligence, and lack of conduct disorder in his past.

I saw J. and his family in therapy for a year and had monthly follow-up sessions with them for the next six months. If A's on a report card and abstinence were our only measures of success, then we couldn't legitimately claim victory with J. But this family came to demonstrate impressive strengths, given J.'s original risk profile and the progress everyone had made. During therapy, J. had moved through the critical developmental phase of ages fifteen and sixteen. He'd become more connected to his family and less vulnerable to negative peer influence. Though he had no intention of giving up his drinking entirely, it was becoming no worse, and though his grades wavered around C's, this, too, was an improvement.

J. planned to stay in school, and he began talking about eventually attending community college. J.'s integrity was intact; he had pride in who he was. While there could always be misfortune as a result of his form of socializing (driving around late at night, partying without adult supervision, spending time in a borderline neighborhood), hopes for his future were still alive. Significantly, J. made the decision to be called Juan, which was a true healing point between Mrs. Haines and her father. Although not a clinical index one can readily measure, it's always important to me when a family seems really happy together, and this they were.

Drug Addiction and Family Discord: Neglect, Denial, Temperament, Learning Disabilities, Favoritism, Marital Problems, Family Alcoholism. Haydn, Linda, and Powell Barrett

Juan Haines was an at-risk adolescent whose prognosis for delinquency took an upturn; Powell Barrett went the distance to drug abuse with a full risk-taking syndrome. It's easy to point the finger at a drug-dependent adolescent whose abusing and abusive behavior is damaging himself and everybody in sight, but this trajectory is often set up early in life.

It's also easy to point the finger at parents who have been incapable of intervening successfully. As obvious as it may appear in theory and in hindsight, it takes a tremendous amount of parent health, awareness, and dedication to rise to the arduous task of diverting trouble when the odds are stacked up for a high-risk situation. There are usually explanations for why parents themselves are unable to mount their energies productively. Stories about children who go off the deep end tend to have some "classic" features in common, but it's the way in which those features intertwine in the absence of protective factors that creates the web of causation and likewise makes each story unique.

Almost a decade ago, I saw Powell Barrett and his family only six times before they dropped out of therapy. I later learned that after they stopped therapy Powell overdosed, was hospitalized, relapsed, and eventually was put in long-term residential care. When I first saw Powell, he was sixteen. Since I considered the Barrett family one of my failed cases, I was surprised to receive a call from Powell nine years later. Although he was now happily married, not drinking, and a father of a toddler, he had some issues he wanted to work on with me because he felt a connection through the few sessions we'd had together years ago. Pleased to hear from him, I was nonetheless puzzled, since what I recalled of his case were my unsuccessful efforts to keep the whole family in therapy to deal with their myriad problems. But there he sat in my office, age twenty-five, responding to my questions, looking dapper and healthy but nonetheless fidgety, rearranging his legs every couple of minutes.

"How do I remember that time in my life?" Powell paused, shuddered, and with an expression of disgust said, "It's mainly a blur. They say for every year you're using, you lose a year of your childhood, which I believe. All I really remember is the pursuit of the high, the con game that would get me out of the house, out of trouble, and on to the next party, the next thrill, the next high. When I look back, I feel a lot of guilt."

"You didn't seem to feel much guilt then," I responded, and we laughed together. I was trying to figure out how much of the drug-abuse cycle Powell now understood. "I remember your feet on my table, your ridiculing everyone in the room and yelling so loudly with your dad that I had to make you both quiet down so the therapists in the side offices wouldn't be disturbed."

Powell snickered and shook his head. "You know, when you're actually in that scene, you have no feelings for anyone. And the fear and hatred you have for yourself is covered up by the drugs — that's the whole idea. Get high so you have no feelings, and if they start creeping in, get higher. God, when I think about the amount of alcohol I consumed, cocaine that went up my nose, and pot I smoked, I just get disgusted. But I was in complete denial, and that denial was only beat by my family's. They were blind. They just didn't want to believe they could have a son as messed up as I was. And to really deal with that, they'd have to deal with everything else — their alcoholism, their marriage, their public image. It was a nightmare."

Powell understood quite a lot — his parents' own disturbing issues, his need to shield himself from his problems and fears with drugs, and the interwoven threads that ran throughout the Barretts' story: denial and its sister characteristic, neglect.

Looking Back

Nine years ago, I was Powell's third therapist. The circumstances that brought this wealthy, high-profile family to consultation were described to me in their first session as follows. Powell and his parents had had a heated argument over Powell's grades. The month was May, and the family (father, mother, Powell, and Powell's older brother) had a six-week European vacation planned for July and August. Sidel Academy, the prestigious school Powell attended, had informed the Barretts their son was about to flunk his sophomore year, and they recommended he take summer classes to make up the work. The Barretts were furious at their son because he refused to "knuckle down." They were also angry that Sidel Academy could not make him do so, given their hefty tuition and the fees they paid for special help for Powell.

On the night of the crisis, Powell and his parents had been slinging bitter insults back and forth over this predicament. Powell and his father began pushing each another around their family room — not an uncommon occurrence. Haydn and Linda had "had a few drinks" as Haydn put it. Trying to intercede, Linda stumbled in between father and son, was thrown against a table, and fell dazed to the floor. While Haydn attended to Linda, Powell made a hasty exit, grabbing the keys to his father's car on his way out. (Powell had his own car but his parents had taken his keys as punishment for his bad grades.) Enraged, Haydn called the police and reported his car stolen. Later that evening a very drunk Powell was picked up and placed in juvenile detention.

One of the first things I pursued in therapy was Powell's substance use. Powell had almost all of the symptoms of drug abuse:

- Possession and use of drugs: Powell was known to drink alcohol regularly to excess and to smoke marijuana. His parents had found paraphernalia in his car and pot in his room. He admitted to experimenting with cocaine and psychedelics a couple of times, though he was suspected of moving toward regular use of these substances.
- Delinquent activity: besides his substance use, Powell's illegal activities had included two shoplifting incidents, pilfering his parents' money regularly, and "stealing" his father's car.
- Decline in school performance: Powell's grades had dropped from a B average in sixth grade to mostly D's and F's by his sophomore year. He had a pattern of truancy and had withdrawn from all extracurricular activities, including athletics.
- Physical deterioration: Powell had lost weight and become indifferent to grooming. He was often tired and depressed.
- Behavioral changes: Powell had lost interest in any friends, except for those also suspected of using drugs and alcohol. He had become angry, hostile, and irritable with his family and was chronically dishonest (failing curfew, lying, stealing).

It was glaringly apparent that Powell had a serious drug problem that warranted immediate treatment. However, the slow development of this problem had lulled the parents into a pattern of knee-jerk reactions.

I had a strong suspicion the Barretts' inaction was abetted by their own alcohol use, but their strong denials shut down these avenues of inquiry. Haydn and Linda had become so used to Powell's problem behavior that it no longer had enough shock value to sustain a long-term solution.

According to his parents, Powell had always been "hell on wheels." Active, demanding, and boisterous, he'd been a tough child for Haydn and Linda to parent, for they tended to be more restrained and introverted in their own temperaments.

In comparison to his high-achieving older brother, Haydn II, Powell viewed himself as dumb. Showing off and getting in trouble became an easy way to distinguish himself. At home and at school, Powell had stirred up trouble over the years and had developed a defensive chip on his shoulder. Powell felt that he was the number-two son to his brother the star. Over the years, feelings of ill will between Powell and his brother, who was nicknamed "Hay," became entwined in their every interaction. When I saw the family, Hay was just ending his freshman year at a good college in southern California, where he had excelled in sports and academics, as he had at Sidel Academy. Haydn and Linda spoke with pleasure of Hay's coming home for the summer and their much anticipated European trip, just as they were bracing themselves for more battling between the brothers.

Although sibling rivalry is common, it becomes a true problem when there is unremitting loathing, as there appeared to be between Powell and Hay. One of the most common factors contributing to significant sibling conflict is overt parental favoritism. In one of the early sessions with this family, I broached the topic of favoritism, since Linda and Haydn showed little awareness of how their preferential treatment of Hay had contributed to Powell's resentment of his brother and Powell's feeling unappreciated within the family. Haydn retorted, "When Powell starts behaving better, he can earn the respect of his parents."

True, from his earliest years, Powell was a less accommodating, less compliant child than his brother. The vicious cycle of favoritism is set off when parents, in their day-to-day interactions with their children, respond more positively toward the child whose temperament is more congenial to the parents and more negatively toward the "different" child. Initially this distinction can be subtle, discrete, and nearly imperceptible — except to the child who feels like a second-class citizen. The least-favored child feels insecure and acts out even more, eliciting greater negativity from the parents, which in turn prompts the child to act out further. These behavioral spirals assume a momentum of their own as the "good" kid, feeding off his parents' praise and positivism, gets better and better, and the "bad" kid becomes angrier and more of a problem.

In any family, siblings can often be identified as relatively easier or harder to parent, but it is our job as parents to arrange ways to help the more challenging child still feel cared for, respected, and supported. As I spoke with Powell and his parents, I had a clear sense that his family didn't like him very much, and he knew it. Perceived rejection and problematic family relationships are associated with adolescent substance abuse; thus, the more I learned about Powell's role in his family, the more concerned I became about the severity of his situation.

Emergency Measures: Attempt and Failure

We commonly make a mental link between neglect and poverty, but other family types — the very rich, dual-working couples, working single parents, and depressed parents at home — can be prone to the same outcome of neglect. For differing reasons, some families with these circumstances divert too much of their energy away from child rearing to other aspects of their lives. Suffering from a great deal of neglect, Powell had been raised mainly by a changing host of nannies, while his father was conducting business worldwide for his lucrative import-export enterprise and his mother was traveling with friends or accompanying her husband on his sojourns. As I observed Powell and his parents, I noticed distance, disengagement, and a dearth of rapport in their relationship. From everything I gathered, Powell lacked a secure and loving attachment to his family. The root of this problem was in the mismatch of temperaments between him and his parents and in his parents' more satisfying experiences with Hay. Temperament and favoritism, strong sibling rivalry, behavioral problems, denial, and neglect were all aspects of the story of this teenager who felt "expendable."

I saw Powell and his family for two evaluation sessions the first two weeks in May, and then I broached the possibility of inpatient treatment. The family instantly rejected this idea. Unable to move the family toward intensive treatment for Powell, I put forth a few strict recommendations (more would follow), stressing the severity of Powell's drug and behavioral problems. I encouraged the family to commit to individual and family therapy, to procure random urine tests to monitor Powell's drug use, and enact some behavioral restrictions and consequences for drug use, which would be consistently enforced with my help. To emphasize the critical nature of their situation and the need for immediate action, I suggested Haydn and Linda forgo an upcoming trip to Singapore. This would enable us to get some work done before July, should they determine it still possible for them to proceed with the family trip to Europe, about which I also expressed some doubts.

Hemming, hawing, and backpedaling made it clear that Haydn and Linda were unwilling to cancel their Singapore trip. Already they were starting to edge their way out of therapy. Since this really was "Powell's problem" (they more or less told me), couldn't I handle it without them? I replied that Powell did have a drug-use problem; evidence of such was plentiful. *I made this well-documented point: an individual treatment approach is absolutely insufficient with teenage drug abusers. For treatment to have any chance of success, the family must be included.*

Insisting their trip was imperative, the Barretts left the city, leaving behind a loose promise they would "definitely" be in touch with me when they returned in two weeks at the end of May. I didn't hear from them again until the fall. Powell was off the hook again. Upon returning from Singapore, the Barretts arranged another reprieve for Powell with Sidel Academy. Through a private tutoring service, Powell would catch up on his work, which would allow them to go to Europe as planned. Essentially, the Barretts reacted to my advice the same way they had reacted to all of the signs and symptoms that should have alerted them to the seriousness of Powell's drug abuse: denial and neglect. By going to Singapore they had spared themselves the pain and misery of addressing their son's problems and their own problems.

Following the crisis created by the failing grades, the fight, the "stolen" car, and juvenile detention, the Barretts had roused themselves into action, initiating therapy with me. But, like so many families with a drug-abusing teen, they vacillated between anger, intense focus on the problem, and harsh punishment, which would be followed by denial, avoidance, and permissiveness. Extreme threats were part of the parental repertoire. Within the last year, Haydn and Linda had threatened but stopped short of sending Powell off to military boarding school, taking their lawyer off his case of shoplifting, and selling Powell's car. Regularly, his parents threatened to take away his allowance or to ground him "for a month," but they rarely followed through. *Each of these episodes of returning to the status quo — the status quo being a distanced, permissive parenting approach — could be called enabling. This is a term used in the chemical dependency field to account for the role of friends or families in maintaining substance abuse.*

The trip to Europe had gone so badly that the Barretts did, indeed, return for four more sessions of family therapy in September. Far from the wonderful adventure it was envisioned to be, the trip was characterized by one argument after another. From the outset I had suspected Haydn and Linda might be alcoholics, but it takes time to confirm substance abuse in some adults. Adults are often highly adept at covering up their drinking patterns, and because family members are invested in maintaining the norm, they keep quiet about secrets. Were we to make any progress with Powell, we would need to uncover his parents' problems, which were driving the neglect, denial, and resistance to treatment.

Immediate therapy goals were to try to keep the option of inpatient treatment open, to help Haydn and Linda set consistent consequences for Powell's behavioral infractions (including substance use), and to generate more compassion among family members. Although Powell's drug issue was our immediate priority, during post-Europe sessions with the Barretts, we began uncovering some uncomfortable issues in Haydn's and Linda's background.

It can be difficult to relate the story of a young man such as Powell without seeming to blame the parents, or, likewise, the adolescent who has brought about a family's suffering. By backing up a generation, we often find a host of contributing factors that are indirectly impacting the teenager. Often there are patterns repeating themselves intergenerationally. *Instead of viewing the drug problem in the teenager in a linear way (that is, what the parents did "caused" the drug abuse), we can examine circular causality.*

Many implicating factors started to emerge in therapy. Haydn felt enormous pressure to succeed in his import-export business, which had been founded by his recently deceased father after World War II. Haydn's own parents had been openly skeptical of his abilities to carry forward the family tradition of prestige and prosperity, so he felt compelled to "out-succeed" his father and prove them wrong. An underachieving son was threatening to him because he saw a part of himself in Powell. He focused what little fathering energy he had on Hay, the heir apparent for the Barrett family business. Linda had married into this wealthy family, but never felt accepted by her "aristocratic" mother-in-law, whom Haydn worshipped. Linda herself had always played second fiddle to her brothers, whom her parents prized. Linda felt abandoned by her husband, who she said "favored" his mother over her, in the same way she had felt abandoned by her parents, who favored their sons over their daughter.

Linda had sought refuge in travel, in her various houses, and in her use of alcohol. Trying to parent a rambunctious Powell had been frustrating and unnerving for her, and she used her wealth to bail herself out, employing nannies around the clock. Although she felt guilty about not devoting more of herself to her sons, she figured her tension and anger wouldn't be good for her children, so she opted out of child rearing, as had Haydn.

Over the years, the parental pattern of anger and abandonment stimulated all of Powell's worst tendencies: his anger, his school problems, his negative role models as peer choices, and his disregard for family rules, policies, and relationships. As these tendencies amplified, he alienated family members further, solidified his role as the "bad kid," and acted as accomplice to his parents' inconsistent disciplinary style. Understanding how certain behaviors and parent-child interactions advance one another and circle through relationships intergenerationally helps us see the complex linkages between parents and children and also helps us avoid blaming any one link.

Nonetheless, because parents are responsible for their children, they usually have to be the ones to commit to changing the patterns, especially when adolescent substance abuse is involved. Because the teenager's mental status is highly impaired by drugs and denial is strong, parents must assume the lead. But Powell's parents evoked a powerful Catch-22: they said they would reach out and support their son when his behavior improved, but his behavior could not improve until they *supported* him in drug treatment.

My last few sessions with the Barretts were an exercise in futility. In family system terms, we would describe the structure of the Barrett family as "chaotic," a term used when there is a high degree of entropy and virtually no parental leadership and limit setting. Although it may sound contradictory, families can be very stable in their chaos, in that the family process can be quite predictable. My efforts to bring about change were met with strong resistance; hence the family's "system stability" was maintained. As is often true, the Barrett's family system would have to collapse completely before patterns would alter. This occurred much later in a fairly catastrophic way, and their system was never rebuilt as an intact family. Though they probably didn't realize it consciously, Haydn and Linda had an active investment in avoiding their family problems: this would mean coming to terms with their marriage and enduring tremendous pain and anxiety over many issues. The Barretts dropped therapy the same way they dropped Powell when he got too hot to handle.

Powell Recalls His Path from the Nightmare to Recovery

What happens to a drug-abusing teenager several years down the line? Where do these kids end up? For many, it's a grim scenario: a high-risk child from an impoverished background becomes a drug abuser, remains untreated, commits crimes again and again to support his habit, and thereby joins a group of young people who make up one of our country's most pressing problems. Powell's wealth had been part of the problem because it afforded his parents enormous neglect, but his family's financial resources also came to his rescue. He had the advantage of a long-term residential drug rehabilitation program to rebuild his life. If Powell had had to burglarize or steal to get money to buy drugs, if he had lived in a neighborhood replete with delinquent role models, if there had been neither tutors nor state-of-the-art treatment centers in his life, he would never have been again sitting in my office at age twenty-five with a promising future ahead of him.

When Powell, fit and prospering, came in for a consultation nine years after our initial encounter, he brought me up to date on his family's story. A year after I first saw him, Powell was hospitalized with a drug overdose and sent to a treatment center out of state where teens can legally be treated involuntarily. Haydn and Linda had again dodged the "mandatory" family program. Powell returned home two months later to the same friends, the same family interaction patterns, and the same problems. He relapsed.

The next step was a highly effective residential care center, which included a solid academic program, an athletic program tapping into Powell's physical strengths, and a topnotch therapeutic program that helped Powell learn to relate to people in authentic ways for the first time in his life. During the time Powell was in treatment, his parents' marriage fell apart. We might speculate that without Powell as a negative focus, Linda's and Haydn's difficulties became more pronounced. *When an ado-*

lescent with the "identified problem" either gets better or leaves home, it is common for parents with deep-seated, unresolved conflicts to experience their own problems more directly and intensely.

For years, Haydn had been having an affair with a woman whom he married almost immediately after divorcing Linda. Linda hit bottom with her alcoholism and was herself hospitalized. Ironically, Linda's and Powell's parallel treatment processes created a bond in their relationship, and they became close for the very first time. Haydn was so humbled by his own midlife troubles, not to mention his mother's criticism of his divorce, that he became much less judgmental toward Powell. Meanwhile, after completing his undergraduate and graduate work, Hay took a position in international banking in Tokyo, distancing himself from his family physically and emotionally. Powell still felt uneasy around his brother — siblings with this kind of history rarely reconcile completely — but he had developed ties with each of his family members he had never thought possible.

If all was as well as it seemed to be, why was Powell once again in therapy with me? People with Powell's history will almost always have residual issues to deal with in the aftermath of their trauma, and it was a true sign of self-awareness that Powell wanted to stay on top of potential problems (in Powell's case, a gambling crisis and an employment decision). Though abstinent for eight years and happy with a wonderful wife and son, Powell was so attuned to his own family history that he feared a slip-up or a recapitulation of a family pattern.

Powell also wanted reassurance that the part he played in the family story was a single part and not the cause of the family's ultimate collapse. While Powell had forgiven his parents, he was having trouble forgiving himself — hence his fears about his potential for addiction. Powell needed to believe he could control his drift toward high arousal and that he could continue to make good decisions for himself and his family. He was no longer just his addiction in operation. Powell hoped to move toward his future in his own way with a relatively clear conscience, no longer hamstrung by his past.

The stories of Juan and Powell take us to the far end of the risk-taking continuum, where biological, emotional, and environmental factors create a fertile environment for problematic risk taking. Harmful risk taking is not likely to erupt inexplicably in a family. Fears that extreme behaviors could happen with any adolescent in any family can create anxiety and rob the average parent of some of the joys of parenting a teenager. Our anxiety can also deprive our children of the freedom they need for normal wing spreading.

There was a time when we could restrain our children in a safety seat, place them in a playpen, or barricade the stairs with a gate. Little by little, we removed the physical barriers and exposed them to a slip or two on the stairs, just as we also taught them about poisons under the sink and electric sockets and eventually took off the safety devices. By adolescence, many of the barriers we impose are admonitions: "You may not." "I can't let you." "It's not all right." All along, like the gates and the socket plugs, our parental goal has been to remove our overt restraints and restrictions incrementally, in synchrony with our children's demonstrated ability to internalize an understanding of the dangers and risks and act of their own accord to keep themselves safe. Some parents will need to hang on to their young child's hand in the parking lot longer, while others can more confidently ease their grip. Likewise, some parents will need to be more diligent in overseeing their adolescent, while others have reason to trust. Despite the open range of risk taking and its potentially dangerous territory, the large majority of teenagers will make it through adolescence safely, especially if they are given opportunities to develop competencies and a healthy independence along the way.

8

Launching

*Goal: Prepare your adolescent for independent life by
helping to build cognitive, emotional, and moral
competencies. Also address your own developmental
challenges so that your adolescent will have a
secure base from which to launch.*

THOUGH raising children can be
deeply preoccupying and endlessly involving, a time will come when
child rearing will no longer be the central feature of our lives. During
adolescence, as our teens extend their wings and become more independent, feelings of loss begin to ease into our parenting, for it becomes
clearer than ever they will eventually go their own way. Launching is not
a single moment in time when a child exits at a set age, but rather an
ongoing developmental process involving the whole family. How parents
react to their young adolescent's new identity and sense of independence
is part of launching. How individuals or couples view the next chapter of
their lives is part of launching.

Any number of issues color our interpretation and experience of a
child's nearing departure. Typically, parents are dealing with their own life
cycle issues — their health, changing looks and bodies, and questions
about the meaning of life. We have to come to terms with how it feels to
look at middle age in the mirror. Moreover, parents are often coping with
their sick or dying parents; rather suddenly there may be no generation
between themselves and mortality. Also central among the issues affecting
launching is a parent's own sense of identity. For all of our necessary

investment in parenting, we must also carve out a meaning of who we are apart from "mom" or "dad." Developing a separate sense of identity while also staying connected to our children is one of the toughest, though most critical, juggling acts of parenting. Parents who face an identity void when their children leave, who have no new possibilities, ventures, or rekindled interests, will necessarily feel greater distress. Dwelling on "the empty nest" (a truly unfortunate description), they are often unable to create a satisfying renaissance for themselves. The "quiet house" becomes a symbol of loss. If anxiety over a child's leaving is unusually high, adolescents can sense it and feel guilty about abandoning their parents, as if they are somehow responsible for taking their parents' job away from them. Siblings who remain at home can miss the sister or brother they fought with tooth and nail and dread the heightened focus on themselves.

Critical among issues affecting launching, married moms and dads must deal with being alone together again as a couple. What will this arrangement feel like? Do they still like each other? Parents who have lost interest in each other may reach a stalemate because the core child-rearing task holding them together has dissipated. Single parents may worry about the prospect of living alone. Whatever the family structure, parents who look to their next stage of life with optimism, albeit with strong tugs at the heartstrings, stand a good chance of moving through the launching transitions.

One of the best ways to view launching is as a developmental task, like getting married, giving birth to one's first baby, or sending a child off to kindergarten. Parent and child will each undergo parallel though separate experiences. As with all developmental tasks, the success of each juncture is hinged to the former process. In other words, we can't move successfully to stepping-stone B without a firm footing on stepping-stone A. Before a child is capable of leaving home, a string of parenting goals must be realized. Tasks to be accomplished include all the goals covered in this book. Has your adolescent internalized a sense of trust and security so he can take on new life adventures? Does he have a sense of identity? Has he been given enough freedom to develop critical competencies and standards of judgment to keep himself safe? Does he have boundaries that will protect him from being overexposed to harms but will also allow interpersonal experiences and relationships to blossom? Has he had the parenting and life circumstances to develop strong character? To launch successfully, the adolescent needs a backpack of developmental "supplies" that are related to previous experience, exposure, and relationships that give him the strength of self to open himself into the world.

Even in the healthiest families, however, a child's departure for college or a job is stressful; late adolescents can become quirky, restless, and moody and so can their parents because this is usually a sad/exciting life stage. When launching is on track, there can be moments of nostalgia as parents mull over the years that have flown by, or even a passing wave of panic because we don't feel quite ready to let go. But parents can also feel a little lighter, in pleasant anticipation of having more energy for younger children or time to pursue their own interests. Most parents describe their last year with their child at home as a strange yet wonderful period. Extraordinary bonds can form with maturing children, just as extraordinary struggles occur as the battles of autonomy and individuation play themselves out. Preparing for the transition of a child's leaving home is rarely smooth, nor should it be. But, when an adolescent launches under steady and extreme duress, or, for that matter, doesn't launch, we look to the whole child and family, for the way in which an adolescent takes wing is inextricably related to and dependent upon the system that nurtured the child.

The Castle Family: Joan and Stan, Celia, Alden, and Daniel

The final vignette of this book traces the Castle family over a period of several years, a time span during which each of their three children left home. I saw the family at three junctures — as it evolved from problematic functioning to coping with minor hitches to full thriving. Initially, the Castles entered into therapy with me because their oldest child, eighteen-year-old Celia, had become depressed and anxious the summer before she was due to depart for college. In the months we worked together, we readjusted family patterns, uncovered family-of-origin issues, and established new goals for each family member. Three years later I saw the Castles again, this time because their middle child, Alden, then a high school senior, was acting out. As is often the case when families restructure — even in the healthiest of ways — the transition is rougher than originally envisioned. In the Castles' second stage of therapy, we ironed out some of the wrinkles that emerged as a result of changes initiated the first go-around. My third intersection with the Castles occurred by chance some years later, when I ran into Joan at her new workplace. She updated me on the family. Because Celia, Alden, and Daniel had each launched in a different way and under different circumstances, their story brings to light many of the major issues that revolve around launching. Their story also illustrates that family functioning can definitely improve when parents take it upon themselves to work on their relationships and their own issues.

Celia's Failure to Launch

It was early July when I first met with the Castle family. Joan, the mom, had called me, expressing her distress over her daughter Celia's symptoms. Celia couldn't sleep, was always tired, and regularly called in sick at her summer job. Daily, she fretted about leaving in September for a college several states away in the Midwest. She didn't think she'd made the right choice. Having applied and been accepted early decision, she felt she'd never adequately explored all her options, even though the college had once seemed like the perfect match and a financial aid package had been awarded to her. She worried about not liking her roommate and living among a bunch of "strangers" in a dorm. She anguished over going through rush but didn't want to eliminate the sorority option. She felt she only did well in high school because it was high school. What if she flunked out? What if she didn't make any friends? What if something happened to her family while she was gone? What if the plane taking her to school crashed? Many of her friends were feeling a little blue and nervous about going away, but Celia's emotions were extreme. Both Joan and Stan were devastated by this turn of events because Celia had always been on track. Joan, in particular, felt wrenched, as Celia tied herself in knots, called herself a loser, and finally reached the decision that she simply couldn't leave home.

At their first appointment, I saw the whole family. Serious, intelligent, kind, and somewhat meek, Stan was a computer ace. About a dozen years ago, he had quit his relatively secure job in the systems department of a large architectural firm to form a software start-up company with a group of three other men. Struggling to bring their product to market, the men had signed personally on a bank loan, and the Castles and one other family had taken out a second mortgage on their homes to meet their share of the payments. For more than a year it had looked as if bankruptcy was inevitable, when, to everyone's relief, an eleventh-hour buyout came from a big computer company. Though the family's financial scare had occurred three years ago, they were still struggling with money issues. Because the family's economic situation was on everyone's mind, the topic crept into the interview early on.

Like her husband, Joan was pleasant and reserved. Celia was similarly quiet. Though verbally unforthcoming in the initial interview, she expressed herself with her tears, which rained steadily throughout the hour. My initial impression of Alden, age fifteen, was that he was the spontaneous extrovert in the family. Again and again, he broke the intensity of the interview with a wisecrack. Twelve-year-old Daniel had a sunny, light-hearted demeanor, but, like many kids his age, showed signs of straddling childhood and adolescence.

After I touched base with each family member, Alden spoke up to depict each family member's role. Dad was "always busy with work." Rarely did he make it home for dinner, and only occasionally would he attend one of the kid's many athletic games. (Alden, in particular, had at least two teams going at any one time.) As for Mom, she "does everything else because Dad is usually burned-out by the time he gets home." Joan appeared to be one of those moms who spends half her life driving a carpool to one practice or game or another and the other half tending to someone else's needs. Up until the last year, Daniel had been Mom's "buddy," riding "shotgun" next to her in the car, but now he preferred to stay in his room and listen to music. Cackling affectionately, Alden referred to Daniel as the "family mascot"; Daniel's grimaced smile revealed both pride and chagrin at being put in this "kid" role by his clearly esteemed older brother. As for Celia, Alden said, "Mom and Celia have their own show. They're two peas in a pod." Celia registered a small snort, while Joan patted her on her shoulder. Joan seemed to be strongly bound to her maternal role. Indeed, much of the description of individual family members was in reference to Joan, as if she were the hub of the wheel.

As a family, the Castles seemed honest, open, and insightful. Everyone seemed to know the rules by which the family worked, though Joan was clearly the most psychologically astute. When everything in a family *looks* to be proceeding normally, it can be helpful to investigate the family's own hunches about what threw things off. Midpoint in the family interview, we reviewed Celia's anxiety about leaving for school; then I posed a question:

LK [to the group]: What are some of your thoughts about why Celia is having such strong reservations about college?

(*I was watching closely to see who would offer an answer, and this time it wasn't Alden.*)

Joan: I've really wondered about my role in this. I look at Celia and wonder whether I've been a good role model for her. Her lack of self-confidence reminds me of my own. No matter how much I reassure her, she still has all these fears about going away. I try to figure out where I went wrong.

(*Predictably, Joan had spoken up, showing a great deal of self-awareness and courage in associating her own lack of self-confidence with her daughter's. Nonetheless, I was uneasy about her willingness to take the rap for her daughter's problem. Fully the mother in the family, she knew she was involved. I decided to address Stan specifically, even though it was obvious to everyone that he was a lot less engaged in the family.*)

LK: Stan, do you have any ideas?

Stan: Well, you mean, more than what Celia herself already said? I mean, you can see for yourself that she feels really bad and confused. She's just too anxious to go.

LK: Yes, you're right. And Joan already mentioned that Celia has always been somewhat anxious, temperamentally speaking, about new endeavors. But, she has always managed to make these transitions, into middle school, to a big high school, to a month-long summer camp. So why now? Do you have any ideas about why she's stuck?

(*Stan knew the refrain about Celia's anxiety, but he lacked experience in excavating deeper psychologic territory. Joan clearly had many thoughts, but I didn't want therapy to mirror the usual family process of having Mom provide all the parenting insights and probing, while Dad remained the outsider, so I continued the focus on Stan.*)

Stan: You're asking me why she's having a tough time leaving home?

LK: Exactly.

Stan: Beyond the reasons we've already talked about? Hmm . . . I think Joan knows Celia better than I do, truthfully.

(*Stan was highly uncomfortable being the family psychology spokesperson, but Joan, Celia, Alden, and Daniel were all figuratively on the edge of their seats, wide-eyed with anticipation because they weren't used to Dad talking about emotional matters. Even Celia's tears had stopped.*)

LK: But, it seems to me that you, as the father, might be in a unique position to view your daughter's coming-of-age process and have some ideas about what's presently causing so much disturbance.

(*I was worried Stan would back away and not take a stab at an answer under the pressure of all those eyes looking at him and wanting to hear from him. It didn't feel like a family where everyone was afraid a dreaded secret would be revealed; this felt like unadulterated hunger.*)

Stan: Well, we've always been a very close family. I guess I should say Celia has been very close to her mother, even though they have their tussles. Maybe the closeness makes it extra hard to leave home. You know, it's been a pretty cozy nest that Joan's built for us.

(*Stan's audience remained attentive.*)

LK: You mention Joan a lot. Are you a part of that coziness too? Do you think it's hard for Celia to leave her relationship with you too?

(*Celia began to sob, and Joan and Stan started to look misty-eyed during this emotionally intense moment.*)

Stan: I suppose, but Joan's really the center. She holds the family together. Well, they joke about me being a workaholic.

LK: Why do you suppose Celia started crying so hard just now?

Stan: I don't know. I guess talking about this is hard on her.

LK: I'm sure you're right about that. (I turn to Celia.) Celia, what made your tears flow just then?

Celia [*laughing nervously*]: I don't know. It's so strange to hear Dad saying anything about the family. We never sit down and talk like this, especially not with Dad. (She looks over at her father.) Don't get me wrong, Dad, but you're hardly ever around, and when you are, you seem like you're in another world.

LK: Celia, when you leave home — whenever that is — do you think you'll miss your dad a great deal?

Celia [tears flowing]: I can't explain it. Yes, I'll miss him, but I miss him now! We just don't have much of a relationship. (She again faces her father. She seems to want to protect him, but she also feels compelled to answer me honestly.) No offense, Dad, I appreciate how hard you work — I really do — but it's like you come home emptied out, and we get nothing.

LK: Have you ever told your dad these things before?

Celia: No, but he knows. And Mom has talked about this a lot.

LK: To whom?

Celia: To Dad, to the boys, to me. Not in a bad way, but it's been a big deal in the family.

LK: But you've never told him yourself how much you miss him? (*Withdrawn and sad, Stan's eyes were down.*)

Celia: What's the point? If he could do anything about it, he would, I suppose, since Mom's always reminding him.

LK [to Stan]: Stan, does it feel any different coming from your daughter?

Stan: It feels awful. I know I'm distant from the family, and I feel terrible about it. But, work drains me, it's true.

(*Stan was overwhelmed. We all felt protective of him in this moment, but I didn't want to reinforce the family assumption that Dad is a lost cause and that trying to connect with him is futile. Stan had come up with the pat family explanation for his absence — work. Knowing his job history, it was likely he had internal conflicts about his near-bankruptcy, but this topic would have to wait since we needed to pursue the theme of connection. Although it's unusual for one person to remain the center of a therapy session for this long, the family clearly needed to hear more from*

Dad. Stan wanted to connect, but he didn't know how. I could tell Joan and I were in sync and that she knew what I was doing.)

LK: It does sound like your work is pretty consuming, but even so, you say that when you arrive home, there's no communication with your wife or your children about your feelings or where this workaholism is taking you. Tell me a little about how you learned about relationships. What was your family like when you were growing up?

Stan: We weren't very close. Especially not like Joan and her family.

LK: Can you tell me why?

(Again, all eyes were peeled on Stan. This was like pulling teeth, but not because Stan was withholding anything, but because he was acutely uncomfortable speaking of emotional matters. His eyes darted nervously, then he obliged.)

Stan: My mother was a volatile woman. My father was a gentle soul who didn't know what to do about it. My sister was my mother's favorite. I frustrated my mother because she always wanted me to excel, never disappoint her like my father did, but I seemed to anyway. My grades weren't high enough. My personality reminded her of my dad's, and then there was my first marriage to Laurie during college. She hated Laurie. The marriage lasted only two years. After that my mother just gave up on me. I don't have much contact with her. My dad died quite a while ago.

LK: How long since you've seen your mom?

Stan: About ten years.

LK: Ten years? That means Celia was eight, Alden was five, and Daniel was two?

(I wanted to raise the implications of that ten-year span for his children — no grandparenting and a significant legacy of disconnection and ongoing loss. Stan was restless. He had reached his limit for now.)

Stan: Yeah, well, it was a very upsetting visit, which is why there hasn't been another. My mother was very critical. We had words. There have been a few phone calls, but not much.

LK: If you don't mind, I'd like to hear the details some time, but I get the gist. You certainly answered one question. You inherited a whole legacy of disconnection.

Satellite Dads

Earnest as the day is long, Stan epitomized a classic pattern among a certain kind of nice guy: they say "yes, sure, can do!" to all the people they want to please, but come home exhausted to their families. They say their families are the most important thing in their whole lives, but the families feel like the lowest of priorities. A full analysis of how Stan filled his day would support his family's view. By tracking his schedule, we'd see that Stan rarely made it to family dinners and even when he was physically present, he was mentally absent. Sometimes he didn't even hear when he was being spoken to. He resembled a caricature of a 1950s dad, isolated with his newspaper and entitled to relax since he's supporting the family financially.

A sweet, well-meaning, never cruel man, Stan had nonetheless withdrawn from his wife and children. Satellite dads come with different temperaments and with different justifications for their disconnection, some more aggressively defensive than others. In extreme cases, some children of these fathers feel truly abandoned because of the lack of connection. Gentle-soul satellite dads like Stan are difficult for adolescents to deal with because the disappointment these kids feel can be mixed up with adoration: the kindness of the father and the vulnerability his quiet suffering implies make it difficult for the adolescent to verbalize negative or ambivalent feelings about the father's behavior.

Although Stan articulated a family-centered priority, he hadn't come through for them. The internal struggle can be very dramatic, if not desperate, for a person in a situation like Stan's. I've had many men in my practice as individual patients or in the husband or father role wrestling so intensely with the demon "success" that they can't see that the family philosophy they espouse is functionally a lie. Having had as a role model a generation of post–World War II men who felt duty-bound to the work ethic, they're floundering in the relationship arena. In therapy, I've heard wives call their husbands on their statements about how devoted they are to their families. These women plead, "Make less money. Let's sell the house. I'll work more or do whatever it takes because we need you." But the demon has a strong hold, rendering them incapable of getting home by 6:00 in the evening, and retaining psychic energy for their families. Wanting to be good fathers, they sometimes feel the pained looks of neglect from family members, but by the end of the day they're empty from their strenuous efforts to be successful.

Stan was suffering from one of the deepest conflicts a man can have: "Am I a failure?" To start his software company, he put his family's livelihood, his integrity, and his dignity on the line, and he nearly lost it all. He described his current work situation with the expression "out of the frying pan and into the fire." As difficult as forming his own company had been, answering to the parent company kept intense heat on him. Echoing in the recesses of his mind were the heavy performance demands of his mother, exacerbating his fear of failure. His father, a mild-mannered, elusive man, remained a passive presence in his childhood. Thus, as with the demon "success," the demon "mom" loomed large inside, and like many people, Stan disconnected from his parents to avoid conflict — a pattern he carried from his family of origin to his family of procreation. Stan took advantage of the family homeostasis; the family seemed to be running all right, though in truth Joan was getting by with little more than Stan's paycheck, until the crisis of Celia's launching made it clear everything was not as fine as it appeared.

One piece of the puzzle of Celia's failure to launch concerned her lack of connection with her father. *When adolescents are lagging behind in some way, already insecure about themselves or their relationships, forging ahead into the world can be frightening.* Hanging by a thread, Celia was not in a position to experience more loss by leaving for school. Without healthy feelings of attachment inside her, Celia felt rudderless as she faced her future. In most families, adolescent girls feel closer to their mothers than their fathers; it has been widely noted that fathers are generally more awkward and confused in their means of relating to their daughters, especially in early and middle adolescence. Many daughters lack relationships with their distant or divorced fathers, especially if the father has moved away or started a new family. Having a distant father does not automatically place the daughter at risk for failure to launch, but in Celia's case there was a frustrated yearning that came from missing someone who was "there, but not really there." As it turned out, Celia's lack of inner security was related both to her disconnected father and to the anxiety she had been absorbing from her mother.

Joan epitomized a syndrome I call the "good-to-a-fault" mom. She had taken the caretaking virtues of nurturance, tolerance, and acceptance to such an extreme that she unwittingly collaborated in a family stasis that affected everyone's growth. Over the first few sessions, we looked more closely at the relationship between Joan and Celia. Though Joan felt somewhat guilty about not contributing to the family income, she believed the family would be best served by her decision to remain on the homefront. After paying taxes and child-care expenses, her take-home pay would have been negligible. Further, she enjoyed creating a nest, which seemed all the more important because of Stan's consuming dedication to work. Because of their financial problems, Joan had been unable to carry out many of her ideas about decorating, but her perennial garden was a wonder, created from cuttings she collected at plant fairs. At one point in therapy, Joan mused, "If only I could do something like that for a living."

When I questioned Joan about this possibility, she explained that she and Stan married with the understanding that she would be the homemaker and he would be the breadwinner. Further probing revealed that Joan was actually terrified of working outside the home. She was convinced she could never find satisfying work. Who would hire her? What qualifications did she have? Would it really be worth it? How would things get done around the house? For years Joan had talked about some type of part-time job, and her plan had been to find something during Celia's senior year. But, then again, her last year with Celia was so precious, and lately, Celia had needed Joan's empathetic listening ear more than ever. In a word, Joan was in a bind: she couldn't really complain about Stan's workaholism because they were all depending on him financially, but, as she mumbled softly at one point, "It's like being married to a zombie." She had settled for trying to be a good sport, accept her plight, and be the best, nurturing mom she could be.

Three implicit "rules" guided Joan's actions. She believed she was a good mom if she, first of all, tended selflessly to her children's needs and responded sympathetically to their problems; secondly, made a comfortable, conflict-free home for her family; and thirdly, didn't bother Stan about his absenteeism because he was already suffering intense pressure. In actuality, Joan needed to rethink each of these "rules."

Out of the goodness of her womanhood and her motherhood, Joan had listened to Celia's scary feelings and vulnerabilities. *Parents who are highly tuned in and attentive to their adolescent's distress sometimes participate in a pattern of circular anxiety with their child.* The more Celia and her mother talked, the more expressive Celia became about her fears, and the more worked up Joan became over what to do about Celia. Joan needed to support and reassure her daughter, not reinforce her travail. Enmeshed with her daughter, Joan lacked a boundary to keep her from absorbing Celia's angst. Likewise, as the child closest to her mother, Celia had been affected by her mother's anxiety over her marriage situation and her feelings of inadequacy. Joan was a reserved, sensitive woman — not a complainer in any sense of the word — but Celia had her antennae out for her mother's disappointed sighs, weak smiles, and moments of reflectiveness.

Joan was experiencing something of a bookend effect in her child rearing; not only was Celia supposedly getting ready to go, Daniel, her youngest child, was entering middle school, which set the stage for his eventual leave-taking. More so than for fathers, mothers often experience a loss of power and status when their last child, who may once have been a "pal," reaches puberty. Unless fathers offer strong support, mothers can become disheartened and disillusioned in their parenting. Through her anxiety and depression, Celia, in a sense, functioned as a spokesperson for her mother's turmoil. The anxiety funneled from mother to daughter and round again. Joan had been on target in the initial interview: her daughter had in a sense inherited her low self-esteem. But we don't want to overlook the fact that Stan, with his "fear of failure" had contributed to Celia's insecurities.

Celia and her mother demonstrate how parents and their adolescents often face parallel developmental tasks. Each needed to find a way to handle her fears, move to the next life stage, and expand her idea of who she was. Self-imposed limitations and self-defeating thoughts held them back. Instead of anxiety, they needed confidence; instead of feelings of loss, they needed to become excited about new beginnings; instead of concerns about separation, they needed to figure out how they could stay connected while also taking on new challenges. So perceptive was Joan to psychological issues that she understood "circular anxiety" quicker than most people. Joan saw that Celia was fixated on vulnerabilities rather than possibilities, and she became determined to change and not share all her feelings with her daughter.

Joan's unspoken second rule was to concentrate on making a pleasant home for her family. This focus, had, however, thwarted her personal development and allowed her to avoid other life concerns that frightened her. *As children grow up, stay-at-home moms often feel compelled to escalate their volunteerism or enter the work force, but role expansion for moms involves personhood much more than job-hood, per se.* Has the mother grown along with her children to fill her life in a satisfying way once the children no longer occupy her every hour? Does she have strong interests and relationships that will keep her from being isolated? What outlets does she have for all the energy previously devoted to child rearing? If a traditional arrangement with Mom at home and Dad as the breadwinner truly works for a couple, then who brings home the paycheck is less of an issue. A division of labor, which can also successfully occur with Dad at home, works optimally when the non-income-producing person knows how to get needs addressed, is respected by the spouse, and shares equal power, regardless of roles. When, instead, mothers are isolated, unemployed, unfulfilled, and confined to rigidly prescribed gender roles, depression and stifled anger can result.[1] In the Castle family, the traditional arrangement had its unspoken flaws: Joan felt devalued in her stay-at-home position, Stan had lost out on the opportunity to be a father, and their marriage relationship suffered from a lack of intimacy.

Joan fit the definition of a type of person often called an overfunctioner. She played partner to Stan's underfunctioning in the home. *An overfunctioning/underfunctioning relationship is characterized by one person doing more and the other person doing less.* In this classic family dynamic (first described by Murray Bowen and elaborated on by Harriet Lerner), each role mutually reinforces the other to maintain a stable pattern, despite the losses to each party.[2] Joan had clearly been the point person for the nest making and the caregiving in the family. She had also been responsible for feeling all the feelings and enacting all the emotional relationships. Again, the boundary issue becomes central. Strong boundaries imply that we are accountable for our share of the family problem solving and relating, but not for all of it. Often, because of gender role prescriptions, women can become overfunctioners with everything related to home — parenting, feelings, calendar logistics, even down to the smallest details like sending thank-you notes or holiday presents to relatives on both sides of the family. There is a fuzzy limitlessness on caretaking and family life, and it can often be overwhelming for women who carry their tendencies to an extreme and define their goodness based on doing everything for everybody else.

Time and again in therapy situations I've heard psychologically aware women acknowledge how they "go along" with an existing problem (for example their husband's alcohol use, anger problems, workaholism, overfunctioning/underfunctioning) and pin the label "codependent" on themselves, often unnecessarily. Certainly, there is a mutuality in most deleterious family patterns. Nonetheless, we want to guard against pathologizing tendencies like caretaking for women and bread winning for men, for most of the generation now parenting were socialized into these gender roles. Many women who came of age during the women's movement find themselves surprised at how highly identified they become with the role of "mother in charge of the domestic world" once they have children. Even if both parents are working, women have been found to do up to 70 percent of the household duties; only when the woman's income is equal to or more than her husband's does the allocation of tasks become more equal.[3] This data suggests that once women cross over to motherhood, caretaking becomes their modus operandi, manifesting itself in parenting, relationships, and domestic duties. While it often makes practical sense for one person to assume the lion's share of caretaking and household responsibilities, if one's rights feel restricted and one feels "squeezed" by the role, problems are likely to surface, as they did with Joan and Stan.

Not only was Joan overburdened in her mother role, she had assumed the position of caretaker for her own mother. As the eldest daughter in a family of five children, she found herself increasingly on her own in looking after her mother, who was in the early stages of Alzheimer's disease. Her father, who was still alive, was, according to Joan, "basically helpless." Because she was accustomed to carrying forth with a stiff upper lip, Joan was initially incapable of expressing her ambivalence. "Well, it's complicated," she said in therapy, evading the issue. It was somehow expected of her — a loyal trust bequeathed to her from her mother. Only two of her four siblings lived nearby — her youngest sister who had marriage problems and a disabled child, and a brother who was busy with his work and family, so "nothing could really be expected of him." Joan's siblings viewed her as the lucky one, which helped elect her to the caretaking role. Despite all her efforts to "do for" her mother, Joan received little in return. "It was always the underdog in our family who got the attention," she remarked. With characteristic pluck she added, "There's nothing to be done about it now. After all, we're all grown up, and mother has Alzheimer's."

Throughout her parents' marriage, her father had had a series of affairs, which her mother patiently endured. Unconsciously, Joan developed a sense that men can't be held accountable emotionally. She was initially attracted to Stan because he was so markedly different from her selfish, philandering father, but functionally, she ended up with the same dearth of emotional energy and connection in her marriage. Like her mother, she let her husband "off the hook" in his husband role. Her unconscious legacy amounted to a credo that men can't be counted on; one might as well give up, be a good sport, keep the family stable by repressing your disappointment in your mate's abandonment, and meet your emotional needs by developing close relationships with your children. Stan, on the other hand, looked to marry someone sweet and compliant, unlike his mom and his first wife. By functioning the way he did — in combination with Joan's mild temperament and her family issues — what he got was another disconnected family, a symptomatic daughter, and a quietly resentful, disappointed wife, who was not altogether different from his own mother.

The most salient problem with overgiving is that it can lead to feelings of victimization or exploitation, which in turn can produce anger or depression. Overfunctioners often think that if they give they'll get back. But what if it's not reciprocal? Joan felt as if her position as the "doer" in relationships had been dealt out to her and she was playing a forced hand. She did not, however, have a temperament that smolders with resentment or rails indignantly. Loyal, duty-bound, and resigned, she had a gracious-to-a-fault goodness, even in her anger. Remaining silent, she harbored an inner despair. "But how would the family get along if I did less around the home?" she questioned. Her ever-repeated rationale for running herself ragged was, "No, but I have to."

Joan's third operating principle was to avoid pressuring Stan for having dropped out of the family. Well handled, a little conflict is not an entirely bad thing, if it productively moves a family out of an unhealthy pattern. Perhaps if Joan had made more of a problem out of Stan's disconnectedness, Celia wouldn't be suffering deeply from father loss. Joan never learned how to communicate her desires or dissatisfactions any more than Stan knew how to communicate feelings. She avoided dealing with Stan's absence in the family, with her own transitional identity issues, and with her feelings of being taken advantage of in her family of origin. As long as she had her hands full with Celia, Joan was able to avert her attention from these problems.

Taking Small Steps

Shortly into therapy, the Castles realized Celia's failure to leave home was a family-wide developmental issue. *If a family hasn't proceeded along its path, adjusting and rearranging to accommodate inevitable life changes, they're in danger of coming to a halt, unsure of where and how to proceed.* Just as Celia was immobilized, unable to take off from her home base, so too were other family members stymied. Therapy became a watershed event, with feelings of all sorts emerging. Not only did Joan see the parallel between Celia's anxiety about her transition and her own anxiety, Joan identified their mirroring lack of self-trust and reluctance to put their own needs "out there." Though Joan feared becoming a demanding woman, she needed Stan to be more intimate with his family; and though Celia felt her mother's need for closeness, she needed to spread her wings. I kidded Joan in therapy that even if she turned up the heat on Stan by half, she was such a gentle person she'd still be much kinder than most people. For Joan, being responsible in a relationship assumed a new form. No longer did she feel she had to accept her plight without complaint. She determined to blaze a new trail and face her challenges so her daughter would believe she could too.

Therapy urged each family member to take small steps rather than grand leaps toward their respective new goals. Joan, Celia, Alden, and Daniel each had to assume individual responsibility for connecting with Stan and vice versa. There was to be no more protecting of Dad: "Don't bother him. He's busy. He's worried about work." In sessions, we worked to remove Stan from his pedestal so his family would no longer see him as distant, uncaring, and impenetrable. Everyone had the psychological skills to appreciate that Dad was suffering from demons related to his legacy of family disconnection. It helped for family members to see him as emotionally vulnerable, wrestling with his issues, rather than neglectful of them. From now on, they might be frustrated with Dad, but they would no longer be depressed by his avoidance.

To break a pattern of overfunctioning, the overfunctioner has to figure out a way not to overgive. The underfunctioner might feel bad about his laxity, whether it be in a family, in a work setting, in a roommate situation, or on volunteer committees. But those who do less usually enjoy some of the benefits of others carrying the weight for them. It takes the overfunctioner to blow the whistle; asking the underfunctioner to "just do more" rarely promotes change. A month after we started therapy, Joan found a part-time job at a floral shop. Necessarily, Stan would need to pitch in more. Joan's siblings would also need to assume a larger share of care for her mother. Joan needed a plan of action that would place a limit on her family/home responsibility, but would not leave her dependent on Stan to come through 100 percent of the time in order for change to occur. *To establish a position of self-care, an overfunctioner needs to protect herself from feeling exploited if the underfunctioner doesn't hold up his end of the bargain; otherwise she continues to be trapped by his underfunctioning.* As motivated as Stan was to reconnect with his family, he had a record of not following through. The family should not be too wooed by his stated resolve.

One example of a self-care position concerned a new rule about family dinners on Tuesday nights. Stan was expected to come home by 6:00 in the evening and help with meal preparation because Joan would not be arriving home until nearly a half hour later. If Stan wasn't there by 6:30, the family would head to the neighborhood deli. Stan would feel all the more responsible to be on time because of their tight budget. Predicting that Stan might slip back into his old pattern, the family formed this plan so they would feel empowered rather than abandoned and hurt, should Stan leave them in the lurch.

Though Stan was a kind and fair person, it took his entire family and the more public forum of therapy to ratchet up his relational skills. Stan made a commitment to initiate more contact with his individual kids and his wife, as did they with him. One of Alden's means of connecting with Dad was to have him arrive a little early to pick him up after baseball practice and watch a few minutes of the practice. Unbeknownst to Stan, however, Alden had prearranged a back-up ride home (his self-care position so he wouldn't feel marooned). Whenever Stan failed to show, he nonetheless suffered the embarrassment of "leaving" his son to find a ride. Daniel looked to his dad to go to the video store with him once a week to pick out a movie, but if he was late, Daniel could go on his own and choose a movie of his own liking for them to watch.

Celia's small step was to attend a local community college and continue to live at home until she felt ready to go elsewhere. I was pleased at how quickly Celia's anxiety and depression improved once therapy was initiated. Excited about her new classes, she felt confident she could excel and eventually finish up at a larger school. She also took a part-time job tending an espresso cart, and generally felt less pressure. Joan, Stan, and Celia agreed that if Celia needed to talk about her vulnerabilities and fears, she should seek out Stan. This move would put some distance between mother and daughter, while also enhancing closeness between father and daughter. During sessions, we practiced active listening, and I urged Stan to share some of his own emotional challenges with Celia. Meanwhile, Joan was under promise to let family members be in charge of their own relationships. Should Stan lapse in his obligations, she had to refrain from rescuing.

In therapy, we made it clear that family members' self-care positions were not "guilt trips" on Dad. The point of all their plans was to facilitate connection, to not give up on Dad even when he disappointed them, and to educate him about the impact of his actions. As Joan launched to the workplace and adopted her new understanding of her mothering responsibilities, Celia likewise successfully launched to a community college. The family entered a transition that would bring Stan closer to his wife and children, move Joan out of her enmeshed position with her children, and provide a healthier environment for Alden's and Daniel's leave-taking down the road.

Variations on Launching

When launching is entirely subverted, it can often be traced to a serious adolescent problem, like delinquency, alcohol or drug dependency, ADHD, depression, anxiety, eating disorders, or developmental delay. Difficulties with launching can also result from a significant family circumstance or problem, like a sudden death of a parent or a contentious divorce that ties all family members in knots. The flip side of failure to launch is an adolescent who perhaps leaves under one of the above conditions, but never comes back to the family. Aside from these extreme problems and situations, it can be difficult to assess whether an adolescent is failing to launch, is launching under fragile conditions and is vulnerable to boomerang, or is merely experiencing some slower version of leave-taking. That a child is still living at home at age eighteen is a crude means of evaluating the launching process. Adolescents do, indeed, achieve autonomy in different ways and on different schedules. Some eighteen-year-olds may remain living at home for an extended period, but are actually proceeding along their course at their own pace; others may leave their families prematurely and be developmentally adrift. Among the various cultures in our country are different patterns and notions about when and under what conditions adolescents can leave home and/or have the freedom to motor under their own power.

Anything an adolescent or family may have struggled with during high school — minor depression, acting out, intense power struggles, family conflict, heavy-duty stressors — can potentially impact or delay launching. Case in point was Celia's transitional crisis. Her difficulty was prompted by her problematic attachments and her subterranean feelings of loss and disconnection within the family at large.

In making judgments about whether an eighteen- or nineteen-year-old is or is not successfully launching, we need to look more at the developmental tasks of late adolescence. Distinctive aspects of this period (which begins during the junior and senior years of high school) include: 1) greater consolidation of personal identity, 2) signs of commitment to a value system, and 3) inklings with respect to one's unique skills and talents and life goals. With the end of high school approaching, late adolescents are usually pondering questions like, "What kind of person am I?" "What am I good at?" "What do I want out of life?"

In late adolescence, we see only the foreshadowings of maturity. Most young adults have a handle but not a firm grasp on identity questions. Many parents are surprised to learn that it is not unusual for children to remain in some oblique way dependent on parents for an extended period. Although individual differences prevail, many young people do not come into their own, in terms of identity consolidation, job or career choices, financial independence, and intimate partnerships until well into their twenties. While age eighteen has legal implications, social maturity is a surer measure of the transition to adulthood than age.

If complete maturity and independence don't usually occur until, say, age twenty-five, what are reasonable launching expectations for an eighteen- or nineteen-year-old? To answer this question, we look to the way in which an adolescent is moving toward personal goals related to the "Who am I?" "What am I good at?" and "What do I want?" questions. Do we see signs of intentionality and direction, whether it be through education, a job, military service, travel, or volunteerism? If an eighteen- or nineteen-year-old is spinning his wheels living at home, not working, not going to school, not contributing in any significant way to the family, we have a clear case of failure to launch.

But, what about a girl who has, say, postponed college, has a job, maybe travels or parties and is fairly responsible around the house and happy? This is a tougher call. She could actually be implementing her current goals: "I want to experience life for a while and not be like my mom, who went straight from high school to college to graduate school and a profession." The parent with a different values system may be the one who deems the situation "poor launching," when, in fact, it's too early to tell. Parents in these situations can legitimately ask for rent and expect compliance with household rules. Judging her a "slacker" may actually reflect the parents' anxiety rather than the daughter's problem. Such parents can feel like they're in a holding pattern along with their child, circling the terminal, waiting for flight directions. To be able to trust and accept that their child is pursuing a course that is right for her (rather than making a mistake and "ruining" her life), parents often need to recall and appreciate the ways their child has demonstrated she has a reliable internal compass guiding her.

Most of us who are now parents were raised during a time when one was either *on* the track to college or a secure job or *off* it. Paths to success seemed more clearly defined. Sometimes parents adopt the template from post–World War II, superimpose it on their children, and react when things aren't going according to that plan. In reality, there is no straight shot to success, but our anxiety has us trying to believe there is. We can get upset when we don't see our kids on the track. More options create more uncertainty. There is a lot of variability in the way kids move out into the world today, which can make parents uneasy.

Attention deficit disorder or learning disabilities, especially if serious, can waylay launching. Because so much child and family energy goes into coping with the natural stressors that accompany learning and school problems (difficulties of group education, tutoring, potential social issues), these adolescents may not be developmentally ready to leave home at age eighteen. Although many colleges have special support programs for kids with learning disabilities, a little breather, if so desired, can be to everyone's advantage. When teenagers have struggled through high school, they often need a couple more years of hands-on parenting, while experiencing the success of, say, employment or part-time community college. Parents can continue to provide needed guidance about budgeting and other forms of self-structure, which is often lacking in kids whose maturity needs a boost. Parents can continue to engender the self-discipline, self-confidence, and self-knowledge necessary for a successful launch. Each adolescent has his own timetable. *If there are signs that a high school senior could benefit from an "extra" something — an extra year at home, at work, or even in a private boarding secondary school — parents should evaluate that option, instead of assuming their child is, by virtue of being eighteen, ready to launch.*

Stage Two of the Castles' Therapy: Alden Is Out the Door

Nearly three years later, the Castles and I reconvened for a therapy tune-up. According to Joan, who expressed herself with a new assertiveness, Alden's behavior was "intolerable and flagrantly disrespectful." Joan was all the more sensitive to potential problems with launching because of her experience with Celia. This time, if something was going to go "wrong," she wanted to catch it early. Alden was violating curfew, partying mid-week, ignoring his family jobs, and threatening to "cut out early." It was March of his senior year, and his grades no longer seemed to count. Though he hadn't officially been accepted, his grade point average and test score index qualified him for admission to the state university of his choice. He had a bad case of "senioritis," whose symptoms include slack-off in schoolwork, cabin fever at home, and ennui. He felt perfectly entitled to stay out, drink, set his own schedule, and call his own shots. Psychically, he was already out the door. "Mom," he would say. "I'll be on my own in six months anyway, so why the curfew?"

Despite family rumblings, when I again saw the Castle family in therapy, they appeared vibrant and engaged. Though Stan continued to grapple with his work schedule, he lived up to his family commitments most of the time. Joan still worked half-time at the same floral shop, but she was taking night classes to expand her business skills. Now away at college, Celia was spending the spring term of her junior year abroad in Edinburgh, Scotland. At age eighteen, Alden was growing his hair and a beard and acting bored, cocky, and impatient with the therapy process. Daniel, who had been generally cheerful and cooperative at age twelve, was brooding and silent, now that he was fifteen.

In our first session back together, Stan spoke up to agree with Joan that Alden needed to be more respectful of family rules and responsibilities. Alden slumped in his chair, grinning like the cat that ate the canary, for he knew freedom was on the horizon. After we talked a while, it became clear that Alden had plenty of room to individuate within the family; I saw no signs of overcontrolling parents. But like many adolescents in the launching mode, he was bucking for independence, trying to get his parents to believe he was a free agent, when, in fact, he still was in high school and he still lived at home. I encourage parents experiencing ornery behavior like this to not ease up too soon in enforcing family rules and expectations. When a senior balks at, say, a rule about letting you know where he's going, claiming no one will be keeping tabs on his whereabouts in a couple of months "anyway," parents can respond, "You're not there yet. That can be something you can do in college."

But within the Castle family, the question remained: Why did Alden feel so entitled to act out? Even Daniel, it seemed, was loosening up on his responsibilities. According to Joan, mounds of sweat-saturated socks were rotting under their beds, though the boys were now supposed to put their own clothes through the wash. Her requests to have the trash emptied were patently ignored. To some extent, Alden had always been a little remiss on his chores, but now Daniel was giving his mother the cold shoulder, which carried a special sting because they had once been so close.

In therapy, Joan protested that Stan wasn't really behind her efforts to have everyone contribute and do his fair share of the household work. "Stan lacks conviction when he talks to the boys, especially when he reprimands Alden. In fact, I think he is actually condoning Alden's misbehavior."

Unconscious Rumblings and Their Unlovely Effects

Daniel's "cold shoulder" to his mom was part of his normal individuation process and not an issue we needed to address. Therapy for him became an opportunity to team with Alden. Together, Alden and Daniel wanted the same things: more independence from Mom and Dad, less parent haggling, and less entanglement in their parents' disputes. In the back of every child's mind is the fear his parents might divorce, which can feel even worse when you mistakenly assume you're the wedge driving them apart.

Because children in a family share the same system, they often bond closer when they feel themselves in a mutual predicament. Alden and Daniel both grumbled when Joan insisted on chores, or made them turn off the TV, or clamped down on messy habits. They had become very close as siblings, which created consequences good and bad for Joan. Appreciating the relationship between her children, Joan felt she was able to back off a little in her parenting. But she felt as if it were two against one because Stan had yet to become a full-fledged member of the parenting team.

In a sense, Alden was the "turf" on which Joan and Stan continued to work out the terms of power in their relationship. Again, Joan was right: Stan was undermining her, maintaining the upper hand by virtue of his "not." Instead of supporting Joan, he was being passive aggressive, either ignoring her cries for help with the boys, or offering weak-kneed reprimands that carried no conviction.

Though we had spent some time on Stan's legacy of disconnection during the first stage of therapy, Stan was continuing to react to problems he had had with his mother; in fact, Alden's acting out and Joan's requests for support set the stage for therapy to deal with Stan's lingering family-of-origin issues. In a very real sense, Stan was identifying with his son, who was kicking up his heels against Mom in a way Stan never had. Because Stan was still fighting the "demanding mom" inside of him, he was at risk for undermining his parenting unity with Joan. *Sometimes, collusion with a child's rebellion means that the parent is unconsciously saying to the child, "Act out for me because I never had a chance."*

What would start out on Joan's part as a reasonable request for Stan to back her discipline would leave them both affronted and offended. Any problem Joan identified would hit Stan's "hot button." All he heard was "You're bad because you're not living up to what's expected of you." Unwittingly Joan became identified with his critical mother and first wife, who had berated him for never being good enough.

Sometimes women become inflamed over their husband's desertion or lack of support and "go after" them with vehemence. In these situations the husband is under attack and is likely to retrench with strong disdain, saying "I'm sick of your grousing and griping." Although I often see this couples dynamic in therapy, it did not apply to Joan and Stan. Joan had too mild a temperament to ever be this way. Nevertheless, she did need to watch out for bringing forty-five years of feeling taken advantage of into their argument. She had a lot of emotion brewing inside. In her requests for parity she needed to contain her emotional upset so that she wouldn't unload accumulated resentment related to her lifelong caretaking excesses onto Stan. Nonetheless, she needed to hold him accountable and *not* buy into his notion of her as too demanding. Stan needed to see the larger picture of what was happening with Alden and Daniel instead of criticizing Joan and throwing her requests back at her.

Since we'd been in therapy together before, Stan quickly saw the light and understood he needed to revisit his reactions to Alden and Joan. Bringing his unconscious identification with Alden to the conscious helped him choose to act differently toward his son. No longer would he play out the same old pattern of fighting back against "the demanding mother." All in all, Alden was launching in a normal way; unlike Celia three years earlier, he would leave on schedule. But unless Joan and Stan worked together to curb his behavior and reinforce family rules, they weren't likely to enjoy the remaining half-year of having Alden at home. Once Joan and Stan began addressing their marital problems and acting in concert, Alden stepped back in line. He had found a hole in the fence because Stan was unconsciously inviting him to transgress, but with that hole patched up, he didn't seem to mind the limitations on his behavior.

An important issue to be tackled concerned Stan's distance from his mother. Because Stan had never resolved his issues with his mom overtly, they operated covertly as his "demon" within. He continued to see himself through his mother's eyes as a loser and a failure. He needed to create new standards for himself and claim, "I'm fine according to *me*." Stan had attempted individuation by marrying during college against his mother's wishes, but because he and his first wife had little in common, they drifted apart. Stan had also attempted to escape his mother's demands by moving three thousand miles away and cutting off contact.

Twenty-five years later the individuation process was far from complete, for Stan continued to grapple with his sense of self-worth. In reviewing Stan's family-of-origin issues, we needed to flesh out a revised view of his now-deceased father, who had been overpowered by Stan's mother. Essentially, Stan had always seen his mother as the "witch" and his father as the "saint," but beneath his father's sweet demeanor was his failure to hold his wife accountable for her hounding of Stan. In therapy, Stan came to see his parents' relationship as more complicated than previously assumed. Though his mother's faultfinding had been excessive, his father, through his vacant stares, had allowed it all to happen.

By becoming stronger as a father, by defining this role as important, and by assessing his career path as "good enough," Stan began to free himself from lingering traps unwittingly laid by both his parents. With Alden's consent, Stan sent his mother an airline ticket and invitation to Alden's graduation. Alden cracked jokes about having primal scream sessions with Grandma, but Stan was determined not to let her little darts sting and not to let her be the judge of his success. The visit had its rough moments, but the family joined forces to keep this seventy-five-year-old woman's needs, issues, and driving objectives in perspective. The visit was declared a success.

Other changes in the family followed. Freed from his family-of-origin traps, Stan became a strikingly happier person, less reactive to his wife, whose requests of him, he realized, had never been unfair. He assumed his share of the household and parenting tasks more willingly, as did the boys. In late summer, Stan left his job and went to work for another software company. (Fortunately, through the selling of his ownership shares, he paid off his remaining debt.) At one time, he had felt driven to be a strategic thinker, a business owner and leader in the computer industry, believing that success in this arena would tame his demons. What finally dawned on him was that his strengths were as a team catalyst and collaborator working with groups of people rather than in the stratosphere of new business development.

During the second stage of therapy, Joan, too, rearranged matters regarding her family of origin. She made plans for her mother, whose Alzheimer's disease was worsening, to spend her days in an adult daycare situation. She delegated assignments (being on call for Dad in evenings, helping him shop, arranging relief care for Dad) to her siblings. Since they knew Joan meant business, they too began doing more of the legwork. Joan took up speed-walking. She was motivated to get in shape because of a special family hike, which would take place over Labor Day weekend, when the whole family would be together, shortly before Alden would leave for his freshman year and Celia for her senior year.

Many parents have commented on the "emptiness" they feel at unloading the station wagon at their child's college dorm or putting her on an airplane with a hug and a wave. There should be "something more," they claim. Some families are creating their own rituals — perhaps a special dinner, where each family member presents the leaving adolescent with some type of representative token, or an event involving the adolescent's larger community. The Castle family determined that their ritual would be a day-hike up Castle Crags. It was Alden who had set himself upon the task of researching and finding a destination that would have a special ring or significance for his family. Everyone was delighted when he found a hike with their family name in a nearby state. Therapy with me ended just prior to the hike, but in my mind, I envisioned the family standing atop the peak of Castle Crags, exhilarated yet exhausted by their climb, looking out together on their new horizons.

Family Friction Pre-Launch

During launching, parents often experience anxiety similar to that of early adolescence. "What's normal?" "What's going to happen next?" Each stage represents a new threshold. As Celia's and Alden's stories illustrate, the way in which an adolescent launches is highly influenced by where he is in his identity development, where the whole family is developmentally, the nature of attachments, and the functioning of the family system. The range of what to expect and what qualifies as normal launching behavior is broad.

Eager to be on his way, Alden represents one end of the normal launching spectrum. *Increased parent-child friction may be nature's way of decreasing everyone's ambivalence about launching.* Joan was anxious about Alden because of what had happened with Celia. When there have been prior hitches or difficulties in launching one's own children (or perhaps even way back when parents themselves left home), there may be heightened concern or reactivity about relatively small indications of going "off track." In most families, the unruly behaviors and habits of a high school senior are more of a nuisance than a true problem. I say the following to many parents experiencing minor parent-child conflicts during launching: "If you choose your top issues, then stand up together to your adolescent and insist that he respect a handful of reasonable household rules, he usually will." That Alden's launching was less difficult than his sister's reflected the family's healthier functioning. Though conflict between Joan and Stan was more evident, they had shed the rigid rules and patterns of denial, fear, and avoidance that once kept family members quiet. Joan felt safe to confront Stan; Stan was ready to tackle issues with his mother; and Alden was flexible and creative enough to include Grandma in his graduation and plan his swan-song hike.

Some adolescents become so overwhelmed by the launching process that they reach the limits of their coping capacity. They begin questioning all their decisions: "What if I hate college? What if it's too hard?" If this is the case, recognize that even though your high school senior looks like an adult, you are still the parent and your child continues to look to you as a secure, reassuring, comforting base. You can speak honestly of feeling a little sad and apprehensive, but avoid exposing all your worries to your struggling senior, who may be barely staying afloat given the undertow of his own anxiety. *A parent's job is to convey faith in the child's competence to solve whatever problems arise; interactions become a dance of nudging, wherein the parent teases out all the good things the child can anticipate, without championing the expectation that college will necessarily be the most wonderful experience of her life.*

Under most circumstances, launching is rarely one thing (only rest-lessness, only reticence) but rather a mixed experience. Typically, the "lasts" — the last football game, the last school play, the last Thanksgiving, the last Mother's Day — can usher in mighty waves of sentiment. A certain antsiness can creep into an eighteen-year-old's behavior, more so with some kids than with others. One mother aptly described her daugh-ter's readiness this way: "She was ready to blow this pop stand her whole senior year. She slept with one foot on the floor." Parents grow weary of their child's loud music and loud friends, of their requests to borrow the car, of their late hours, dirty dishes in their rooms, and monopolizing of the phone — a syndrome sometimes referred to as "dirtying the nest." Thus harbingers of change gradually work their way into the relationship.

Issues during the senior year vary, depending on the child's next planned step, how the parents feel about it, and whether the teenager and the parents have conflicting values and expectations. If, for example, a daughter wants to enter the military but the parents have always had their hearts set on her proceeding straight to college, problems will arise if the parents can't align their vision with their child's particular dreams. Most healthy parents know who their child is by the time she reaches age eighteen and — perhaps with a sigh or two behind closed doors — are able to accommodate their child's needs.

For those applying to college, the first half of the senior year can be one of the toughest of all child-rearing phases because of the inherent stresses of the application process. On the one hand, parents' hearts go out to their seniors, who are bombarded by every distant relative and neigh-borhood acquaintance with the question, "Where are you applying to school?" On the other hand, an adolescent's procrastination can be infuri-ating, especially if he saunters into the bedroom late at night, just before applications must be mailed, asking to have his essay proofread. Parents should keep in mind that sometimes procrastination is an adolescent's way of dealing with the stress of leaving home.

Because adolescents who are applying to college are under so much pressure, parents will want to make sure their behavior isn't exacerbating that pressure. We can subtly help our adolescents stay abreast of the time line; we can encourage them to work with their guidance counselor; we can make sure they have all the necessary tools and a quiet place to expedite the application process; and we can listen to whatever messages they may be sending us regarding how much support they need. But, in the end, it's their process.

One of the best ways we can help our adolescents manage these stressful months is to get a grip on our own anxiety. This is sometimes easier said than done because our anxiety often springs from our love and concern. *Some of our parental anxiety has its roots in our efforts to try to control our adolescent's exit to make sure they land in a place that will keep them safe and happy. A lot of the anxiety parents feel can be understood as a type of grieving over the anticipated loss.* Without question, this is an unsettling, challenging time for most parents, who sometimes feel a little helpless and sometimes a little overwrought. As a coping mechanism, some parents go so far as to form a support group to exchange information and get it out of their systems in their child's absence.

Once the frenzied months of the college application process have been conquered, parents are likely to experience more of what psychologists call rapprochement, a stage characterized by the rebridging of adolescents to their parents. Though rapprochement can be thrown into eclipse during the first half of the senior year, this phase typically begins around age sixteen; prior to that point, most teenagers are working so hard to figure out a non-cloned identity for themselves they necessarily distance from their parents. Once a teenager begins to come into his own person, privacy is no longer as critical. Particularly during their senior year, adolescents may talk openly with their friends in our presence, revealing parts of themselves previously shut off from parents. They may actually extend an invitation to do something together or ask for advice. During rapprochement, the relationship becomes less of a one-way street. What happens to adolescents during this stage is that they begin integrating their commitment to themselves and their independent identities with their commitment to a mature relationship with their parents. This change can occur anywhere between the ages of sixteen and twenty-one. It feels all the more welcome to parents who have struggled with the challenges of identity exploration.

Seniors will, nonetheless, cut their parents off on some matters, especially those we want to lecture on before they go. I've held workshops with high school seniors and parents, usually broken down into a session with only the parents, a session with the teenagers, and a session with both. Top on the list of parental concerns are sexual issues such as AIDS and date rape. Teenagers in launching workshops muse long and hard over these and other complex issues: How will I know who to trust? What is going to happen to my parents? How can I keep myself from partying too much? Will my friends change and become distant to me? Who will I be after my freshman year? What will that last minute with my parents feel like? But, when the teenagers regroup in the workshop session with their parents, they tend to revert to their eyeball-rolling, uncommunicative, disinterested stance on these issues. Though these teenagers are older and though many share some of the same concerns as their parents, they nonetheless often deny their parents access to these fears.

Whatever prior practice we've had separating from our children — sending them off to visit relatives, to overnight camps, to exchange programs — can help with launching. Through such experiences, we've learned how to perform the ritual of the loving good-bye, to contain our anxiety, and to trust that they will have the means to keep themselves safe in our absence. Nonetheless, one mom who launched her second son — yet still had two children remaining at home — attested to the poignancy of the send-off: "I thought I'd wrapped my heart around my sleeve the first time with my oldest son, so I went waltzing into the airport with my second son on his way to college thinking that this wouldn't be so bad. But, I put my arms around him and broke into tears and I thought, this is still hard the second time around. Someone ought to tell you that saying good-bye never gets any easier."

A Picture of Health: The Castle Family Revisited

By happenstance, I saw Joan Castle some three or four years after the family had concluded their second stage of therapy. Having left her job at the floral shop where she first began part-time work, Joan now managed the shop I visited to purchase flowers. Though she was busily preparing for a wedding she was doing the next day, she spoke so engagingly of her family and their changing lives that we became engrossed in a conversation. She had transformed herself from the subdued, scared woman who initially entered therapy with me into a confident, thriving individual.

As Joan readied my order, she rattled on enthusiastically about her children and her husband. Not only had Celia finished college, she was teaching in Edinburgh, Scotland, where she'd done linguistic work during her college junior year and formed some fast friendships, to one young man in particular. When Celia would return to the States was very up in the air. Alden was a college senior, majoring in environmental science, but it was Daniel's news that surprised me, because of the nonplused, accepting way Joan delivered the update on her son. During his junior and senior years of high school, Daniel had become intensely interested in video production. Having recently graduated from high school, he was taking a year off, living at home, working in a video store, doing some filming with a group of young people. Though Joan and Stan hoped he would go on to college sooner or later, they understood he needed some time to decide how serious he was about video work and to figure out his own path. Though Daniel's launching was far from the direct process most parents hope for, Joan and Stan were able to stay composed for a couple of key reasons. This was their third child, and experience can help us keep a cool head and perspective. Moreover, Joan and Stan had worked very hard in therapy, and had developed greater resources for coping with uncertainty.

With a wave of her hand, Joan laughingly explained that she and Stan still had a tiff now and then over one of the issues we'd worked on in therapy — budgeting problems, his inability to come home as scheduled, and delegation of housekeeping tasks. But as she put it, "We work these out along the way." They were looking forward to visiting Alden at his college's family weekend soon and extending their trip a few days to see some sights together. I asked whether they had kept up their ritual of climbing Castle Crags together over Labor Day weekend. Indeed, the hike took place each year, though not everyone made it every year. All in all, Joan radiated a new flexibility and lightness of being. She spoke with enjoyment of her current work, her more fluid relationship with Stan, and her new opportunities for friendships and other activities, but she did often miss her children. Just before I left the shop, Joan commented, "You know, they're always inside of you, and you're always inside of them. There's a closeness there. Actually Stan said that the other day."

As I walked out the door, flowers in arm, I mused on how this family, which had once functioned only adequately, now illustrated the numerous traits psychologists associate with family health. With or without therapy, families can achieve a level of higher functioning, but the question of where a family will go with changes always remains. What had occurred in the Castle family was powerful and impressive, for they took what they learned during therapy and continued growing. Family health is a perpetual state of becoming. In a sense, you never "get there" or reach an end in that journey, but at any point in time we might stop the ongoing videotape of life and see the freeze-frame photograph of what family health looks like.

I saw in Joan *an acceptance of the complexity and ambiguity of life*. Though Daniel was not headed straight to college, she trusted he would be O.K. How different this attitude was from her emotional pins and needles over Celia's situation seven or eight years ago. Likewise, she was unruffled by the fact that Celia, with whom she had once had an enmeshed relationship, was now living abroad in Scotland for an indefinite period. Joan seemed to have a similar acceptance in her marriage. Her relationship with Stan wasn't perfect; they continued to tussle over their differences, but what they had together was definitely "good enough." Likewise, her *greater comfort with ambivalence* was evident; family members had their strengths and weaknesses, which would stir up feelings both negative and positive, but Joan was comfortable rather than afraid of the ambivalent mix of life. Because there was no longer reason to deny or cover up issues, the family would deal with their problems head-on — a clear path to enhancing health. Importantly, though Joan and Stan still had their minor differences, there seemed to be *equal power between parents*.

The manner in which Joan had told me of the family's carrying forward of their traditional yearly hike made it clear the Castles experienced a *joy and comfort in being together*. In the family as a whole, there was *a conscientious balance of self-care and care of others*. Having enhanced her feelings of self-worth through her work as a florist, Joan was nurturing her need for a productive life, yet she also remained attentive to her husband and children, without overfunctioning. *Boundaries were appropriate and clear.* Joan had explained to me that she and Stan were "a team, more now than ever." Recently, they had both agreed to not pay out extra cash to Daniel for some lunch money he had "charmingly" requested. She had chuckled as she described the scams Daniel attempted and the extras he tried to wheedle because he was the last kid at home and knew his parents' soft spots. In their smooth handling of ongoing child-rearing snags that will occur with any teen, Joan's and Stan's *warmth, authority, and good communication skills* were evident.

As for things between Joan and Stan, Joan had remarked, "Stan is still late a lot, with his appointments hither and yon, but that's his problem. If I'm supposed to go somewhere with him, but he's running late, I just take my own car. Sometimes it comes in handy because he's more social than he looks and wants to stay later than I do, especially if I need to come into work early for a big event." This attitude illustrated a *balance of autonomy and connectedness.* Though Joan enjoyed being out with Stan, she felt entitled to engineer her own schedule.

There was *flexibility in family and individual functioning,* which allowed for change, negotiation, and more enjoyment in life. "I've learned not to sweat the small stuff," Joan had said. Joan's enhanced trust in self and others allowed her to be more open and accepting, not in her old way of tolerating a problematic status quo or avoiding conflict; rather, she had a greater freedom to confront problems when necessary, but she also chose her issues judiciously. As she described each of her children's undertakings, I saw an *encouragement of independence and separate identities.* She genuinely appreciated the different paths her children were pursuing, and she *valued each family member for who he or she uniquely was.*

Though her child-rearing years were largely behind her, Joan exuded *an optimism about change,* as she embraced the "unknown" of the future. She was excited about what she was doing and how everyone was growing and developing. Her former fear and anxiety had been supplanted by a forward-looking confidence and trust in her children. Stan, too, had exercised extraordinary courage in facing his issues and making a radical change in his work situation. Joan's and Stan's expanded views of life, their freedom, courage, competence, and security were striking. And, their sound characters and strengths were reflected in their children.

A generation ago, a hallmark theme of adolescent development was separation. Indeed, literature on adolescence stressed this notion. Although our adolescents need to differentiate from us and become their unique selves, the word "separation" implies a severing of the relationship. An emphasis on our children becoming other than us does not reflect the fact that they stay connected to us, nor does it account for the continuity of the relationship after adolescence. More current thinking in adolescent development acknowledges the critical nature of feelings of attachment to psychological well-being.

Launching is the preparation of the individual throughout adolescence for the initial takeoff for independence. Our adolescents usually come back to us — some more than we might desire — and stay in contact with us. The relationship continues, but with less proximity. Less contact often means less anxiety for us, less mutual exposure to bad habits, and less active parenting. But we never stop being parents. Raising healthy children is all about connecting with them, and then, because they have a part of us inside them and we have a part of them inside us, allowing them to be free and take flight on their own strong wings. With a secure attachment and a responsive family stretching to accomplish the parenting goals of this book, an adolescent has the best possible chance of achieving a safe and good passage through adolescence, through launching, and through life.

Notes

___

Introduction

1. Offer, P., E. Ostrov, and K. Howard. *The Adolescent: A Psychological Self-Portrait* (New York: Basic Books, 1981). Brandenburg, N. A., R. M. Friedman, and S. S. Silver. "The Epidemiology of Childhood Psychiatric Disorders: Prevalence Findings from Recent Studies," *Journal of American Psychiatry* 29 (January 1, 1990): pp. 76–83.

1. "Trust Me"

1. E. Erikson, *Childhood and Society, Second Edition* (New York: W. W. Norton & Co., 1963).
2. J. Bowlby, *Attachment and Loss: Attachment,* Volume I, 1969; *Separation,* Volume II, 1973; *Sadness and Depression,* Volume III, 1980 (New York: Basic Books). M. D. S. Ainsworth, M. C. Blehar, C. Waters, and S. Wall, *Patterns of Attachment: A Psychological Study of the Strange Situation* (Hillsdale, N.J.: Lawrence Erlbaum Associates, 1978). M. Ainsworth and J. Bowlby, "An Ethological Approach to Personality Development," *American Psychology* 46 (1991): 333–41.
3. S. Fraiberg, E. Adelson, and V. Shapiro, "Ghosts in the Nursery," *Journal of the American Academy of Child Psychiatry* 14 (1975): 387–421.
4. M. Main and N. Kaplan, "Security in Infancy, Childhood and Adulthood: A Move to the Level of Representation," *Monographs of the Society for Research in Child Development* 50 (1985): 66–104.
5. S. Minuchin, *Families and Family Therapy* (Cambridge, Mass.: Harvard University Press, 1974). M. Bowen, *Family Therapy in Clinical Practice* (New York: Jason Aronson, 1978). Although family systems theory has been refined and revised over the last two decades, Minuchin and Bowen laid much of the groundwork.
6. Stanley Turecki with Leslie Tonner, *The Difficult Child* (New York: Bantam Books, 1989). Mary Sheedy Kurcinka, *Raising Your Spirited Child* (New York: HarperPerennial, 1991).
7. N. Boyd-Franklin, *Black Families in Therapy: A Multisystems Approach* (New York: Guilford Press, 1989).

8. Paul C. Rosenblatt, Terri A. Karis, and Richard C. Powell, *Multiracial Couples: Black and White Voices* (Thousand Oaks, Calif.: Sage Publications, 1995).

2. Adjusting Control and Freedom

1. W. Robert Beavers and Robert B. Hampson, *Successful Families: Assessment and Intervention* (New York: W. W. Norton & Co., 1990). The original research was written by J. M. Lewis, W. R. Beavers, J. T. Gossett, and V. A. Phillips, *No Single Thread: Psychological Health in Family Systems* (New York: Brunner/Mazel, 1976).
2. Diana Baumrind, "Authoritative vs. Authoritarian Parental Control," *Adolescence* 3 (1968): 255–72.

    Diana Baumrind, "Effective Parenting During the Early Adolescent Transition," in *Family Transitions,* P. A. Cowan and M. Hetherington, eds. (Hillsdale, N.J.: Lawrence Erlbaum Associates, 1991.)

    In approach and theoretical bases, Baumrind's delineation of parenting style into authoritative, authoritarian, and permissive typologies varies significantly from the work of Beavers, whose background is object relations/systems. One can only surmise how the Baumrind/Beavers categorizing of families overlaps; it logically follows that Baumrind's authoritative family would be Beavers's optimal family and her authoritarian family would be Beavers's midrange or borderline dysfunctional family, for they are both rule bound and rigid. Baumrind's permissive family is also vulnerable to midrange or more serious dysfunction because of the implicit lack of structure.
3. S. I. Powers, S. T. Hauser, J. M. Schwartz, G. G. Noam, and A. M. Jacobson, "Adolescent Ego Development and Family Interaction: A Structural-Developmental View," in *Adolescent Development in the Family: New Directions for Child Development* 22, H. D. Grotevant and C. R. Cooper, eds. (San Francisco: Jossey-Bass, 1983).
4. Salvador Minuchin, *Families and Family Therapy* (Cambridge, Mass.: Harvard University Press, 1974): 54.

3. A Self of One's Own

1. Carol Gilligan, *In a Different Voice: Psychological Theory and Women's Development* (Cambridge, Mass.: Harvard University Press, 1982).
2. J. E. Marcia, "Development and Validation of Ego Identity Status," *Journal of Personality and Social Psychology* 3 (1966): 551–58.
3. Daniel Offer, *The Psychological World of the Teenager* (New York: Basic Books, 1969). Daniel Offer, E. Ostrov, and K. Howard, *The Adolescent: A Psychological Self-Portrait* (New York: Basic Books, 1981).

4. G. Remafedi, J. A. Farrow, and R. W. Deisher, "Risk Factors for Attempted Suicide in Gay and Bisexual Youth," *Pediatrics* 87 (1991): 869.
5. D. C. Haldeman, "The Practice and Ethics of Sexual Orientation Conversion Therapy," *Journal of Consulting and Clinical Psychology* 62 (1994): 221–27.
6. J. E. Marcia, "Identity in Adolescence," in *Handbook of Adolescent Psychology*, J. Adelson, ed. (New York: John Wiley & Sons, 1980).

4. Navigating Character

1. Carol Gilligan, *In a Different Voice* (Cambridge, Mass.: Harvard University Press, 1982). Lawrence Kohlberg, *Essays on Moral Development, Vol 1: The Philosophy of Moral Development* (1978) and *Essays on Moral Development, Vol 2: The Psychology of Moral Development* (San Francisco: Harper & Row, 1984).
2. Thomas Lickona, *Raising Good Children* (New York: Bantam Books, 1983).
3. L. H. Williams, H. S. Berman, and L. Rose, *The Too Precious Child: The Perils of Being a Super-Parent and How to Avoid Them* (New York: Atheneum, 1987).
4. A. J. Cherlin, F. F. Furstenberg, P. L. Chase-Lansdale, K. E. Kiernan, P. K. Robins, D. R. Morrison, and J. O. Teitler, "Longitudinal Studies of Effects of Divorce on Children in Great Britain and the United States," *Science* 252 (1991): 1386–89. P. Amato and B. Keith, "Parental Divorce and the Well-Being of Children: A Meta-Analysis," *Psychological Bulletin* 110 (1991): 26–46.
5. E. M. Hetherington, "Coping with Family Transitions: Winners, Losers, and Survivors," *Child Development* 60 (1989): 1–14.
6. Molly Reid, personal communication from research gathered for the following study: Molly Reid, Sharon Landesman, Robert Treder, and James Jaccard, "'My Family and Friends': Six- to Twelve-Year-Old Children's Perceptions of Social Support," *Child Development* 60 (1989): 896–910.
7. E. Greenberger and L. Steinberg, *When Teenagers Work: The Psychological and Social Costs of Adolescent Employment* (New York: Basic Books, 1986).
8. Robert Coles, *The Moral Life of Children* (Boston: Houghton Mifflin, 1986).

5. The Social Kaleidoscope

1. David Elkind, *Children and Adolescents: Interpretive Essays on Jean Piaget* (New York: Oxford University Press, 1974).
2. Lyn Mikel Brown and Carol Gilligan, *Meeting at the Crossroads: Women's Psychology and Girls' Development* (Cambridge, Mass.: Harvard University Press, 1992).
3. K. Chernin, *The Hungry Self: Women, Eating, and Identity* (New York: Times Books, 1985).
4. M. T. Sadker and D. Sadker, *Failing at Fairness: How America's Schools Cheat Girls* (New York: Charles Scribner's Sons, 1994).

5. Terri Apter, *Altered Loves: Mothers and Daughters During Adolescence* (New York: St. Martin's Press, 1990).

6. J. C. Coleman, *Relationships in Adolescence* (London: Routledge & Kegan Paul, 1974).

7. J. R. Rabinor, "Mothers, Daughters, and Eating Disorders: Honoring the Mother-Daughter Relationship," in *Feminist Perspectives on Eating Disorders*, P. Fallon, M. Katzman, and S. Wooley, eds. (New York: Guilford Press, 1994).

8. L. B. Mintz and N. E. Betz, "Prevalence and Correlates of Eating-Disordered Behaviors Among Undergraduate Women," *Journal of Counseling Psychology* 35 (1988).

6. The Slippery Slopes of Sexuality

1. E. Donnerstein, "Porn: Its Effect on Violence Against Women," in *Porn and Sexual Aggression,* N. W. Malamuth and E. Donnerstein, eds. (Orlando, Fla.: Academic Press, 1984): 53–84. U.S. Surgeon General, "Report of the Surgeon General's Workshop on Pornography and Public Health," *American Psychologist* 42 (1987): 944–45.

2. F. F. Furstenberg, J. Brooks-Gunn, and S. P. Morgan, *Adolescent Mothers in Later Life* (New York: Cambridge University Press, 1987). M. Zelnik and Y. J. Kim, "Sex Education and Its Association with Teenage Sexual Activity, Pregnancy, and Contraceptive Use," *Family Planning Perspectives* 14 (1982): 117–26.

3. S. Panzarine and J. Santelli, "Risk Factors for Early Sexual Activity and Early Unplanned Pregnancy," *Maryland Medical Journal* 36 (1987): 927. C. Chilman, *Adolescent Sexuality in a Changing Society, Second Edition* (New York: John Wiley & Sons, 1983). M. Zelnik, J. F. Kantner, and K. Ford, *Sex and Pregnancy in Adolescence* (Beverly Hills, Calif.: Sage Publications, 1981).

4. M. P. Kuss and S. L. Cook, "Finding the Facts: Date and Acquaintance Rape Are Significant Problems for Women," in *Current Controversies on Family Violence,* R. J. Gelles and D. R. Loseke, eds. (Newbury Park, Calif.: Sage Publications, 1993): 104–19. G. Cowan and R. Campbell, "Rape Causal Attitudes Among Adolescents," *The Journal of Sex Research* 32 (1995): 145–53.

5. J. Goodchilds and G. Zellman, "Sexual Signaling and Sexual Aggression in Adolescent Relationships," in *Porn and Sexual Aggression,* N. M. Malamuth and E. Donnerstein, eds (Orlando, Fla.: Academic Press, 1984): 233–43.

6. H. I. McCubbin, A. Cauble, and J. Patterson, eds., *Family Stress, Coping, and Social Support* (Springfield, Ill.: Charles C. Thomas, 1982).

7. The Wide-Open Range of Risk Taking

1. D. Baumrind, "A Developmental Perspective on Adolescent Risk-Taking in Contemporary America," in *Adolescent Social Behavior and Health*, Charles E. Irwin, Jr., ed. (San Francisco: Jossey-Bass, 1987).
2. L. D. Johnson, P. M. O'Malley, and J. G. Bachman, *Drug Use Among American High School Seniors, College Students and Young Adults, Vol. I, High School Students*. DHHS Publication No. ADM 91–1835 (Washington, D.C.: National Institute of Drug Abuse, U.S. Printing Office; 1993).
3. Jonathan Shedler and Jack Block, "Adolescent Drug Use and Psychological Health: A Longitudinal Inquiry," *American Psychologist* 45, no. 5 (May 1990): 612–30.
4. National Research Council, *Losing Generations: Adolescents in High-Risk Settings*. Co-published by the American Psychological Association and the National Academy Press, Washington D.C., 1995. Martha Straus, *Violence in the Lives of Adolescents* (New York: W. W. Norton & Co., 1994).
5. Richard Jessor, "Risk Behavior in Adolescence: A Psychosocial Framework for Understanding and Action," in *Adolescence at Risk: Medical and Social Perspectives*, D. E. Rogers and E. Ginsburg, eds. (Boulder, Colo.: Westview Press, 1992).
6. D. Stanton and T. Todd, *The Family Therapy of Drug Abuse and Addiction* (New York: Guilford Press, 1982). L. Kaplan and J. Girard, *Strengthening High-Risk Families: A Handbook for Practitioners* (New York: Lexington Books, 1994).
7. M. Ho, *Family Therapy with Ethnic Minorities* (Newbury Park, Calif.: Sage Publications, 1987).
8. M. Rutter, "Resilience in the Face of Adversity: Protective Factors and Resistance to Psychiatric Disorder," *British Journal of Psychiatry* 147 (1985): 598–611. N. Garmezy, *Stress-Resistant Children: The Search for Protective Factors* (Elmsford, N.Y.: Pergamon Press, 1985).

8. Launching

1. S. Schwartz, "Women and Depression: A Durkheimian Perspective," *Social Science in Medicine* 32 (1991): 127–40.
2. Harriet Lerner, *The Dance of Intimacy* (New York: Harper & Row, 1989). M. Bowen, *Family Therapy in Clinical Practice* (New York: Jason Aronson, 1978).
3. Arlie Hothschild, *The Second Shift* (New York: Avon Books, 1989).

Resources for Parents

Adolescent Development

Elkind, David. *All Grown Up and No Place to Go: Teenagers in Crisis.* Reading, Mass: Addison-Wesley, 1984.

Steinberg, Laurence, and Ann Levine. *You and Your Adolescent: A Parent's Guide for Ages 10–20.* New York: HarperCollins, 1990.

Attachment

Bowlby, J. *A Secure Base: Parent-Child Attachment and Healthy Human Development.* New York: Basic Books, 1990.

Attention Deficit Disorder

Hallowell, Edward M., M.D., and John J. Ratey, M.D. *Driven to Distraction.* New York: Simon & Schuster, 1994.

Hartman, Thom. *Attention Deficit Disorder: A Different Perception.* Penn Valley, Calif.: Underwood-Miller, 1993.

Body Image/Eating Disorders

Chernin, K. *The Hungry Self: Women, Eating, and Identity.* New York: Times Books, 1985.

Siegal, M., J. Brisman, and M. Weinshel. *Surviving an Eating Disorder: New Perspectives and Strategies for Families and Friends.* New York: Harper & Row, 1988.

Wolf, N. *The Beauty Myth: How Images of Beauty Are Used Against Women.* New York: William Morrow Co., 1991.

Boys' Development

Phillips, Angela. *The Trouble with Boys: A Wise and Sympathetic Guide to the Risky Business of Raising Sons.* New York: Basic Books, 1994.

Caron, Ann F. *Strong Mothers, Strong Sons: Raising the Next Generation of Men.* New York: HarperPerennial, 1994.

Discipline

Bluestein, J. *Parents, Teens and Boundaries: How to Draw the Line.* Deerfield Beach, Fla.: Health Communications, 1993.

Nelson, J., and L. Lott. *Positive Discipline for Teenagers: Resolving Conflict with Your Teenage Son or Daughter.* Rocklin, Calif.: Prima Publications, 1994.

Divorce

Ahrons, C. *The Good Divorce: Keeping Your Family Together When Your Marriage Comes Apart.* New York: HarperCollins, 1994.

Everett, C., and S. Everett. *The Healthy Divorce: For Parents and Children.* San Francisco: Jossey-Bass, 1994.

Drug/Alcohol Use

Gaetano, R. J., with J. J. Masterson. *Teenage Drug Abuse: One Hundred Most Commonly Asked Questions About Adolescent Substance Abuse.* Union, N.J.: Union Hospital, 1989.

Schwebel, Robert. *Saying No Is Not Enough: Raising Children Who Make Wise Decisions About Drugs and Alcohol.* New York: Newmarket Press, 1989.

Emotional Development

Goleman, Daniel. *Emotional Intelligence.* New York: Bantam Books, 1995.

Family Systems

Lerner, H. G. *The Dance of Intimacy.* New York: Harper & Row, 1989.

Lerner, H. G. *The Dance of Anger.* New York: Harper & Row, 1985.

Napier, A. Y., and C. Whitaker. *The Family Crucible: The Intense Experience of Family Therapy.* New York: Harper & Row, 1978.

Scarf, Maggie. *Intimate Worlds: Life Inside the Family.* New York: Random House, 1995.

Gay/Lesbian Issues

Fairchild, B., and N. Hayward. *Now That You Know.* New York: Harcourt, Brace, Jovanovich, 1981.

Griffin, C., M .J. Wirth, and A. G. Wirth. *Beyond Acceptance.* Englewood Cliffs, N.J.: Prentice-Hall, 1986.

PFLAG, Inc. P.O. Box 20308, Denver, CO 80220. (303) 321-2270.

Girls' Development/Mother-Daughter Relationships

Apter, Terri. *Altered Loves: Mothers and Daughters During Adolescence.* New York: St. Martin's Press, 1990.

Caron, Ann F. *Don't Stop Loving Me: A Reassuring Guide for Mothers of Adolescent Daughters*. New York: HarperPerennial, 1991.

Brown, Lyn Mikel, and Carol Gilligan. *Meeting at the Crossroads: Women's Psychology and Girls' Development*. Cambridge, Mass: Harvard University Press, 1992.

Marone, Nicky. *How to Father a Successful Daughter*. New York: McGraw-Hill, 1988.

Orenstein, Peggy. *School Girls*. New York: Doubleday, 1994.

Launching

Coburn, K. L., and M. L. Treeger. *Letting Go: A Parent's Guide to Today's College Experience*. Bethesda, Md.: Adler & Adler, 1988.

Littwin, S. *The Postponed Generation*. New York: William Morrow Co. 1987.

Okimoto, J. D., and P. J. Stegall. *Boomerang Kids: How to Live with Adult Children Who Return Home*. Boston: Little, Brown, 1987.

Moral Development

Coles, Robert. *The Moral Life of Children*. Boston: Houghton Mifflin, 1986.

Damon, W. *Higher Expectations*. New York: The Free Press, 1996.

Glenn, H. S. *Raising Self-Reliant Children in a Self-Indulgent World*. New York: St. Martin's Press, 1988.

Lickona, Thomas. *Raising Good Children*. New York: Bantam Books, 1983.

Parent–Child Relationships

Fishel, Elizabeth. *Family Mirrors: What Our Children's Lives Reveal About Ourselves*. Boston: Houghton Mifflin, 1991. (Reissued in paperback in 1994 as *I Swore I'd Never Do That!*)

Kirshenbaum, M., and C. Foster. *Parent/Teen Breakthrough: The Relationship Approach*. New York: Penguin, 1991.

Miller, Alice. *The Drama of the Gifted Child: The Search for the True Self*. New York: Basic Books, 1981.

Polarization

Taffel, Ron. *Why Parents Disagree and What You Can Do About It: How to Raise Great Kids While You Strengthen Your Marriage*. New York: Avon Books, 1994.

Rape/Trauma Recovery

Ledray, L. E. *Recovering from Rape*. New York: Henry Holt & Co., 1986.

Warshaw, R. *I Never Called It Rape*. New York: Harper & Row, 1988.

School Achievement

Bruns, Jerome. *They Can But They Don't: Helping Students Overcome Work Inhibition.* New York: Viking Co., 1992.

Gardner, Howard. *Frames of Mind: The Theory of Multiple Intelligences.* New York: Basic Books, 1993.

Greene, L. J. *Kids Who Underachieve.* New York: Simon & Schuster, 1986.

Rich, Dorothy. *MegaSkills: How Families Can Help Children Succeed in Schools.* Boston: Houghton Mifflin, 1988.

Sex Education (for Parents and/or Teenagers)

Bell, R. *Changing Bodies, Changing Lives, Revised Edition.* New York: Vintage Books, 1988.

Calderone, M. S., and E. W. Johnson. *The Family Book About Sexuality, Revised Edition.* New York: Harper & Row, 1989.

Comfort, A. *The New Joy of Sex.* New York: Pocket Books, 1991.

Fenwick, E., and R. Walker. *How Sex Works: A Clear, Comprehensive Guide for Teenagers to Emotional, Physical, and Sexual Maturity.* New York: Dorling Kindersley Limited, 1994.

Gordon, S., and J. Gordon. *Raising a Child Conservatively in a Sexually Permissive World, Revised Edition.* New York: Simon & Schuster, 1989.

Harris, R. *It's Perfectly Normal: Changing Bodies, Growing Up, Sex and Sexual Health.* Cambridge, Mass.: Candlewick Press, 1994.

Leight, L. *Raising Your Child to Be Sexually Healthy.* New York: Rawson, 1988.

McCoy, K., and C. Wibbelsman. *The New Teenage Body Book.* New York: The Body Press/Perigee Books, 1992.

Wattleton, F., with E. Keiffer. *How to Talk to Your Child About Sexuality.* A Planned Parenthood Book. Garden City, N.Y.: Doubleday & Co., 1986.

Siblings

Dunn, J., and R. Plomin. *Separate Lives: Why Siblings Are So Different.* New York: Basic Books, 1990.

Klagsbrun, F. *Mixed Feelings: Love, Hate, Rivalry, and Reconciliation Among Brothers and Sisters.* New York: Bantam Books, 1992.

Stepparenting

Kaufman, T. *The Combined Family: A Guide to Creating Successful Step-Relationships.* New York: Plenum Press, 1993.

Visher, E. B., and John Visher. *How to Win as a Step-Family, Second Edition.* New York: Brunner/Mazel, 1991.

Temperament

Chess, S., and A. Thomas. *Know Your Child: An Authoritative Guide for Today's Parents.* New York: Basic Books, 1987.

Kurchinka, Mary. *Raising Your Spirited Child.* New York: HarperPerennial, 1991.

Turecki, Stanley, with Leslie Tonner. *The Difficult Child, Revised Edition.* New York: Bantam Books, 1989.

Zimbardo, Philip, and Shirley Radl. *The Shy Child.* New York: McGraw-Hill, 1981.